International Corporate Personhood

This book tracks the phenomenon of international corporate personhood (ICP) in international law and explores many legal issues raised in its wake. It sketches a theory of the ICP and encourages engagement with its amorphous legal nature through reimagination of international law beyond the State, in service to humanity.

The book offers two primary contributions, one descriptive and one normative. The descriptive section of the book sketches a history of the emergence of the ICP and discusses existing analogical approaches to theorizing the corporation in international law. It then turns to an analysis of the primary judicial decisions and international legal instruments that animate internationally a concept that began in U.S. domestic law. The descriptive section concludes with a list of twenty-two judge-made and text-made rights and privileges presently available to the ICP that are not available to other international legal personalities; these are later categorized into 'active' and 'passive' rights. The normative section of the book begins the shift from *what is* to *what ought to be* by sketching a theory of the ICP that – unlike existing attempts to place the corporation in international legal theory – does not rely on analogical reasoning. Rather, it adopts the Jessupian emphasis on 'human problems' and encourages pragmatic, solution-oriented legal analysis and interpretation, especially in arbitral tribunals and international courts where legal reasoning is frequently borrowed from domestic law and international treaty regimes. It suggests that ICPs should have 'passive' or procedural rights that cater to problems that can be characterized as 'universal' but that international law should avoid universalizing 'active' or substantive rights which ICPs can shape through agency. The book concludes by identifying new trajectories in law relevant to the future and evolution of the ICP.

This book will be most useful to students and practitioners of international law but provides riveting material for anyone interested in understanding the phenomenon of international corporate personhood or the international law surrounding corporations more generally.

Kevin Crow is Assistant Professor of International Law and Ethics at the Asia School of Business, Malaysia, and International Faculty Fellow at the MIT Sloan School of Management, United States. His research focuses on corporate subjectivity, private authorship of public international law, and the ways in which understandings of economic and institutional morality as well as beliefs regarding 'the natural' inform legal and market logics.

International Corporate Personhood

Business and the Bodyless in International Law

Kevin Crow

Routledge
Taylor & Francis Group
LONDON AND NEW YORK

First published 2021
by Routledge
2 Park Square, Milton Park, Abingdon, Oxon OX14 4RN

and by Routledge
605 Third Avenue, New York, NY 10017

Routledge is an imprint of the Taylor & Francis Group, an informa business

British Library Cataloguing-in-Publication Data
A catalogue record for this book is available from the British Library

Library of Congress Cataloging-in-Publication Data
Names: Crow, Kevin, Law teacher, author.
Title: International corporate personhood : business and the bodyless in international law / Kevin Crow.
Description: Milton Park, Abingdon, Oxon ; New York, NY : Routledge, 2021. | Includes bibliographical references and index.
Identifiers: LCCN 2020053821 (print) | LCCN 2020053822 (ebook) | ISBN 9780367231941 (hardback) | ISBN 9780429288746 (ebook)
Subjects: LCSH: Persons (International law). | Corporation law.
Classification: LCC KZ3925 .C76 2021 (print) | LCC KZ3925 (ebook) | DDC 346/.066—dc23
LC record available at https://lccn.loc.gov/2020053821
LC ebook record available at https://lccn.loc.gov/2020053822

ISBN: 978-0-367-23194-1 (hbk)
ISBN: 978-0-367-69494-4 (pbk)
ISBN: 978-0-429-28874-6 (ebk)

Typeset in Garamond
by Apex CoVantage, LLC

For Leonie and Korbinian

Contents

Impossibility Unlikelihood Possibility Potentiality Likelihood Actuality

Introduction
The status quo

International corporate personhood (ICP) describes the phenomenon of a transborder legal personality to which an expanding arsenal of international legal rights exclusively belong and from which an expanding arsenal of private normative legal rules flow. Toward the goal of defining and theorizing this phenomenon, this book offers two primary contributions, one descriptive and one normative. The descriptive section sketches a history of the emergence of the ICP and discusses existing analogical approaches to theorizing the corporation in international law. It turns to an analysis of the primary judicial decisions and international legal instruments that animate internationally a concept that began in U.S. domestic law. The descriptive section concludes with a list of twenty-two judge-made and text-made rights and privileges presently available to the ICP that are not available to other international legal personalities; these are later categorized into 'active' and 'passive' rights. The normative section begins the shift from *what is* to *what ought to be* by sketching a theory of the ICP that – unlike existing attempts to place the corporation in international legal theory (to which I am heavily indebted) – does not rely upon analogical reasoning. Rather, it adopts a Jessupian emphasis on 'human problems' and encourages pragmatic, solution-oriented legal analysis and interpretation, especially in arbitral tribunals and international courts where legal reasoning is frequently borrowed from domestic law and international agreements. It suggests that ICPs should have 'passive', or procedural, rights that cater to problems that can be characterized as 'universal' but that international law should avoid universalizing 'active' or substantive rights which ICPs can shape through agency. It suggests that, with all of their problems, ICPs remain the most flexible, adaptive, and often the most powerful international legal personalities. It argues that, if barriers such as 'purpose' and 'constituency' can be redefined, ICPs are the international legal forms that are finely suited and underutilized to realize radical change in areas such as environmental protection and cross-border wealth distribution.

Fleur Johns – whose work richly informs my own – wrote in 1993 that transnational corporations were 'invisible' to international law because of the discursive practices elevated by the field.[1] In the nearly two decades since, the most prominent developments in corporate subjectivity to international law have come not from international law per se, but from 'guiding' frameworks, internal corporate policies, and regional 'best practices' standards. In all efforts, increased ability to collect and monitor data has been more crucial as a catalyst for 'catching' corporate misbehavior than international law.

So why write about business and the bodyless ICP in international law? Why does international law matter to this picture and why should we care about defining and theorizing the international corporate person? The topic is worth addressing because these legal personalities organize international economic activity through value chains through constructs so pervasive they come to be perceived as 'natural', like markets and competition; they direct and internally regulate production and thereby shape labor and opportunity across geographic space; they accumulate spoils of production but decide which State redistributive efforts to acknowledge through legal structures within States that cumulatively transcend States; they shape the international law affecting States, influence the engagement of States with international law, and exercise growing control over the ways in which human beings experience life, even indirectly through interactions and entanglements with States. While the rise of Corporate Social Responsibility (CSR) and Environmental, Social, and Corporate Governance (ESG) initiatives – and even the rise of Business and Human Rights – might be understood as making the corporation 'visible' through soft but serious engagement with hard international law, discussions around these initiatives usually do not address the ways in which ICPs themselves create the terms of engagement, not just between State and corporation but also amongst States. In sum, this topic is worth addressing because ICPs are legal phenomena with immense power to reshape the human condition in manners both positive and negative.

Examples abound. Let us begin with five illustrative vignettes from the past five years. In 2016, in the International Centre for the Settlement of Investment Disputes case of *Urbaser v. Argentina*, an international arbitral tribunal found that, although a human right to water could be read into Argentina's commitments under international law, the corporation Argentina contracted to provide that water was under no positive obligation to provide it.[2] Although the case indicated that an ICP could potentially incur a positive obligation not to breach a contract with a State that involved fulfilling a State's duty to its citizens, in this case, the ICP was free to terminate public services so long as it did not actively obstruct the State's duty to provide those services.

In 2017, after revelations that Exxon scientists had known about the corrosive effect of their product upon global climate change for two decades and that the company had nevertheless pressed the narrative that climate change was a 'hoax' through lobbying and marketing activities, the attorneys general of the U.S. States of Massachusetts and New York subpoenaed Exxon as part of investigations on behalf of their citizens, asking whether Exxon had knowingly concealed the risks of its product from customers. Rather than pursue the many procedural and tort-based defenses available to halt the investigation or defend their name, Exxon filed civil rights lawsuits against the attorneys general, claiming a political right to silence about climate change.[3]

In 2018, the U.S. Department of Justice indicted Jho Low and one of his collaborators at Goldman Sachs for Low's efforts to wash an estimated USD 1.3 billion stolen from Malaysia's national development fund. Although Low is a natural person, his case provides a good inroad for those interested in understanding the legal technologies available to the ICP: his use of international legal forms was slapstick and unsophisticated yet shockingly successful. Although official evidence has yet to see trial, numerous records indicate that Low was able to syphon the Malaysian people's money into private and offshore accounts through haphazard use of offshore shell companies that owned firms and opened bank accounts in various States and through various intermediaries, often posing as his own colleagues or employees through fake email addresses.[4] This limited range of legal technologies jury-rigged by Low enabled him to steal public funds while publicly flaunting it for eight years; imagine what a natural or legal person with polished offshore expertise could do with a complete arsenal of international financial technologies and the means to use them.

One might draw parallels to Apple, the world's first trillion-dollar company, that made 2019 the tenth year in a row during which it paid no taxes. In doing so, it utilized some of the same transactional techniques Low used, and both did so legally. It was the source of funds rather than the means of moving them that pushed Low into criminality. Intent notwithstanding, Apple's sophistication cannot be compared to Low's. Apple used a far broader combination of legal technologies – offshore trusts and subsidiaries, transfer pricing, creative income channeling, and aggressive lobbying – to ensure that the excess of $250 billion kept as cash on hand would avoid government coffers. One example: unlike natural persons, for whom Statelessness is almost invariably accompanied with conditions of suffering and hardship, Apple's Irish holding company and another of its Irish subsidiaries chose Statelessness for its financial benefits. Because Irish tax law allows Statelessness, and because U.S. tax law requires that a State be listed in order to attach taxation, Apple was able to access a privilege of taxless Statelessness that belongs only to similar firms.[5]

Finally, in 2020, Airbus agreed to pay more than 3.6 billion euro collectively to the UK Serious Fraud Office (SFO), the U.S. Department of Justice (DOJ), and France's Parquet National Financier (PNF) as part of a deferred prosecution agreement (DPA) to avoid prosecution in those States for bribes Airbus paid to various airlines and officials, mostly in South Asia and Africa. The agreement also required Airbus to disclose information about the individuals to whom it furnished bribes, and this resulted in several of those individuals facing criminal charges in their own States. Only legal persons can incur the prosecutorial immunity of DPAs – international heavy-hitters like Goldman Sachs, Siemens, Standard Bank, or Rolls-Royce, to name a few[6] – while natural persons can be prosecuted for receiving the payments furnished by those legal persons, often as a result of information disclosed through DPAs.

The common thread through these five vignettes is the phenomenon of corporate personhood as it relates to multinational corporations and as it appears in international courts or domestic courts dealing with international law. Corporate law is primarily a domestic animal; there is no public international company law, competition law, tort law, or tax law. But there are common practices and a collection of near-universal principles emerging from multiple jurisdictions and in international courts with respect to the concept of legal personhood. Corporations are universally treated by legal systems as "legal persons" that exist separately and independently of their directors, officers, shareholders, or other natural persons with whom the corporate person interacts. This legal person, the corporation, can own property, enter into contracts, commit torts, and hold an ever-increasing pallet of rights. The liabilities it incurs are separate from those of its shareholders and its assets are separate from shareholder assets. Although this set of conditions is often referred to as 'limited liability', the reality necessitated by the structure is that shareholders have no liability. These shareholders can be either natural and legal persons. A shareholder's possession of shares does not equate to a classic 'ownership' interest but rather to the possession of intangible rights created by the corporate form, such as the right to receive dividends (economic rights) or to vote on shares (political rights). Shareholders acquire shares either by purchasing them when they are initially issued or by purchasing them from another shareholder. The latter form of acquisition is vastly more common than the former, so the common-sense intuition that purchasing stocks directly contributes to the capital of a corporation is usually false.

To claim that these legal themes are common across most commercial jurisdictions is uncontroversial. But there is far less clarity as to what is meant by a corporation's fiduciary duties to its shareholders, whether a corporation's 'purpose' is to maximize profits, and whether corporations should pursue only the interests of shareholders (which is assumed to be 'increasing profits') as opposed to 'stakeholders' or to the public at large. These are all themes addressed in the following pages as they relate to the primary focus of the book: the distinct form of 'corporate personhood' that emerges from the converging phenomena of post-WWII interdependent globalization and the post–Cold War proliferation of international economic law. This is what I refer to as the ICP: a legal person composed of persons, transnationally fluid in form and in ownership, transcending States yet receiving form from States – a person that overlaps at times with the individual and at times with the State, yet accrues rights available to neither.

The aim of this book is twofold and the aims correspond with the book's contributions. The first aim is descriptive. It seeks to define the ICP and situate it in the broader history of the corporation and amongst existing theories of corporate personhood and international legitimacy (Chapter 1). It analyzes the treatment of the ICP in various international courts and texts, taking great care to emphasize the role of the ICP in generating the law that governs it rather than viewing it solely as a product of law (Chapters 2 and 3).

The second aim is normative. After demonstrating that the ICP is a distinct legal creature for which domestic understandings of corporate personhood or corporate rights are inadequate to explain, the book aims to establish a theory of the ICP in international law drawing on Hume and Hohfeld as well as Kurki's concepts of 'passive' and 'active' rights (Chapter 4). It then demonstrates that ICPs are unlike any other subject of law in their capacity to make law applicable only to disjointed parts of the whole subject or 'person', underscoring the inapplicability of analogical reasoning to the bodyless and borderless (Chapter 5). It finally concludes with a discussion on the implications of the ICP – its past, its present, and its theoretical application – for sovereignty, for the corporate veil, and more generally for visions of international law that emphasize the primacy of the State rather than the individual.

Chapter 1 (The emergence of international corporate personhood) begins with definitions and distinctions before embarking on a survey of corporate legal evolution in three phases: the magistrate phase; the public charter phase; and, finally, the personhood phase. It reviews existing understandings of the corporation as analogous to either individuals, States, or international organizations with respect to its relationship to international law and sets out a series of existing 'incarnations' of the ICP, which inform how we might understand, *inter alia*, the separation of ownership and control. It sets the stage in broad terms, leaving most of the technical details to Chapters 2 and 3, and the theoretical components to Chapter 4.

Chapter 2 (The international corporate person in international law: judge-made law) tracks the process through which what began as a nominally para-Statist organization in the immediate post-WWII period became increasingly para-Individual over time and across space. It focuses on judicial decisions that have moved the needle on the ICP's form and function; and divergent views regarding the source of authority for creating new rights or obligations for corporations. In this chapter, I argue that international investment law has enabled a fundamental transition in international legal practice primarily through its collapsing of natural persons and legal persons into the single category of 'investor'. In a survey including but not limited to international investment law, Chapter 2 seeks to identify the most influential judicial decisions and arbitral awards from which international law's relationship to the international corporate person derives.

Chapter 3 (The international corporate person in international law: texts and practices) is similar in structure to Chapter 2 but, rather than focusing on judicial decisions and opinions, it analyzes international agreements and other texts that comprise 'black letter' international law. Whereas texts can (and do) create explicit or implicit rights and differences, texts and the absence of texts can also create practices which become 'rules' solidified by inertia or normative forces more than deliberate intention. The picture that emerges from these two chapters is at once amorphous and technical, but it is important to document and understand the status quo to move toward a more cohesive theory if the ICP. One primary emphasis of these two chapters is the private sector's influence on the creation of public international law.

Chapter 4 (Theorizing international corporate personhood) addresses two of the major issues raised by the preceding chapters: corporate constituency and the evolution and weaponization of the public–private divide in international law. It suggests that the work of Philip Jessup offers a helpful analytical lens that can empower lawyers to reimagine legal analysis in a way that serves 'peoples' rather than sovereignty and – the Mr. Hyde to sovereignty's Dr. Jekyll – the corporate veil. It argues that 'passive' rights should be assigned to corporations only as they serve the public good, globally defined, and that 'active' rights should be assigned only as they can be attached to corresponding duties to the publics which a given ICP's actions affect. One of the primary contributions of this book is in the final section of Chapter 4, where I draw on Chapters 2 and 3 to compile a list of twenty-two passive and active rights and privileges ascribed exclusively to ICPs, available to no other legal form. This process of working backward from rights themselves, and situating them within 'active' and 'passive' contexts, provides a useful analytical framework for applying a more cohesive and accountable theory of the ICP going forward.

Finally, **Chapter 5** (Political bodies and the bodyless) focuses to a greater degree on present forms and functions of the ICP. It demonstrates that ICPs are unlike any other subject of law in their capacity to make law applicable only to disjointed parts of the whole subject or 'person'. Justifications for ICP treatment are inconsistent with the treatment of 'things' that either have agency or have bodies but not both; trends in international courts show tensions in the concept of personhood as accorded to corporations and the dissolving lack thereof with respect to nature, animals, and AI. After exploring these trends, I argue that understandings of the ICP as para-individual or para-State have created and sustained international liability structures that do not reflect the legal reality of ICPs or MNEs more generally. Finally, I gather inspiring ideas from a number of scholarly threads (old and new) that are relevant for reform. Throughout this effort, the argument maintains that the ICP can be (and sometimes is) reappropriated by natural humans as vehicles for positive change. Indeed, in many ways, ICPs are more flexible and more adaptive than traditional 'sovereigns' and other international legal personalities; some can mobilize a store of wealth and various forms of power far outmatching many States. As such, ICPs have potential to rapidly address some of the world's greatest challenges; definitions of purpose and attachment to narrow constituencies nevertheless limit the radical utility of ICPs as a legal form.

The analysis throughout this book pushes the reader to think critically on the idea of 'sovereignty', both as a barrier to resolution of global problems such as inequality and climate change, and as a close cousin to the corporation, especially with respect to the corporate veil. The book concludes with a critical discussion regarding the future of corporate purpose and aspirations for law and humanity along these themes. It stresses that by compartmentalizing obligations to tort law and aspirations to criminal law, by distinguishing between passive and active rights, and by globalizing passive rights while regionalizing active ones, international corporate regulation and international law more generally can move beyond coercive universalizing claims to morality or economic justice while internationalizing redistributive and dispute settlement procedures that allow regionalized conceptions of morality and economic justice to flourish.

Notes

1 Fleur Johns, *The Invisibility of the Transnational Corporation: An Analysis of International Law and Legal Theory*, 19 Melb. U. L. Rev. (1993–1994).
2 *Urbaser S.A. v Argentine Republic* (ICSID Case No. ARB/07/26) Award (8 December 2016).
3 See e.g., Michael Hiltzik, A New Study Shows How Exxon Mobil Downplayed Climate Change When It Knew the Problem Was Real, *Los Angeles Times* (22 Aug. 2017).
4 For a journalistic account of Low's escapades, see Tom Wright & Bradley Hope, *Billion Dollar Whale: The Man Who Fooled Wall Street, Hollywood, and the World* (2018).
5 See e.g., Fair Tax Mark, Report, The Silicon Six and Their $100 Billion Global Tax Gap (2019), available at https://fairtaxmark.net/wp-content/uploads/2019/12/Silicon-Six-Report-5-12-19.pdf (accessed 4 June 2020).
6 See generally Organisation for Economic Co-operation and Development (OECD), Resolving Foreign Bribery Cases with Non-Trial Resolutions: Settlements and Non-Trial Agreements by Parties to the Anti-Bribery Convention (2019).

Chapter 1

The emergence of international corporate personhood

While the concept of corporate personhood – a corporation as a bearer of human rights – has been fermenting in the United States for well over a century, the concept of ICP is of relatively recent vintage. The aim of this chapter is to track the emergence of the ICP to better understand the various theories we might adopt in conceptualizing the ICP's relationship to existing international legal frameworks. To do this, a helpful first step is to back away from the conventional view on international law which conceptualizes the discipline as primarily concerned with relations between States. As many passages in this book show, the conventional view is not only increasingly irrelevant because of innovations in treaty and case law, it is also based on fundamental misconceptions.[1] International law and some form of international corporation were born in virtually the same instant; one might even think of the state and the incorporated Church as zygotic legal twins, created quite intentionally to occupy two distinct aspects of organizational governance (**II.**). Against this backdrop, and in broad strokes for now, the chapter will follow the major transformations in the corporate form through time, from the Dutch East India Company to Westphalia the 1600s to the first industrial revolution to the post-WWII period to the present, drawing a red line from what began as a legal insulation for churches and universities, and what spent seasons as catalyst for colonization, public servant, capital agent, to what finally became a politically-empowered legal person. The zygotic twins of yesteryear became evolved to private chartered corporation and state rather than church and state (**III.**). However, the legal contours and associated rights and obligations of the corporate person are unclear, particularly in the international context. While Chapter 3 will spend considerable time exploring precisely what these contours are (and aren't), this chapter explores three primary theories of the corporation in international law, extracts three primary theories on corporate personhood primarily from Anglo-American and European law, and finally links these threads together in describing the emerging concept of international corporate personhood (**IV.**, **V.** and **VI.**). With these points aired, the chapter concludes with a discussion on the natural persons that compose the ICP and the international agreements that affect them (**VII.**).

Before we embark, however, this journey will require a shared understanding of a few essential definitions and two essential distinctions (**I.**).

I. Definitions and distinctions

Legally defining international corporate forms and activity can be confusing. There are many terms used to refer to business enterprises that act in more than one jurisdiction; this section will set out a cluster of the most common concepts and acronyms for current and future reference as you progress through this book. The most common of term is Multinational Corporation (MNC) and a close second is Transnational Corporation (TNC). These entities can engage in Direct Investment (DI), Foreign Investment (FI), or both (Foreign Direct Investment, or FDI). They can also participate in Corporate Groups (CGs) and Corporate Networks (CNs). I set out legal definitions for each of these in subsection **I.a**. The term that I use with greatest frequency in this book is one that comes from the field of economics: Multinational Enterprise (MNE). Like the economists, I use the term 'enterprise' rather than 'corporation' to refer to the any multinational corporation, network of corporations, corporate groups, subsidiaries, or other business arrangements with some form of centralized control, but the term does not refer to any specific legal form. The ICP can be an MNC or a TNC and it can make up part of an MNE, and all of these corporate forms can possess International Legal Personality (ILP). However, while the ICP always possesses an ILP, as a legal category, the ICP has characteristics which are distinct from other ILPs. Much ink has already been spilt over the treatment of ILPs generally, but while the ICP may possess some of the general characteristics of most ILPs, it is also distinct from any other form. I endeavor to make this distinction crystal clear in subsection **I.b**.

a. Definitions

The first use of the term Multinational Corporation has been attributed to David E. Lilienthal who, in April 1960, gave a paper to the Carnegie Institute of Technology on 'Management and Corporations 1985' which was later published under the title 'The Multinational Corporation'. Lilienthal defined MNCs as 'corporations . . . which have their home in one country but which operate and live under the laws and customs of other countries as well'.[2] The typical economist's definition of a 'multinational enterprise' is any corporation which 'owns (in whole or in part), controls and manages income generating assets in more than one country'.[3] The separation of ownership and control is an essential feature of the modern MNE. Another important feature to note is the direct control over investments, rather than simple portfolio investment. Yet it allows for a conceptualization of international economic activity broader than the typical parent–subsidiary legal relationship.

In its most recent definition, operational since 1978, the UN Commission on Transnational Corporations in Word Development drew a distinction between 'multinational corporations' and 'transnational corporations'. While I will not be using this distinction in this book, many UN documents consider enterprises owned and controlled by entities or persons from one country but operating across national borders as 'transnational', whereas enterprises owned and controlled by entities or persons from more than one country are considered 'multinational'.[4] The now shelved UN Code of Conduct – which will be discussed at greater length in Chapter 2 – collapsed this distinction into TNCs, stressing control as the defining factor.

The OECD book *Guidelines on Multinational Enterprises* goes one step further, loosening the requirement from control to coordination:

> [Multinational Enterprises] usually comprise companies or other entities established in more than one country and so linked that they may coordinate their operations in various ways. While one or more of these entities may be able to exercise a significant influence over the activities of others, their degree of autonomy within the enterprise may vary widely from one multinational enterprise to another. Ownership may be private, state or mixed.[5]

According to this definition, the ability to coordinate activities between enterprises in more than one country is the salient factor defining an MNE. Other factors are not decisive. The definition is, therefore, broad enough to encompass both equity and nonequity based direct investment, regardless of the legal form, or ownership, of the undertakings. The OECD definition is the one I adopt going forward. The ICP, by contrast, focuses on a specific characteristic of the MNE. Namely, the characteristic of being bound to international law as a subject – as a holder of rights and as a bearer of duties or obligations.

The final two definitions are necessary to describe the organizational structures of MNEs: Corporate Groups and Corporate Networks. CGs are typically characterized by a hierarchical structure in which one firm exercises control over other firms in a multinational group. The most common example of this is when one firm owns a majority of voting shares in another firm, but control can arise from a variety of arrangements, including from minority shareholdings. For example, circular holdings might create equality between three firms, but it could be that two of them are dependent in some other way upon the third. Two quick examples: if A holds 40% of B, B holds 40% of C, and C holds 40% of A, but all three firms share common management and A provides services without which B and C could not operate, A controls B and C; or if A holds 40% of B and B holds 40% of A, but both firms share common management and hold controlling shares in C, D, and E, then A and B jointly control C, D, and E. The key factor that distinguishes a CG from a CN is this hierarchical element of control.

CNs are systems of contracts, medium-term commitments, or repeated transactions. In the case of Networks, the element of control is notably absent. Moreover, the varied members or ICPs that can make up a Network do not need to share any joint purpose. Presumably, they all share the aim of being profitable, but they are not coordinated toward that aim together. They are rather using each other to achieve that aim. Contrast this with a Group which might operate a controlled member at a loss so long as it increases the profits for the Group as a whole.

b. Distinctions

The ICP is legally (if not physically) distinct from the MNE. It is a term I introduce to describe a post-millennial phenomenon in international law. Most of the aforementioned conceptualizations were settled in the late 1970s and early 1980s, before the U.S. concept of corporate personhood began to manifest widely and internationally through the auspices of arbitral awards concerning international trade and investment agreements. Many scholars have wrestled with the question of what duties corporations might owe to States or to individuals under international law, and these are important parts of my concept of the ICP, but what I add to the conversation here is the phenomenon of judge- and self-made rights owed to corporations through international law. As we have seen, the conventional definitions of the MNE are primarily concerned with ownership and control. Because these definitions come from economically focused organizations, they concern themselves with how corporate property and corporate liability can be structured on the international stage, that is, under which circumstances can a home state parent company be said to 'control' a host state subsidiary, thereby opening a path to parent liability for a claimant in the host state? MNE definitions are therefore focused on the transactional, territorial, and property-based aspects of international business organizations. By contrast, the ICP is a term that describes the phenomenon of profit-driven corporate forms acquiring rights of two types: (1) rights historically accorded only to natural persons on the international stage, for example, social and political rights in international law; and (2) rights that belong only to ICPs, not to natural persons, States, or any other form of legal personality, for example, access to deferred prosecution agreements under international anti-corruption law. Both persons and things can have passive rights (rights exercisable by another on behalf of a right-holder), but only persons can have active ones (rights exercisable an one's own behalf linked to the ability incur responsibility for one's actions). Not all MNEs are 'persons' in the sense that they can collectively or individually choose to access international rights and incur responsibilities or duties; the ICP describes the subcategory of MNEs that can do so.

I will use both terms – MNE and ICP – frequently throughout this book. The MNE describes a category into which an enterprise falls when its controversies revolve around ownership and control, and the acquisition or transfer of property and capital. The ICP describes the process of acquisition or the characteristic of having acquired, not property or capital, but legal abstractions – rights and duties. Of course, concepts of property, ownership, and control play an important role in how we theorize the ICP, but the ICP itself is more of a concept than a category.

The ICP *must possess* an ILP but it is also *legally distinct* from the ILP, which includes States and any other actors that can be considered subject to the *in personam* jurisdiction of international law. As such, the ILP describes the category of actors into which the ICP falls, that is, the ICP is a type of ILP. The literature on non-State ILPs tends to describe entities that are concerned with the acquisition and use of rights under international law.[6] As with most ILPs, it is difficult to determine precisely how rights might correlate to accompanying obligations under international law in the case of business enterprises. The seminal case on non-State ILPs – the International Court of Justice's (ICJ's) *Reparations for Injuries* Advisory Opinion – sets out a four part test to identify a non-State ILP: (1) an independent or autonomous existence, (2) the ability to possess international rights or obligations, (3) the actual possession of those rights and obligations, and (4) the ability to enforce rights on the international plain. There is no international treaty that explicitly defines the contours of the ICP, but judges and arbitrators in recent years increasingly find that MNEs possess an ILP. And as I demonstrate in this book, some have gone so far as to treat them conceptually as ICPs.

The ILP primarily describes 'States, armed groups, and individuals,'[7] with the ICP falling under the category of 'individuals'. However, the rights and obligations accorded to ICPs distinct from other organizational and natural individuals.[8] As a judge-made phenomenon, the ICP features dimensions never statutorily accorded to business enterprises; they are treated in some ways as human but never fully human. Chapters 2, 3, and 4 detail the legal and theoretical dimensions of this phenomenon, but for now let us simply note four important elements that render ICPs distinct from other ILPs:

(1) The purpose of any ICP primarily is to serve the interests of its shareholders, which are often themselves ICPs whereas the ILP is presupposed to possess a primarily political personality. Obviously, the ICP is also a political actor but it does not hold any legally prescribed political power and its reasons for engaging in politics spring solely from its economic interests.

(2) Although domestic laws governing corporations often (if superficially) require corporations to serve a definable public purpose, and while ILPs exist often to serve interests of a defined public (even if global), the ICP in its entirety serves no fixed definable public and therefore has no definable public purpose (though it could serve a public purpose if the public were defined).

(3) While ILPs such as states or the UN have fixed avenues through which they can exercise influence on international law, ICPs have no fixed process for this, and therefore exercise influence in a variety of un- or under-regulated, opaque channels.

(4) Quite distinct from ILPs such as States, which are established as subjects of international law and can therefore incur theoretically inescapable obligations to legal and natural persons, an ICP can expand, contract, and reshape at will, creating, dissolving, distancing, or redefining its obligations to other ILPs and to the citizens of any given state in which it may operate.

II. The corporate trinity: state, Church, company

While the emergence of both the present international legal order and the cluster of legal technologies that give form to the ICP are relatively recent phenomena, understanding MNEs requires that we view them as emerging to a degree from the multinational corporate model set out by the Dutch East India Company (VOC) and the British East India Company (BEIC) around the turn of the 17th Century and the birth of the modern Westphalian State around 1648.[9] The colonial corporation and the Westphalian State can both be understood as divisions of a more centralized sovereignty that was characteristic of Feudalism. The increasingly diverse sources of legitimacy of authority for State, Corporate, and Church actors can be seen as driving these divisions. In very broad strokes, the State increasingly gleaned authority from its ability to defend its public, that is, the public interest, from external and internal hostilities; the corporation gleaned its authority from its ability to enrich the State, that is, territorial extensions of sovereignty and police power amplified for the VOC and BEIC as tax revenues proved vast; and the Church gleaned its authority from God, who also gave the King unconditional authority to rule through Divine Right (in contrast to the conditional rule granted by China's Mandate of Heaven).[10] While by now the Church has drifted away from this holy trinity of public organization, the dance between the corporation and the State – and the ways in which law grafts form onto them – is ever vibrant.[11] The Westphalian system can therefore be viewed as setting into motion a compartmentalization of the legal responsibilities and duties of public entities within a polity, including (at that time) the corporation. One might say the Church, the State, and the Company were all corporations that served the discreet spiritual, security, and economic needs of a polity, respectively.

It is therefore puzzling that, for many years, the corporation remained largely absent from most histories of international law's authorship. Fortunately, some recent work on Grotius, scholars at the Salamanca School, Oppenheim, Vattel, and other 'Great Men' of international law has brought to the fore many of the corporate and private monetary interests that undergirded the professed 'universal' principles of these thinkers.[12] These principles furnished justification for the advent and expansion of colonialism, conceptions of property that transferred resource wealth from the poor to the rich, and in many cases facilitated a slow transfer of legal authority from State to Business Enterprise. The experience of the VOC and the BEIC as evolving from corporate form to para-State to empire before ultimate dissolution provides a hindsight overview of the many State-to-MNE dances that are presently occurring, though with compartmentalized interests across a far broader range of companies and actors.[13] Both the VOC and the BEIC – and, later, the Virginia Company – used the corporate form to pursue profit interests free from disruptions caused by changes in ownership; unlike partners, shareholders were interchangeable. And all three companies progressed from small shareholder groups petitioning the State for charters to extend and exercise sovereignty to para-States with private militias and vast political influence. Fascinating histories on each of these companies are referenced in the endnotes.[14] But here I wish to briefly review a few of the 'Great Men'–sponsored legal principles that formed the bedrock of these international commercial conquests. The oldest school that is thought to have influenced (if not founded) modern international legal thought is Salamanca, whose influential Thomist theologian jurists included Francisco de Vitoria. In the 1530s, Vitoria was the first international legal scholar to draw a distinction between personal morality and commercial morality. He did so by posing the following question to his students:

> You are a captain of a ship full of grain, and you are headed to a port in a country where there has been famine for a long time. You arrive at the port and you see the people coming with their money in their hands, and they want to buy the grain that is in your ship. You, as the captain, know that in the distance of two days of sailing, there are tens of other ships on their way to this same port, loaded with grain as well. Do you have the duty to disclose to your clients what you know?[15]

Vitoria answered this question in the following way:

> If you are ordinary men and women, then of course you have to tell these starving people that there are other ships with grain coming. This means that the price of your grain will go down, down, down, down. But that is your duty to the people closest to you. [But i]f you are a commerçant, a merchant, then, well, it is not that clear.[16]

In doing so, Vitoria drew a distinction between personal and commercial morality. On this view, there is a 'natural law' that governs morality between natural persons and another that governs economic relations and commercial transactions.

As an early career advocate and lobbyist for the VOC, Grotius built from Vitoria's notion that commercial transactions or, more specifically, free trade at sea was a natural right endowed by God. Freedom of trade understood as freedom of the seas took on a salvationist quality: monopolies over the seas led to war, but free trade over sea would unite the world in peace.

Thus, Grotius found that war was just where it served to correct violations of this freedom, and by the same token, private property could not be confiscated on the mere grounds that it belonged to a non-Christian people. The VOC therefore could justifiably attack Portuguese merchants whose crown claimed monopoly over the seas; it could also enter into trade relationships with non-Christian peoples, which was previously thought to be sacrilegious.[17] This 'economic theology' (as Giorgio Agamben has called it) both complements and wrestles with Carl Schmitt's 'political theology' of the State – the claim that Sovereignty from the monotheistic worldview: the Sovereign parallels the notion of an omnipotent God and all organs of the State reflect secularized institutions of the Church.[18] The economic theology Grotius espoused in the service of the VOC viewed a global freedom of commercial exchange as a secularized embodiment of 'heaven on earth', salvation – freedom defined in liberal terms is the highest value and goal.[19] Grotius's economic theology in turn influenced Adam Smith's understanding of economic forces (as evidenced by frequent citations to Grotius), who in turn influenced the construction of legal and economic knowledges that inform the structure of our present. Indeed the turbulence we witness at the WTO or amongst Western and Eastern political theologies in our time is not new.[20] Liberal free trade and sovereign protectionism have been involved in a hydraulic relationship almost from the outset.

For Vattel, economic morality reflected human morality: a product of responses to emotional needs. Writing in the mid-1750s, Vattel's characterizations of human beings as being fundamentally self-interested predated Smith's rational choice theory by about two decades, and Smith also paid credence to Vattel through citations. Vattel's foundational text took human needs rather than divine law as the starting point for developing a theory of legitimacy for the international legal order. His key innovation was the characterization of the State a 'moral person', that is, endowed with moral faculties of intellect and will.[21] However, Vattel's view of the individual was considerably more nuanced than his initial economist followers understood – Vattel did not view individuals as individually seeking to increase pleasure in a vacuum but rather understood them as simultaneously internal and external actors. That is, individuals could be simultaneously motivated by two self-interested rationales – one that sought to maximize internal happiness and another that sought to maximize the happiness of the community. This understanding, for Vattel, transferred also to the State, which he understood as acting simultaneously in internal self-interest (for its citizens) and external communal interests (for the good of humanity through peace and economic prosperity). Within this framework, morality, reason, love, and other human values were responses to emotional needs determined more by time and circumstance than adherence to any objective moral or 'natural' law.[22] This analogy was convenient in an age of colonization and conquest: just as Vattel's natural law held that individuals had an internal duty to preserve and protect themselves and an external interest in perfecting the community for individual interest, States had an internal duty to protect and perfect themselves but no external duty to protect others.[23] In fact, the external interest in perfecting was valid only insofar as it served the internal duty to perfect.[24] Thus, States should strive to act internationally in a manner that maximizes internal perfection and external harmony with that goal. For Vattel, each State was a 'corporate "nation-person"' endowed with its own unique moral nature. And each corporate nation-person was bound to serve that unique moral nature and treat external relations as faculties in service to that goal.[25] It is difficult to understate the influence of Vattel's text upon U.S. constitutional 'founding fathers' such as Jefferson, Adams, Hamilton, and Madison.[26]

More recently, Martti Koskeinnemi has convincingly argued that Vattel, Grotius, and the Salamanca thinkers cannot really be said to have 'founded' international law in the modern sense.[27] Koskeinnemi places the 'founding' more directly in accession to texts that share international understandings of subjectivity and legal personality, especially the laws of war texts that bubbled up in the mid-1800s. These texts distinctly understood international law as the law governing relationships between States. But States themselves were referred to as 'corporations' or even 'corporate persons' with regularity in English treatises on international law up until the first World War (in line with the Organic Theory of corporate personhood described in a following section).[28] This use of 'corporations as States' was not due to a lack of familiarity with business corporations. In texts such as William Edward Hall's 1890 classic *Treatise on International Law* or even earlier in Emer de Vattel's 1758 foundational *The Law of Nations (Le Droit Des Gens)*, passages on the personality of the state vis-à-vis other international actors exude the impression that lawyers of the 18th and early 19th century found the greatest legal distinctions between corporations and States in technocratic administration rather than in the theoretical underpinnings of the entity, for example, sovereignty.[29] States and businesses often appear as two different types of corporations – different but complementary sovereigns. The 'dizygotic relationship' of the corporation to the State seems assumed. Perhaps this was because British and American corporations of the time were in fact less legally distinct from the State than the corporations of today. That is, the legal (if nominal) purpose for both entities was to serve the public.

So what changed? At least part of the answer lies in an interpretive departure from a traditional understanding of how the legal technology of the corporation interacts with the concept of sovereignty. As mentioned, the legal evolution of both states and corporations were linked to the early Christian Church. The Church was both the earliest known instance of what could be called a corporate person and what many historians consider a catalyst to the advent of the territorial State in the modern international system (though this account has been valiantly contested).[30,31] As the story often goes, the extraterritorial rights of Christians to practice their religion in non-Christian territories was one of the central issues that spurred the Thirty Years War, which in turn led to the Peace of Westphalia. This was the treaty that first separated territory from religion, resulting in what international relations scholars have traditionally (even if mythically)[32] identified as the birth of modern sovereignty, and by the same coin, the advent of international law. For as long as there have been States possessing Westphalian sovereignty – that is, territorial sovereignty coupled with the principle of non-interference in domestic affairs – there have been rules governing the relations between them. These rules compartmentalized the Church-as-corporation: while it held sway as a legal actor within the international system, it held no sovereignty in the territorial sense. Like the State, it was composed of persons, but unlike the State, the persons from whom it was composed acceded to its authority through belief rather than by virtue of birth or physical location. In other words, as a corporation, the Church had *imperium* (authority over people) without *dominium* (authority over territory or things). In this original sense, it is unclear whether the corporation's authority derived from the State or the State's authority derived from the corporation, that is, the Church. Perhaps the Westphalian concept of sovereignty most clearly attaches to the ability to create and enforce law,[33] regardless of whether that ability is tied to a particular territory.

What changed in the mid-19th century was that Courts began to treat corporations less as 'personalities' and more as 'people'. This phenomenon began in the United States shortly after the Civil War as a result of an off-the-cuff headnote in a court reporter's note to an 1886 judicial opinion concerning the 14th Amendment.[34] That headnote did not accurately describe the opinion but was nevertheless cited as authoritative in subsequent cases which eventually led to the corpus of cases that today enshrine the U.S. concept of corporate personhood: corporations can enter into contracts, access legal remedies, and exercise rights in the same way natural persons can. Whereas domestically, at least in the United States, this concept allows corporations to be treated as citizens, internationally the corporation is often understood as an entity that is closer to the State. As I argue in the coming chapters, however, the corporation's 'personhood' and the State's 'legal personality' are perhaps better understood as overlapping sovereignties with different constituencies. This argument draws much inspiration from Joshua Barkan,[35] whose book *Corporate Sovereignty* acutely demonstrates that both corporate 'personhood' and State 'personality' are rooted in a power that belongs exclusively to sovereign entities: the power to choose to exempt oneself from law.

Another factor that drove change was the rise of shareholder primacy, especially after WWII. Whereas corporations were once thought to serve a public purpose – indeed were at one point only created and sustained if they could prove that they served a public purpose[36] – corporate models changed as publicly traded companies emerged and shareholders became more numerous and more diverse. No longer were shareholders small groups of wealthy investors who put up large sums of money to support corporate ventures. In the United States, the rise of public trading, the Securities Act, the Securities Exchange Act, and the establishment of the Securities and Exchange Commission (SEC) in the interwar period enabled much broader sourcing of capital by centralizing public trading law and requiring disclosure of material information.[37] Now shareholders no longer needed to share a plan, purpose, nationality, class, or form; they no longer needed to share any interests at all apart from one: making money. Whereas during the colonial era shareholder status belonged only to small groups of capitalist elites, it now became increasingly accessible to the public. Moreover, rather than thinking of shareholder status as the status of owning an 'interest' in a company, shareholders began to think of themselves as collectively owning the company itself. Thus, in the 1930s, two law professors – Adolph Berle and Merrick Dodd – publicly hashed out the question of corporate purpose in relation to shareholders in the pages of the *Harvard Law Review*, Berle arguing that a corporation was the property of the shareholders and, as such, should serve their economically construct 'best interest', Dodd arguing that corporations are publicly constructed economic institutions and, as such, they should concern themselves with the economic interests of employees, customers, and the public at large. Amongst the interwar corporate community in the United States, building on the 1919 Michigan case of *Dodge v. Ford* and a string of Delaware cases,[38] Berle's arguments held more sway. Berle's scholarship, the Michigan case, and a string of subsequent cases reinforced shareholder primacy at the same time as they affirmed the business judgment rule for managers, maintaining a strict separation between ownership and control. By the 1970s, the shareholder primacy theory of corporate governance had become the accepted (if not the legal) truth. Perhaps this was best encapsulated in Milton Friedman's famous 1970 essay, 'The Social Responsibility of Business is to Increase its Profits'.[39] In that essay, and in the midst of the Cold War, Friedman argued that the idea that corporations have any purpose apart from increasing profits is not only undemocratic because it supports what would amount to a unilateral tax on shareholders, it is also 'socialist' because it 'involves the acceptance of the socialist view that political mechanisms, not market mechanisms, are the appropriate way to determine the allocation of scarce resources to alternative uses'. True to form, Friedman did not seem to grasp that the market mechanisms to which he refers are themselves politically constructed.

Today, shareholder primacy is internationalized. Although ICPs have different constraints in different States, and although CSR movements supported by big institutional investors like Blackrock have promoted stakeholder rather than shareholder primacy,[40] the dominant view remains that an ICP's primary purpose is to increase profits for shareholders. And although, as Vitoria has shown, international law has always held dual moralities for humans as opposed to merchants, the ICP's landscape today has changed since the pre-WTO fledgling-ICSID days of Friedman (let alone Vitoria). On the international stage, ICPs create internal normative legal orders much like

States yet operate in economically constructed 'self-interest' in social and economic contexts that transcend the State. They are supranational specters of the political State that both shape and are shaped by it. When a State subsidizes its airplane manufacturers or its farms,[41] or when a State requires that cans of tuna caught with non-ecofriendly nets be labelled,[42] or when a State bans the sale of Seal pelts,[43] or when a State bans online gambling while permitting physical casinos,[44] another State's ICPs will be harmed by those actions and that those ICPs can petition that State to file a request for WTO consultations. At the same time, almost half of the world's international trade takes place within ICPs, and discrimination within that space is within the control of the ICP, even if the structure of a foreign ICP enables it to undercut all domestic players in a given State.[45] International trade law cannot touch an ICP whose supply and global value chains (GVCs) span the globe and whose internal trade enables it to bring together individual parts at a lesser cost than any domestically operating producer. In these and similar ways, ICPs encompass economies that transcend States but can mobilize international law through States to undermine domestic legislation that harms ICPs, even if the domestic legislation serves the public interest. Shareholders thus serve as a sort of alternate constituency for State action through the proxy of the corporation. These ICP shareholders are often scattered throughout the globe, are often ICPs themselves, and are often detached from the political actions of the ICP, whether by geographic, political, or cultural distance, or by ignorance of the fact that they are even shareholders in a particular ICP, which the advent of wealth management firms readily facilitates. In sum, ICPs have political power without commensurate attachment to a definable political community. The geographic, economic, ideological, and physiological dispersement of shareholders creates in the place of genuine political interest singular sets of interests that are predefined or assumed by corporate managers and directors.

III. A brief history of corporate personhood in three phases

Understanding how the international corporate person functions today requires a basic knowledge of its ancestors beyond the Church – namely, colonial companies. While legal historians continue to debate the precise characteristics and significance of international corporate form at different times, what follows is what I venture to call a 'broad strokes consensus' on three major phases in international corporate development. These phases are broad summaries, with time periods sometimes overlapping, intended as background to provide greater Context for the present concept of the ICP.

a. The Magistrate Charter Phase: pre-1850

The 16th and 17th centuries saw the advent and evolution of the joint-stock corporation – a legal technology that allowed for owners of a company to buy and sell portions of ownership (usually represented by a certificate) building upon earlier single-ownership or fixed-partnership models.[46] Following from this basis, because portions of ownership could be transferred without any effect on the existence of the company, the corporation narrowed its proximity to the structure of the Church, both possessing varying shades of immortality. The Chartered Company was one important type of joint-stock corporation. It is particularly notable because it facilitated much of the extraterritorial legal framework underpinning the European colonial era. This phase in the development of the MNE – the Magistrate Charter Phase – is characterized by direct, explicit linkage to a 'home state', not just through use of its capital, but also through use of its monopoly on violence. Chartered corporations were partially owned by the state, could extend the police powers of the state, and could call upon the state to dispatch military force. I am here using the language of modern-day international investment law, in which the 'home state' is the state in which an investor is headquartered or based while the destination state of the investment is referred to as the 'host state'. This language highlights the red line between today's MNEs and the earliest MNEs, even though 'home states' no longer explicitly vest extraterritorial sovereign powers through Royal Charters to companies abroad.

Many histories of the modern multinational corporation place its first incarnation to the mid–19th century United States, and therefore, they leave out earlier colonial forms of international corporate engagement.[47] These included the English and Dutch East India Companies mentioned in the Introduction, and other major 16th- and 17th-century companies such as the Muscovy Company, the Hudson's Bay Company, and the Royal African Company. One conventional narrative regarding these companies from UK and U.S. academics, at least until very recently, was that the colonial-era companies could not be considered MNEs. That narrative assured its audience that MNEs could divorce themselves from any link to the legally-blessed company structures of the past because modern MNEs are defined by two distinguishing characteristics: (1) a volume of international transactions to which the colonial-era companies failed to rise and (2) a managerial hierarchical structure in which direction of and control over the company are decided by larger groups of professionals rather than small numbers of owner–managers.[48] The conventional narrative also distinguishes colonial-era corporations from present ones. As the argument goes, modern commercial intercourse is characterized by contract rather than coercion: although colonial-era companies certainly transacted with their 'home state', the volume of contracted transactions on record is markedly lower than even the smallest MNEs of today. Moreover, although colonial-era companies were often (though not always) headquartered in their 'home state', they simply lacked the communicative and technological infrastructure to exert direct control over company activities in the 'host state'.

That part of the mainline narrative is misleading for at least two reasons. First, it depends upon a definition of transaction that assumes each transaction would be facilitated by a separate contract, with definite volumes of goods, services, and other parameters prescribed. But this simply is not how colonial-era companies conceived of transactions.[49] Rather, companies in a host State would enter into single contracts with a parent in the home State, and on the basis of this guarantee a vast (albeit difficult to specify) volume of individual transactions cross borders.[50] And second, although it is true that colonial-era managers often owned a significant share in the companies whereas modern MNE managers rarely own more than an insignificant number of shares, the lack of legal technologies aligning management incentives with corporate goals without granting significant shares did not prevent these companies from developing complex and hierarchical management structures connected directly to the home State. The hierarchies reached across States, with day-to-day operations delegated to onsite managers with major strategic decisions concentrated in home State management. The historical context was different, so obviously these companies were not structured precisely like modern MNEs, but similarities are nevertheless clear. As Carlos and Nicholas note:

> For the Hudson's Bay Company, each factory was managed by a chief factor, who carried out the trade with the Indians, managed the day-to-day operations of the post, and oversaw the general workers, or servants. One chief factor, answerable to the Court of Directors in London through the correspondence committee, was appointed with control over all the factories on the bay. The English East India Company's Court was served by subcommittees for accounts, buying, private trade, presidencies, shipping, and treasure; the Dutch East India Company has committees for receipts, equipment of ships, accounting, commerce, and correspondence. The home-based managers of the Dutch company corresponded with the Batavia [present-day Jakarta] Government, and those of the English company corresponded with President [sic] and his Council in each of the company's separate trading regions in Asia; these in turn controlled local managers in branch factories.[51]

The colonial-era companies thus provided foundational characteristics that foreshadowed modern MNEs in a number of ways, *inter alia*, cross-border transactions through sales or production branches in two or more countries;[52] administrative hierarchical structures that dispersed authority efficiently toward the goal of easing cross-border transactions;[53] and ownership structures that ensured exportation of capital or 'profit' from 'host' state to 'home',[54] or to be redirected as seen fit by 'home' state management.[55]

Most of the colonial joint-stock giants had disbanded or substantially downsized by the turn of the 19th century, with the notable exception of the BEIC which held out until 1858. Apart from these giants, few firms in the United States or Europe had widespread international operations until the mid-1850s. While American firms actively sought and benefitted from export markets – notably European markets for slave-produced cotton and tobacco[56] – few sought to transplant operations or production to other states. In fact, some American firms – such as those whose revenue depended on intellectual property appropriated from European counterparts (e.g., American publishing houses printing Charles Dickens novels) – benefitted from a legal landscape that allowed uncompensated use of foreign property, and therefore had little or nothing to gain by expanding markets abroad.[57] Moreover, as the next subsection details, until the early- to mid-1900s the partnership form was preferable to the corporate form for business ventures in the United States and the UK unless the business venture served a clear public purpose. When the first modern MNEs emerged onto the scene in America, the cross-border activity was largely limited to transactions between the United States and one or a few countries in Latin America. Perhaps because early U.S. citizens tended to view the corporate form with some suspicion,[58] it took the better part of a century for the U.S. corporation's initially strict 'public purpose' charter to evolve into the post-WWII MNEs that dominate the world today. In the words of the 1837–1838 Pennsylvania delegation to the *Dartmouth College* decision, from which the modern tension between corporate and State power flows:[59] 'Whatever power is given to the corporation, is just so much power taken away from the State, in derogation of the original power of the mass of the community'.[60]

b. The public charter phase: 1850–1945

Although it inherited the legal technology of the corporation from the UK, the growth of the 1850s ICP in the 20th century is a story that revolves around the United States. The first characteristic of the modern corporate form – a joint stock company with tradable shares made available to the general public – arose statutorily in the UK in 1844;[61] when some U.S. states added limited liability to this form in the early 1850s and when the UK added it in 1855,[62] the modern corporation was born.

Initially, in the United States and elsewhere, corporate charters were only granted to those business enterprises that could demonstrate some specific public purpose. The justification for limited liability was simple: the law wished to incentivize business organizations to undertake the financial risk necessary to innovate and execute large infrastructural projects. Legal personality and limited liability enabled corporations to specialize and improve within the bounds of the public purpose for which they were created. When a corporation no longer served a public purpose, governments could – and often did – revoke a corporation's charter. Different U.S. states had different manners of determining 'public purpose' (sometimes more political than practical) and the practice of revoking public charters had largely faded by the early 1900s. This trend aligned with a series of Supreme Court decisions that favored a proliferation of access to the corporate form: increasing the number of small businesses that could incorporate meant that the benefits of limited liability would not be hoarded by a powerful few.[63] The early corporate form in this way incorporated a check on the concentration of its own power, but its proliferation had the effect of generalizing the 'purpose' of the corporate form. 'Public purpose' could be broadly construed; after all, any innovation or attempt to generate economic activity could be construed through some lens as a benefit to the public.

The structure described in the first phase – magistrate charters granted to colonial companies – continued to influence corporate structure as it crystalized in domestic law across the globe. Indeed, to this day, the colonizer–colonized relationship remains an important determinant for whether international trade, investment, and cross-jurisdictional corporate operations will flounder or flourish. Indeed, the United States continues to benefit by proxy to the Crown's colonial engagements. In business literature concerned with the international expansion and 'administrative distance',[64] some studies have shown that characteristics such as common commercial language, common legal system characteristics, common polities, regional trading blocs, and other features facilitated by a historically colonizer–colonized relationship made international trade about 900% more likely, amongst other metrics.[65]

By the early 1900s, corporate law in all of the world's major commercial jurisdictions (mostly colonizers and former colonizers) had converged around a set of core legal innovations: (1) legal personality, including the authority to bind the firm to contracts and to bond those contracts with assets that belong to the firm rather than property of individual owners; (2) limited liability for owners and managers; (3) shared ownership by investors of capital; (4) delegated management under a board structure; and (5) transferrable shares, creating a sort of immortal form of ownership.[66] While debates regarding corporate purpose and the legal structure of corporate ownership have swung largely between the three poles of labor, state, and shareholder primacy, the five core innovations listed previously remain largely unchallenged in international legal systems.[67]

Quietly at first, the ICP was born during the 'public charter' period in U.S. jurisprudence. While corporate law in the United States is largely the *de jure* domain of States and *de facto* domain of Delaware, the question of to whom or to what constitutional rights are owed is a question that belongs to the U.S. Federal Courts, that is, the District and Circuit Courts and the Supreme Court. A few years after the U.S. Civil War ended in 1865, the U.S. Congress adopted the Reconstruction Amendments to the U.S. Constitution – the 13th Amendment abolished slavery and involuntary servitude (except for those convicted of a crime) and the 15th Amendment sought to secure voting rights for previously enslaved men.[68] The 14th Amendment today is a famous fixture in American constitutional jurisprudence largely because of its Equal

Protection and Due Process clauses; less famous, perhaps, is the choice of the word 'persons' to indicate the beneficiaries of those clauses. The full text of Section 1 of the 14th Amendment reads:

> All persons born or naturalized in the United States, and subject to the jurisdiction thereof, are citizens of the United States and of the State wherein they reside. No State shall make or enforce any law which shall abridge the privileges or immunities of citizens of the United States; nor shall any State deprive any person of life, liberty, or property, without due process of law; nor deny to any person within its jurisdiction the equal protection of the laws.[69]

Setting aside the controversies that gave rise to the Amendment, the question of to whom the text itself applied was relatively uncontroversial until all but one of its drafters had died. However, the final living drafter – a lawyer by the name of Roscoe Conkling, whose close ties to the Southern Pacific Railroad Company were well known – changed the course of history when he cited excerpts from his diary to convince an 1882 Supreme Court that the word 'persons' rather than 'men' or 'human beings' was chosen deliberately so that the rights enshrined in the 14th Amendment would apply to corporations as well as to freed slaves.[70] As legal historian Adam Winkler puts it:

> [E]veryone knew when it was ratified in 1868 [that] the amendment's guarantees of equal protection and due process were designed to secure the rights of the newly freed slaves and protect them from discrimination by the states. Nearly a decade and a half later, however, in December of 1882, the esteemed Roscoe Conkling told the justices the Fourteenth Amendment was also written to protect the rights of corporations like his client, the Southern Pacific Railroad Company.[71]

The text of the case itself – *Santa Clara County v. Southern Pacific Railroad Company*[72] – included no dispositive legal discussion on the definition of 'person', yet the summary written by the court reporter and included with the published case asserted Conkling's definition as law. And just as many footnotes and dicta have proven in common law courts to overshadow the legal reasoning in case from which they sprung (what I anecdotally call 'reasons without reason'), so too did the court reporter's understanding of what unfolded in *Southern Pacific* overshadow the actual law discussed in subsequent opinions. In *Santa Clara*'s day, court reporters drafted summaries that were 'headnotes to the opinions of this Court [but] not the work of this Court. [They] are simply the work of the Reporter, giving his understanding of the decision, prepared for the convenience of the profession'.[73] The relevant part of the summary reads:

> The defendant Corporations are persons within the intent of the clause in section 1 of the Fourteenth Amendment to the Constitution of the United States, which forbids a state to deny to any person within its jurisdiction the equal protection of the laws. One of the points made and discussed at length in the brief of counsel for defendants in error was that "corporations are persons within the meaning of the Fourteenth Amendment to the Constitution of the United States." Before argument, Mr. Chief Justice Waite said: "The Court does not wish to hear argument on the question whether the provision in the Fourteenth Amendment to the Constitution which forbids a state to deny to any person within its jurisdiction the equal protection of the laws applies to these corporations. We are all of the opinion that it does."[74]

Absent a careful reading of the entire *Southern Pacific* decision, a busy lawyer skimming summaries for relevant law would likely understand that the question was thus decided, that the definition of 'person' was uncontroversial. But the truth was that the Chief Justice had merely directed lawyers to argue other, less-controversial points in the case.[75] Nevertheless, through subsequent decisions that relied on the summary rather than the legal opinion, 'person' came to include corporations without any foundation in solid legal argument.[76] In this way, corporate personhood can be described as judge-made law in the purest sense – not in *Southern Pacific* itself but in the cases that cited *Southern Pacific* as the source of corporate personhood – because it is a legal concept entirely lacking a statutory basis; it is a legal fiction crystalized and perpetuated (but not devised) by judges. About a decade later, in the now infamous case of *Plessy v. Ferguson*,[77] the same Court interpreting the same Amendment found that racial segregation was not unequal within the meaning of the equal protection clause as mere separation did not necessitate inequality amongst races.

For a long while, the corporate personhood decisions confined themselves to obscure corners of American corporate law. There was little demand for legal structures governing international corporate forms; the MNE in those days was either an enterprise spanning fewer than a handful of jurisdictions or a colonial enterprise. Moreover, the interwar period – with its massive economic depressions and political instabilities – stalled the expansion of the MNE and therefore its legal development. One study sampling the UK's largest 448 MNEs in the decade preceding WWII found that 31% of multinationals had operations in only one country apart from its home State. Nevertheless, the seeds of the international corporate person, with all of their potential to hold, create, and activate international rights, were planted during this phase.

The Corporate Charter Phase can thus be summarized as a convergence of two movements. On the one hand was a movement toward defining corporate purpose in broader terms. This movement served the interests of smaller organizations insofar as it granted limited liability to a larger variety of business endeavors and served the interests of larger organizations insofar as it allowed them to diversify the nature of their operations. On the other hand was a movement toward full legal personality for corporations in virtually all the world's major commercial jurisdictions. Before this era, resistance toward full personality was often rooted in the uncomfortable dissonance between granting fictional legal entities personality without granting personality to humans, such as women, immigrants, felons, and slaves. In the United States at least, the Civil War eroded resistance to that idea. In fact, the very Amendment which sought to assign full legal personhood to freed slaves also created it for corporations, even though the Supreme Court never addressed the question head on. But it was not until the post-WWII era – with the advent of private-sector personhood in the 1950s and exploding in the 1990s, and the rise of shareholder primacy in the 1970s moving to dominance in the 1980s – that corporate personhood manifested fully in U.S. corporate law and internationalized through U.S. corporate power and legal influence.

c. The personhood phase: post-1945

While both the modern MNE and the concept of corporate personhood began in the mid-1850s United States, they did not begin to merge until the post-WWII period. As late as 1949, in a *Columbia Law Review* article, Justice Douglas reaffirmed in passing a faulty understanding of precedent that continued to guide post-WWII decisions on corporate rights: the 'natural truth' that corporations were 'persons' according to the 14th Amendment.[78] The internationalization of this process occurred initially through the collapsing 'legal persons' and 'natural persons' into the single category of 'investor' in international investment agreements, starting with the first bilateral investment treaty between Germany and Pakistan in 1959 (an early example of public law curated by private-sector brokers such as Hermann Abs of Deutsche Bank,[79] discussed later in this book).[80]

Corporate personhood as presently understood did not emerge with *Southern Pacific* but did emerge from similarly obscure, initially non-binding roots. Before WWII, U.S. Supreme Court jurisprudence maintained the 'clear distinction' between corporate and natural persons.[81] For instance, in the 1906 case of *Hale v. Hankel*, Justice Brown described the corporation as 'a creature of the state' that received 'certain special privileges and franchises', contrasted with natural persons who 'owe no duty to the State to divulge [their] business'.[82] During the Lochner Era – most famous for its brazen insistence on freedom of contract to the extent that restrictions on working hours and child labor were held unconstitutional – the Court consistently held that corporate persons were entitled only to rights associated with property, not to political rights such as free speech or freedom of association.[83] While the

Court also made this property-political distinction when it came to the rights of natural persons, it did not categorically deny either set of rights to natural persons. Corporations began to acquire political rights through a process similar to their acquisition of 'personhood' – Footnote 4 in the famed 1938 Supreme Court case of *United States v. Caroline Products* set out in dicta different standards of scrutiny the Court ought to apply to different types of cases (it would take about two decades for the dicta to reappear as binding precedent in *Brow v. Board of Education*).[84,85] Volumes have been written on the Court's shift from the protection of private property rights to the protection of public political rights during the post-WWII era and particularly during the Civil Rights Movement in the 1950s and 1960s. One consequence of this shift was that corporations – through cases such as *NAACP v. Button*,[86] *Grosjean v. American Press*,[87] and *Virginia Pharmacy Board v. Virginia Citizens Consumers Council*[88] – were able to attain similar levels of constitutional protection. The process started with news corporations fighting laws that suppressed speech (e.g., *Near v. Minnesota*)[89] but set a precedent that began to collapse the public-private divide. The corporation was no longer solely a public entity, a creature of the State, granted privileges rooted in its service to the public. It was also a private entity, a bearer of rights, and these applied to all corporate persons, regardless of form or product. In chronological order, the most important post-WWII cases that led from *Southern Pacific* to the political-rights-holding present of the corporate person – ones that have been extensively analyzed by other scholars[90] – are *Buckley v. Valeo*,[91] *First National Bank of Boston v. Bellotti*,[92] *Austin v. Michigan Chamber of Commerce*,[93] *Boy Scouts of America v. Dale*,[94] *McConnell v. Federal Election Commission*,[95] *Federal Election Commission v. Wisconsin Right to Life*,[96] *Citizens United v. Federal Election Commission*,[97] *United States v. Sourapas and Crest Beverage Co.*,[98] *Western Tradition Partnership v. Attorney General of Montana*,[99] and *Burwell v. Hobby Lobby*.[100] The summary result of these decisions is that corporations today have many of the same political rights as natural persons, but two important caveats remain. First, if an organization is private or closely held, then the rights of the organization prevail over the rights of its employees. This was the case in *Boy Scouts of America*, where the non-profit organization excluded Dale on the basis of its First Amendment right to freedom of association prevailed over Dale's; and it was the case with *Hobby Lobby*, in which the closely held corporation's 1st Amendment right to practice its religion prevailed over the rights of employees entitled to contraceptives through the Affordable Care Act. Second, if the right claimed by the corporation is not one that is exercisable as a group right, the Court may find that the corporation does not hold that right. This was the case in *Sourapas* where the Court found that a corporation could not exercise the 5th Amendment right to self-incrimination because that was an 'individual right'. At their core, these are theoretically contradictory understandings of what a corporate person is, as discussed in the 'Three Conceptions' section that follows.

Against this backdrop, it is fair to conclude that corporate personhood did not emerge as a friend to the powerful but as a legal tool mobilized to break up powerful monopolies, cartels, and trusts and to access, via the 14th Amendment's Due Process clause, the arsenal of political rights set out in the 1st, 4th, and 5th Amendments. Notwithstanding these roots, the acquisition of human rights without the usual constraints associated with being human proved useful to large MNEs over time. The phenomenon puts lawyers in a bind: on the one hand, critics of the ICP who call for duties to match the rights in a sense legitimate the rights ICPs have acquired – legitimate the legal (liberal) category of 'personhood' for corporations in the first place.[101] (To be clear, I use the term ICP to describe a phenomenon within the category of MNEs, not in order to endorse the assignment of liberal economic values to legal fictions.) On the other hand, those who insist that officiating international duties through law would lead ICPs to (legitimately) claim and create more international rights are often forced to accept 'veil piercing' as a legitimate shield to international corporate liability. Issues such as these will be discussed further in Chapter 4; more than anything, they highlight the need for a clear and broadly held articulation of 'purpose' – not corporate purpose per se but ICP purpose specifically.

Questions of personhood and purpose are closely intertwined insofar as differing conceptions of the former create different sets of contradictions with respect to the latter. For example, one can think of the rights associated with corporate personhood as flowing from and reflecting the rights of the shareholders, in which case speech rights and special taxation rules for the corporation make sense but criminal sanctions do not. Conversely, one can think of the corporation as a person distinct from shareholders with human rights all its own, in which case criminal penalties are consistent with the law's treatment of other human rights holders, yet other legal technologies like pass-through taxation or circular ownership create dissonance in the analogy.

The conventional view in public international law is that the corporation is a 'personality' but not a 'person'. Most of the world's domestic jurisdictions treat corporations in this way even while international courts erode that understanding. (A description of this erosion occupies much of the next two chapters.) This view understands the MNE as something closer to a para-State or para-Institution (i.e., an organization representing a shared community of interest), but not so much a para-Individual. It is within this understanding that shareholder primacy holds the most theoretical sway, but shareholder primacy within this understanding nevertheless needs an update considering the internationalized nature of the MNE. The idea that shareholders share any common interests is a misnomer, and the globalized and multilayered nature of their interests does not necessitate 'profit' as the only suitable broad abstraction upon which 'purpose' can be built. Moreover, corporate interdependence calls for a more nuanced understanding of shareholder interests; the global supply chains utilized by virtually every large corporation, even those whose operations are bound to a single jurisdiction, can produce economic and social ripple effects that sacrifice the future for the quarterly 'now'. For these reasons and many others, experts should be involved in the determination of purpose in every case, and the entity most suited to ensure experts are involved (at present) is the State, which in turn creates friction with international legal principles of (corporate) sovereignty (e.g., in the form of veil piercing) and regulatory autonomy if the MNE is understood as a para-State.

Globally, calls for a larger State role in guiding corporate purpose and action gained traction in the immediate post-War period. Amongst the major commercial jurisdictions, socialist-leaning and Asian jurisdictions were the most likely to adopt such a model – Japan, France, and most of 1960s Southeast Asia provide good examples. This model looked particularly convincing in the early-to-mid 1980s. However, alongside the rise of Thatcherism in the UK and Reaganism in the United States, following the collapse of the Soviet Bloc toward the end of the 1980s and the Asian Financial Crisis in the early 1990s, the shareholder primacy model rose to the status of 'conventional wisdom' or even 'natural truth' in many Western jurisdictions – some even called this model 'The End of History for Corporate Law'.[102] As of this writing in mid-2020, COVID-19 appears to have fractured the logical structures upon which shareholder primacy was precariously perched.[103] Nevertheless, while serious challenges to the model have been mounted and while important discussions regarding 'purpose' flourish particularly in European jurisdictions,[104] the shareholder primacy model – what one might call 'Friedman's Dream'[105] – won out over its competitors, particularly after the fall of the Berlin Wall and the rise of International Investment Law's (IIL) so-called 'second generation' of investment agreements in the 1990s. As of 2020, shareholder primacy remains the dominant model taught in business and law schools,[106] and thus, reflects the dominant understanding of 'purpose' amongst corporate lawyers and managers.

IV. Three conceptions of the ICP

There are three common 'para-conceptions' of the corporation in international legal texts and discussions which I will draw on repeatedly throughout this book.[107] These are (1) para-individualist, (2) para-Statist, and (3) para-institutionalist.

a. Para-individualist

The individualist conception represents the ICP in terms of its ability to bear rights and responsibilities under international law in its own name. The ICP's 'point of access' to international law in this conception is through the State, and specifically, through nationality. On this view, when an ICP seeks to access rights accorded to it under international law, it must do so through the State in which it is organized, for example, the right of diplomatic protection. Conversely, when an ICP breaches an international duty, those who suffer from the resulting harm must seek redress through domestic law, as in breach of contract.

In international law, Anglo-American interests have pressed courts to 'integrate the corporate unit "with a wider legal fabric that assumes individual actors, makes them responsible, and seeks to facilitate their development"'.[108] Yet the ICP resists clean individualization for several reasons. For one thing, it takes on what Otto von Gierke called a 'group-will', a will that does not replicate any individual will but can only belong to a collective unit. This is especially apparent in corporate profit-maximizing behavior. For another thing, by their very design ICPs have access to options available to no other individual. They can freely opt in and out of various nationalities, seek taxation benefits from one State, contract benefits from another, and labor laws in still another. As Johns puts it, 'Such "housing" of global corporate activity in the legal order of one or more nation state(s) is acknowledged to be a matter of convenience or approximation, as is a corporation's treatment as being equivalent to other nationalized persons'.[109]

Despite these problems and many others it is the para-individualist conception of the ICP that has facilitated the corporate acquisition of rights typically accorded only to humans under domestic systems (as in the United States and the European Union) and the acquisition of new international rights accorded only to ICPs (as the example of international anti-corruption law demonstrates in Chapter 3).

b. Para-statist

As we have already seen, the para-State conception of the corporation is likely as old as corporations themselves, but recent years have seen a growth in ICP acquisition of what some have called 'State-like' powers.[110] For example – and borrowing three categories of power from Joseph Nye[111] – in terms of economic power, some ICPs post revenues far greater than the gross domestic product of many States;[112] in terms of military power, private contractors have long outnumbered military personnel in conflict zones such as Iraq and Afghanistan,[113] and the same contractors could very well be parts of corporate groups or networks with contracts in other conflict zones; and in terms of 'soft' power, ICPs like Google, Apple, Huawei, Twitter or Facebook have more global persuasive capital than many individual States, especially when it comes to selective information dissemination through algorithmic design, unilateral suppression of speech, exclusive access to large data sets, or forms of influence associated with marketing and public relations campaigns. In recognition of such vast powers, a crowning feature of the para-Statist conception is that the ICP – like the State – can or should be a direct subject of international law independent from the legal apparatus of the State.

Many international lawyers continue to assume the primacy of the State, and as such, the reactions to the 'contracting out' of State functions to ICPs have largely sought to restore 'normalcy' by reasserting the power of the State. On this view, the rigid divides between 'private' and 'public' law are assumed to be necessary if not correct, even natural, and therefore must be restored: the State has a monopoly on violence, the State's legal relation to individuals is vertical not horizontal, and corporations are creatures of sovereign concession.[114] That said, even within these parameters, there are para-State efforts to attach obligations from international law to corporations through the nexus of the State. For example, the field of Business and Human Rights that has blossomed out of the 2011 United Nations Guiding Principles (UNGPs or 'Ruggie Framework') understands the ICP very much in para-individualist terms yet conceptualizes the ICP as responsible for assisting the State in complying with its international obligations. This approach has the benefit of pragmatic expedience since it aligns with the uncontroversial view that States are obliged to protect the rights of their citizens under certain international agreements. I will further discuss the UNGPs and similar efforts in the next chapter.

c. *Para-institutionalist*

The institutionalist perception views the ICP as a nexus of contracts. Like the United Nations, which is the product of shared agreement between Members created to pursue more efficient or effective diplomatic outcomes, the para-Institutionalist ICP is an act of contractual will created across borders to serve the interests of its creators.[115] On this view, the ICP has rights and duties that it creates for itself through agreement, and its international responsibilities – like, say, adopting CSR policies – are the product of internal choice as to how best to achieve the outcomes it desires. In this way, para-institutionalism can be thought of as a hybrid between the previous two conceptions. That is, it is para-individualist insofar as it views domestic law as its access point to international law rather than a direct subject to international law, but para-Statist insofar as it views internal corporate governance as a form of constitution-making.

V. Three incarnations of the ICP

Although born predominantly out of Anglo-American understandings of the corporate form, international lawyers have long struggled to understand how and whether to treat MNEs as subjects to international law.[116] Although there is broad recognition of the importance of analogical reasoning,[117] there is a lack of consensus on how to analogize corporations; different conceptions gain favor in different fields of international law. This book suggests that the ICP is a judicial and arbitral response to these struggles. The ICP draws on a longstanding tradition of MNEs as duty-bearers with respect to States and (sometimes) individuals, and it utilizes an existing category under international law – in other words, the para-individual – to attribute rights to these entities. However, the waters muddy considerably around two questions: (1) precisely which rights ICPs are owed and (2) how (or whether) they correspond to duties. Much of the existing literature addresses the multinational corporation as an 'international legal personality' in the same boat as non-governmental organizations (NGOs) and inter-governmental organizations (IGOs). However, the ICP is distinct from these entities in a number of ways which render it more analogous to a constituent than a 'stakeholder'. The ICP can be a bearer of human rights and can be responsible for upholding them; the ICP is a person that is itself composed of persons, both legal and natural;[118] the ICP can own private property and at the same time is private property;[119] it can be held responsible for decisions but often cannot be found to have had intent.[120] While all of these considerations are perhaps easier to explain once the idea of international corporate constituency is accepted, I will first focus narrowly on describing constituency itself. Thus, setting aside questions regarding the relative power of individual shareowners, the proper line between the public and the private, and the multitude of legally blessed parent–subsidiary and voting arrangements under which publicly traded ICPs can operate, this section sets out three dominant theories on how to conceptualize the international corporate person as a person composed of persons and discusses the implications of each for corporate constituency. Professor Eric Orts categorized these in relation to U.S. firms in his book *Business Persons: A Legal Theory of the Firm*;[121] later I expand his observations on existing literature to relate more directly to the ICP.

a. The organic or 'real entity' theory

Modern versions of the organic theory of corporate personhood are often traced back to the writings of the German legal philosopher Otto von Gierke, who bore great influence on Hayek. (Hayek's work provided crucial intellectual justifications for the reformation of post-Cold War international economic law.)[122] Gierke viewed the corporation as 'an objectively real entity, which any well-developed child or normal man must perceive: the law merely recognizes and gives legal effect to the existence of this entity'. To Gierke and his followers, those who declared the corporation fictitious were committing a logical error akin to declaring that 'a river is fictitious, the only reality being the individual atoms of oxygen and hydrogen'.[123] Corporations take on a will and reality distinct from the sum of their members, described sometimes in supernatural terms: '[c]ommunities of spirit and purpose, will and action . . . psychical realities which the law recognizes rather than creates'.[124] Law does not grant personhood so much as it recognizes personhood's objective existence. Perhaps because many of those who advanced the organic theory were thinking primarily of the identity and rights of religious associations rather than business corporations,[125] the theory contests the primacy of the State and, in doing so, maximizes the corporation's autonomy. On this view, perhaps the ICP is analogous to a church whose god is the global market and whose congregation is shareholders. Put another way, the question of whether international law explicitly recognizes or defines its parameters is irrelevant to its existence.

b. The positivist or concession theory

The positivist theory of corporate personhood views the corporation as a legal construction whose parameters are wholly contained by states. It has only those attributes of personhood (rights, duties, etc.) that the law chooses to grant to it. This view emerged from English common law, which described the corporation as a sort of law-made god (rather than a church recognized by law as in the organic view): the corporation is 'invisible, immortal, [resting] only in intendment and consideration of the law'.[126] Early U.S. constitutional jurisprudence also understood corporate personhood in this way.[127] In the landmark 1819 decision *Dartmouth College*, the U.S. Supreme Court, found that '[a] corporation is an artificial being, invisible, intangible, and existing only in contemplation of law. Being the mere creature of law, it possesses only those properties which the charter of its creation confers upon it, either expressly, or as incidental to its very existence'.[128] Just as gods and money can outlive people but would cease to exist in pragmatic terms if people ceased to believe in them, ICPs can outlive States but would cease to exist in pragmatic terms if States ceased to animate them. Thus, on this view, the ICP and its parameters are purely a construction of State consent – a claim perhaps most convincingly illustrated through the structure of international investment law as discussed in the following chapters.

c. The proxy or institutional theory

The proxy theory holds that ICPs deserve recognition as legal persons because they are composed of and act on behalf of natural persons. Whereas the organic theory draws 'a sharp distinction between the corporate entity and the shareholders',[129] the proxy theory collapses that distinction. And whereas the positivist theory understands corporate rights as created by the State and thereby revocable, the proxy theory views them as inalienable to the extent that its incorporators' rights are inalienable. To draw an example from U.S. jurisprudence, in his *Hobby Lobby* opinion, U.S. Supreme Court Justice Samuel Alito argued that the purpose of the 'fiction' of corporate personhood is to 'provide protection for human beings': 'A corporation is simply a form of organization used by human beings to achieve desired ends . . . When rights, whether constitutional or statutory, are extended to corporations, the purpose is to protect the rights of these people'.[130] On this view, the ICP has no will, no intention, and no moral capacity; it is simply a proxy for the people beneath the corporate veil. The ICP is therefore a proxy for other constituencies: alternately the ICP's parent company, the ICP's board of directors or officers, or the ICP's shareholders, depending on the structure of the ICP.

VI. The separation of ownership and control

Publicly traded firms are owned by shareholders. But individual shareholders do not control firms in any meaningful sense unless ownership reaches critical voting mass. In one version of the corporate story, ownership and control became separate in law to increase firm efficiency. That is, a structure in which most shareholders have little or no control over the management decisions of the firm arose in response to collective action problems associated with reactive decision making. The hierarchical structure of control can respond more rapidly to market forces than a vast sea of shareholders with differing opinions on what to do next. Notwithstanding such explanations, the origin of ownership-control separation is difficult to trace; wisdoms that were conventional up until the turn of the 21st century have now been contested or dispelled. For example, Adolf Berle and Gardiner Means's seminal *The Modern Corporation and Private Property* argues that legal, organizational, and technological developments in the late 19th and early 20th centuries eroded the power and influence of stockholders, and this led to the emergence of large, diffusely held enterprises controlled by professional managers or minority interests.[131] This explanation was accepted in the corporate governance literature for most of a century, but recent work has shown that the ownership-control divide emerged much earlier; it was already present in the early decades of the 19th century, long before the development of modern industrial enterprises and even before the emergence of railroads.[132]

The theoretical underpinnings of separation are also difficult to pin down. If the separation of ownership and control emerged in order to decrease reactive shareholder decisions and thereby increase efficiency, it has done a poor job of serving that aim. From at least the early 1800s to the present, publicly traded organizations often fall into a situation in which large minority shareholders gain effective control over a firm thereby bulldozing the interests of the diffuse majority of the shares. Today, institutional whales such as Black Rock, Vanguard, and State Street regularly use large minority blocks to exercise influence (if not control) that is disproportionate to that of the diffuse majority.[133]

Nevertheless, Berle and Means's typology of control remains a useful for general characterization: they distinguish between '(1) control through almost complete ownership, (2) majority control, (3) control through legal device without majority ownership, (4) minority control, and (5) management control', where each type represents successively greater degrees of separation between ownership and control. Chapters 3 and 4 will explore the significance of this phenomenon in international corporate structure in the context of the ICP's relationship to international law. Just as veil piercing in MNE structure holds an analogy to the sovereign immunity held by States, the separation of ownership and control in publicly traded MNEs is analogous to the separation of powers between the branches of many State governments. And as Chapter 3 will show, the dual MNE features of ownership separation and the ability to easily reorganize or transfer assets and liabilities amongst multiple independently 'controlled' entities has important implications for veil piercing as well.

VII. Discussion: a person composed of persons

In stepping back and taking a broad view on the emergence of the ICP, as this chapter has done, one striking subtext is that legal discussions on the ICP's rights and obligations under international law tend to overlook employees as constituents or rights holders in the international realm. An overwhelming majority of the scholarship revolves around corporate obligations to 'the public' as represented by the State, or obligations to shareholders of a given ICP, MNE, or international corporate group.[134] For this reason, I think it is helpful to introduce the concept of constituency as it relates to the ICP. The ICP occupies a space in which it serves as a constituent to a broader transnational legal apparatus – especially in international economic law – but it can also be understood as composed of constituents. When considering the latter form of constituency, existing domestic and international legal structures tend to assume or at least privilege the analogy that shareholders are the constituents of a corporation. Shareholders own an interest in the corporation much as citizens 'own' an interest in their polity, and both shareholders and citizens can exercise influence over the political and strategic direction of the larger organization through the practice of voting. But the analogy is a particularly poor fit for large ICPs because it can serve to ignore the interests of vast numbers of employees who in fact compose the economic output of the ICP but who are not shareholders.

This is not to say that employees of corporations have always been ignored by international agreements, but international tribunals have yet to explore such issues in detail. Perhaps because international tribunals have barely begun to treat corporations as subjects of international law, when considering corporate obligations under international law, arbitrators, judges, and academics alike have focused on obligations to the States in which they operate, and by extension, 'the public'.[135] While shareholders have enjoyed access to international arbitration through international investment agreements, employees typically must rely on domestic tribunals to redress grievances. So long as an ICP is compliant with domestic regulations where a grievance occurs, there is little opportunity for employees to access international adjudication.[136] Thus, when it comes to the rights of employees, initiatives to internationally regulate labor standards have come from multilateral initiatives rather than judicial decisions.

The two primary initiatives to internationally standardize the conduct of labor relations by ICPs are the OECD Guideline on Employment and Industrial Relations (OECD Guideline) and the International Labour Organization's Tripartite Declaration of Principles on Multinationals and Social Policy (ILO Declaration). The progression of these initiatives – and particularly the ILO Declaration – manifest broader patterns in the corporate history outlined here insofar as the progression reflects the arduous and amorphous relationship between labor and capital or between working- and managerial-class interests. That is, a legal form that sets out to maximize benefit to the public becomes a catalyst through which capital carves out 'minimum standards' owed to the public. For example, just as a corporation's initial *privilege* of limited financial liability was justified by the benefit it would produce for the public in exchange of the liability the public absorbed on its behalf, the ILO's initial mission as conceived under Part XIII of the 1919 Treaty of Versailles was rooted in the notion that no State could achieve uniformly just and equitable labor conditions unless every State did so. While it accepted that corporations and States would not immediately produce equitable working conditions, it did so only insofar as it was temporally impossible. Creating possibility was the goal. To that end, it declared that sustained peace after WWI was impossible without decent wages and humane conditions in all of the world's increasingly interdependent States. Subsequent events suggest that Part XIII was right on that point, though the Versailles Treaty famously missed the mark on several others.

The consolidated international institutions set up under the United Nations following WWII faced increasing pressure from the economic and labor demands particularly from former colonies in the 1960s. Efforts to restructure international economic relations so as to correct for asymmetries of wealth and other forms of power between Western States and the Global South began around 1955 at the Bandung Conference culminated in the New International Economic Order (NIEO) through a series of UN Resolutions in the 1970s.[137] The story of the NIEO, though at turns both inspiring and tragic, is beyond the scope of the book, but it is worth mentioning that it ultimately failed to gain buy in from Western powers during a surge of Hayek and Friedman-fueled corporatism in the 1970s. It was in this corporatist climate – during which Friedmanian sentiments that the 'social responsibility of business is to increase its profits' first took hold in mainline political thinking[138] – that the ILO Declaration was finally adopted in 1977.[139] What began as a developing country–led initiative pressing for a binding international code for MNEs wound up as 'a non-binding tripartite declaration of principles concerning multinational enterprises and social policy' that provided no follow-up machinery or accountability for State Parties. While the 1980s brought a series of revisions requiring reviews, reports, and a procedure to interpret provisions, the ILO Declaration has never provided any direct international judicial access to workers. Similarly, the OECD Guideline stops short of providing judicial remedies to States or workers when corporations fail to provide the labor conditions codified in the agreement. Since the OECD Guideline is a part of the more general OECD Guidelines on Multinational Enterprises, I will discuss its mechanisms more thoroughly in Chapter 3, but for now let us simply note that it is non-binding and non-judicial in nature.[140] The end result of the consolidation efforts was, inter alia, to decline recognition of any special rights for workers under international law – combatants and cultural groups could claim rights under various international declarations and agreements, but 'the worker' was folded into the larger category of 'the public'.

The emergence of the ICP is the emergence of an entity that international law understands as serving shareholders but whose power is checked by States. The rights it holds are rights that serve its shareholders and the obligations it owes are to the domestic publics capsuled within the States in which it operates. If it owes any duties to the 'global public' – if such a thing can be said to exist[141] – it owes them not to humanity but to the 'international community', which is traditionally understood as a collection of diplomatic stances espoused by States. Workers are lost in this picture. Whereas the OECD Guideline is jointly addressed by Member Countries (predominantly Western countries) to MNEs operating within their territories, the ILO is addressed to governments, advocacy groups, and MNEs operating in both home and host countries. Largely because of resistance from MNE representatives during negotiations, both agreements are voluntary in nature, apply to national and multinational corporations, and assert the primacy of national law. Indeed, the ILO Declaration states:

> All the parties concerned by this Declaration should respect the sovereign rights of States, obey the national law and regulations, give due consideration to local practices and respond relevant international standards.[142]

This passage ties several of the themes from the beginning of this chapter to several of the themes addressed in the next two chapters. The first theme is that, like many international agreements, although it is addressed in part to ICPs as a 'concerned party', its language does not reflect the ICP's multiple constituencies or acknowledge that the ICP is itself constituent. In doing so, like many agreements, it implies that an ICP holds a passive rather than an active role in creating and sustaining both domestic and international legal structures. A second theme is that, like in many international agreements, the concept of sovereignty is addressed only in the context of State rights, but experience shows that State sovereignty over territories (*dominium*) and corporate sovereignty over things (*imperium*) are not as neatly severed as the language of the text seems to presuppose (the history of Royal Dutch/Shell Group in Nigeria provides a poignant example of this). A final theme to note is that, as in many international agreements, the ILO Declaration's language requires 'respect' for the 'relevant international standards' that apply to the ICP but does not provide any perspective on the practical ramifications of that requirement. At least theoretically, this language invokes an understanding of the ICP's position in international law that reaches well beyond the four corners of the ILO Declaration; it theoretically accords MNEs a duty to respect international standards. The ILO Declaration is, of course, only one small part of the international legal frameworks that can potentially apply to ICPs – other frameworks include the UN Guiding Principles, various OECD initiatives, and international investment agreements considered as 'corporate law'. The application of such frameworks depends largely upon a fuller understanding of how to conceptualize the position of the ICP in relation to international law. For these reasons among others, I spend considerable portions of the next two chapters discussing the concepts of constituency, sovereignty, and property as they relate to the ICP, and I attempt to theorize the ICP more clearly as well as its position within international law more generally.

Notes

1 See seminally Antony Anghie, *Imperialism, Sovereignty, and the Making of International Law* (2005); see also L Eslava & S Pahuja, The State and International Law: A Reading from the Global South, *Humanity Journal* (2020).
2 Quoted in D K Fieldhouse, The Multinational: A Critique of a Concept in A Teichova et al (Eds.), *Multinational Enterprise in Historical Perspective* (1986).
3 N Hood & S Young, *The Economics of the Multinational Enterprise* (1979); J H Dunning & S Lundan, *Multinational Enterprises and the Global Economy* (1992).
4 See e.g., C D Wallace, *Legal Control of the Multinational Enterprise* (1983).
5 OECD Guidelines for Multinational Enterprises Concepts and Principles (27 June 2000), par. 3, available at www.oecd.org/daf/investment/guidelines/mnetext.htm. For the old version of this paragraph, see OECD Guidelines 1991 Review (Paris 1992) at p. 104; also reproduced in The OECD Guidelines for Multinational Enterprises (Paris 1994, 1997).
6 M Noortmann, A Reinisch & C Ryngaert (Eds.), *Non-State Actors in International Law* (2015); A Bianchi, The Fight for Inclusion: Non-State Actors and International Law, in U Fastenrath, R Geiger, D-E Khan, A Paulus, S von Schorlemer & C Vedder (Eds.), *From Bilateralism to Community Interest: Essays in Honour of Judge Bruno Simma* (2011); E Roucounas, The Users of International Law, in M H Arsanjani, J Katz Cogan, R D Sloane & S Wiessner (Eds.), *Looking to the Future: Essays on International Law in Honor of W. Michael Reisman* (2011); R Higgins, *Problems & Process: International Law and How We Use It* (1994); and A Clapham, *Human Rights Obligations of Non-State Actors* (2006).
7 A Kjeldgaard-Pedersen, *The International Legal Personality of the Individual* (2018).
8 See K Crow & L Lorenzoni-Escobar, International Corporate Obligations, Human Rights, and the *Urbaser* Standard: Breaking New Ground?, *Boston University Int'l L. J.* (2016); K Crow, International Law and Corporate Participation in Times of Armed Conflict, *Berkeley J. Int'l L.* (2019).
9 For a seminal history and critique dealing with this narrative, see Martti Koskenniemi, *From Apology to Utopia: The Structure of International Legal Argument* (1989).

10 See e.g., Anthony Carty & Janne Nijman (Eds.), *Morality and the Responsibility of Rulers: European and Chinese Origins of a Rule of Law as Justice for World Order* (2018).
11 See e.g., Alexander Hertel-Fernandez, Who Passes Business's "Model Bills"? Policy Capacity and Corporate Influence in U.S. State Politics, *Perspectives on Politics* (2014). See also Katarina Pistor, *The Code of Capital: How the Law Creates Wealth and Inequality* (2019).
12 See generally the work of Janne Nijmann, but particularly Images of Grotius, or the International Rule of Law Beyond Historiographical Oscillation, *Journal of the History of International Law* (2015).
13 I describe these processes in greater detail in Chapters 3 and 4.
14 See Philip Lawson, *The East India Company: A History* (2013); William Dalrymple, *The Anarchy: The Relentless Rise of the East India Company* (2019); Om Prakash, *The Dutch East India Company and the Economy of Bengal, 1630–1720* (2014); Louisa Balk, Frans Dijk & Diederick Kortlang, *The Archives of the Dutch East India Company (VOC) and the Local Institutions in Batavia (Jakarta)* (2007); Adam Clulow, *The Dutch and English East India Companies: Diplomacy, Trade and Violence in Early Modern Asia* (2018).
15 This is a paraphrasing of Vitoria, provided by Martti Koskenniemi in an interview with Demitri van den Meerssche for Opinio Juris, Interview: Martti Koskenniemi on International Law and the Rise of the Far-Right, (12 Oct. 2018), available at http://opiniojuris.org/2018/12/10/interview-martti-koskenniemi-on-international-law-and-the-rise-of-the-far-right (accessed 5 May 2020).
16 *Id.*
17 Johannes Thumfart, On Grotius's Mare Liberum and Vitoria's De Indis, Following Agamben and Schmitt, 30 *Grotiana* 65 (2009).
18 *Id.* For impact on current legal and political philosophy, see Katrina Forrester, *In the Shadow of Justice: Postwar Liberalism and the Remaking of Political Philosophy* (2019).
19 *Id.*
20 See e.g., Anthony Carty & Janne Nijman (Eds.), *Morality and the Responsibility of Rulers: European and Chinese Origins of a Rule of Law as Justice for World Order* (2018).
21 Ben Holland, The Moral Person of the State: Emer de Vattel and the Foundations of International Legal Order, 37 *History of European Ideas* 438 (2012).
22 Keon Stapelbroek & Antonio Trampus, *The Legacy of Vattel's Droit Des Gens* (2019).
23 Emer de Vattel, *The Law of Nations* (1758).
24 *Id.*
25 Lisa Ford & Tim Rowse (Eds.), *Between Indigenous and Settler Governance* (2013).
26 *Id.*
27 See e.g., Martti Koskeinnemi, Imagining the Rule of Law: Rereading the Grotian 'Tradition', 30 *EJIL* 17 (2019).
28 William Edward Hall, *Treatise on International Law* (1890).
29 *Id.* See also Emer de Vattel, *The Law of Nations* (1758).
30 Andreas Osiander, Sovereignty, International Relations, and the Westphalian Myth, 55 *International Organization* 251–87 (2001).
31 See e.g., Richard Coggins, Westphalian State System, in Iain McLean & Alistair McMillan (Eds.), *The Concise Oxford Dictionary of Politics* (2009).
32 See e.g., Andreas Osiander, 'Sovereignty, International Relations, and the Westphalian Myth', 55 *International Organization* 251–87 (2001). Osiander sets out several compelling alternative narratives to Westphalia and disputes the accuracy of the conventional one.
33 See generally e.g., Joshua Barkan, *Corporate Sovereignty* (2013). Barkan argues that those who view law as a restraint on corporate power misunderstand its nature as a legal creation that itself creates law.
34 See Adam Winkler, *We the Corporations: How American Businesses Won their Civil Rights* (2018).

35 Joshua Barkan, *Corporate Sovereignty* (2013).
36 *Id.* See also David Kershaw, *The Foundations of Anglo-American Corporate Fiduciary Law* (2018).
37 See generally e.g., Grégoire Mallard & Jérôme Sgard (Eds.), *Contractual Knowledge: One Hundred Years of Legal Experimentation in Global Markets* (2016).
38 The Honorable Leo Strine, The Dangers of Denial: The Need for a Clear-Eyed Understanding of the Power and Accountability Structure Established by the Delaware General Corporation Law, *Wake Forest L. Rev.* (2015).
39 Milton Friedman, The Social Responsibility of Business is to Increase its Profits, *New York Times Magazine* (13 Sept. 1970).
40 Larry Fink, A Fundamental Reshaping of Finance (Letter to CEOs), available at www.blackrock.com/corporate/investor-relations/blackrock-client-letter (accessed 20 May 2020); Doug Sundheim & Kate Starr, *Making Stakeholder Capitalism a Reality, Harv. Bus. Rev.* (22 Jan 2020).
41 For an overview of the U.S.–EU aircraft saga, see Timeline: Highlights of the 16-Year Airbus, Boeing Trade War, *Reuters* (15 Feb 2020); on agricultural subsidies, see e.g., WTO, DS267, *US – Upland Cotton*, AB Report (2008).
42 WTO, DS381, *US – Tuna II*, AB Report (2018).
43 WTO, DS401, *EC – Seal Products*, AB Report (2014).
44 WTO, DS285, *US – Gambling*, AB Report (2005).
45 See World Bank, Arm's-Length Trade: A Source of Post-Crisis Trade Weakness, *Global Economic Prospectus* (June 2017); see also Sol Picciotto, *Regulating Global Corporate Capitalism* (2013).
46 Ann M. Carlos & Stephen Nicholas, Giants of an Earlier Capitalism: The Chartered Trading Companies as Modern Multinationals, 62 *The Business History Review* 398 (1988)
47 *Id.*
48 See e.g., Alfred Chandler & Bruce Mazlish, *Multinational Corporations and the New Global History* (2005); Mira Wilkins, The Free-standing Company, 1870–1914: An Important Type of British Foreign Direct Investment, *Economic History Review* (1988).
49 *Id.*
50 *Id.*
51 Ann M. Carlos & Stephen Nicholas, Giants of an Earlier Capitalism: The Chartered Trading Companies as Modern Multinationals, 62 *The Business History Review* 398 (1988). Citing E. E. Rich, *The Hudson's Bay Company, 1620–1740* (1958); K Chaudhuri, *The Trading World of Asia and the East India Company, 1660–1760* (1978); K Glamann, *Dutch-Asiatic Trade, 1620–1740* (1981).
52 *Id.*
53 *Id.*
54 See Paz Tolentino, *Multinational Corporations: Emergence and Evolution* (2001).
55 Thomas R. Tørsløv, Ludvig S. Wier & Gabriel Zucman, The Missing Profits of Nations, National Bureau of Economic Research (NBER), Working Paper No. 24701 (2019).
56 See generally Sven Beckert, *Empire of Cotton* (2014); Sven Beckert & Seth Rockman (Eds.), *Slavery's Capitalism* (2016).
57 Susan K. Sell, *Private Power, Public Law* (2003).
58 See Naomi R. Lamoreaux & William J. Novack (Eds.), *Corporations and American Democracy* (2017).
59 *Trustees of Dartmouth College v. Woodward*, 17 US 481 (1819).
60 *Id.*
61 Phillip Blumberg, The *Law of Corporate Groups: Substantive Law* (1988).
62 *Id.*
63 Adam Winkler, *We the Corporations: How American Businesses Won their Civil Rights* (2018).

64 Pankaj Ghemawat, Distance Still Matters: The Hard Reality of Global Expansion, *Harvard Business Review* (Sept. 2001).
65 Jeffrey A. Frankel & Andrew Rose, An Estimate of the Effect of Common Currencies on Trade and Income, 2 *Quarterly Journal of Economics* CXVII (May 2002).
66 Henry Hansmann & Reinier Kraakman, The End of History for Corporate Law, Olin Center for Law, Economics, and Business, Discussion Paper No. 280 (2000).
67 *Id.*
68 See generally Kurt Lash, *The Reconstruction Amendments: The Essential Documents, Vol. 1* (2020).
69 U.S. Const., Amendment XIV, Section 1.
70 *Id.*
71 Adam Winkler, *We the Corporations: How American Businesses Won their Civil Rights* (2018).
72 *Santa Clara County v. Southern Pacific Railroad Company*, 118 US 394 (1886).
73 Loren P. Beth, *John Marshall Harlan: The Last Whig Justice* (1992), 164–165. For background on Bancroft Davis, author of this particular report, see James W. Ely, *The Chief Justiceship of Melville W. Fuller, 1888–1910* (1995), 49. For Davis's controversial list, see Charles A. Beard and Alan F. Westin, *The Supreme Court and the Constitution* (1912), 17–18.
74 *Santa Clara* (1886).
75 Adam Winkler, *We the Corporations: How American Businesses Won their Civil Rights* (2018).
76 For other arguments along these lines, see Morton J. Horwitz, Santa Clara Revisited: The Development of Corporate Theory, *West Virginia L. Rev.* (1985–1986); Gregory A. Mark, The Personification of the Business Corporation in American Law, *University of Chicago L. Rev.* (1987).
77 *Plessy v. Ferguson*, 163 US 537 (1896). This decision established the 'separate but equal' doctrine.
78 William O. Douglas, Stare Decisis, 49 *Columbia Law Review* 735 (1949).
79 For a thorough history of Deutsche Bank that includes sections on the fascinating career of Abs, see Werner Plumpe et al, *Deutsche Bank: The Global Hausbank, 1870–2020* (2020).
80 It should be noted that there are those who credit the post-WWI cluster of the U.S. Friendship, Commerce, and Navigation Treaties as the first bilateral investment treaties, but these were not binding instruments providing specific causes of action and venues through which to seek remedies. For a history with this view, see Kenneth J. Vandevelde, *The First Bilateral Investment Treaties: U.S. Postwar Friendship, Commerce, and Navigation Treaties* (2017).
81 *Hale v. Hankel*, 201 US 43 (1906).
82 *Id.*
83 E.g., *Hale v. Henkel*; *Northwestern National Life Insurance Company v. Riggs*, 203 US 243 (1906).
84 *Brown v. Board of Education*, 347 US 483 (1954).
85 *United States v. Caroline Products Co.*, 304 US 144 (1938).
86 *NAACAP v. Button*, 371 UUS 415 (1963).
87 *Grosjean v. American Press Co.*, 297 US 233 (1936).
88 *Virginia Pharmacy Board v. Virginia Citizens Consumers Council*, 425 US 748 (1976).
89 *Near v. Minnesota*, 283 US 697 (1931).
90 For an overview, see e.g., Stephen Wilks, *The Political Power of the Business Corporation* (2013); see also Adam Winkler, *We the Corporations: How American Businesses Won their Civil Rights* (2018).
91 *Buckley v. Valeo*, 424 US 1 (1976).
92 *First National Bank of Boston v. Bellotti*, 435 US 765 (1978).
93 *Austin v. Michigan Chamber of Commerce*, 494 US 652 (1990).

94 *Boy Scouts of America v. Dale*, 530 US 640 (2000).
95 *McConnell v. Federal Election Commission*, 540 US 93 (2003).
96 *Federal Election Commission v. Wisconsin Right to Life*, 551 US 449 (2007).
97 *Citizens United v. Federal Election Commission*, 558 US 310 (2010).
98 *United States v. Sourapas and Crest Beverage Co.*, 515 F.2d 295 (9th Cir. 1975).
99 *Western Tradition Partnership v. Attorney General of Montana*, 567 UUS 516 (2012).
100 *Burwell v. Hobby Lobby*, 573 US 682 (2014).
101 For foundational examples, see e.g., Felix S. Cohen, Transcendental Nonsense and the Functional Approach, *Colum. L. Rev.* (1935); Martin Wolff, On the Nature of Legal Persons, *L. Q. Rev.* (1938).
102 Henry Hansmann & Reinier Kraakman, The End of History for Corporate Law, Olin Center for Law, Economics, and Business, Discussion Paper No. 280 (2000).
103 See e.g., Martin Whittaker, Is COVID-19 Killing Shareholder Primacy?, *Forbes* (9 April 2020), available at www.forbes.com/sites/martinwhittaker/2020/04/09/is-covid-19-killing-shareholder-primacy/#124a31735661 (accessed 9 April 2020).
104 See e.g., CFA Institute, *Corporate Governance Policy in the European Union* (2016).
105 See Milton Friedman, The Social Responsibility of Business is to Increase its Profits, *New York Times Magazine* (13 Sept 1970).
106 But this is beginning to quake. See Alissa Kole Amico, The Pandemic is a Litmus Test of Stakeholderism, Harvard Law School Forum on Corporate Governance (4 May 2020), available at https://corpgov.law.harvard.edu/2020/05/04/the-pandemic-is-the-litmus-test-of-stakeholderism (accessed 20 May 2020).
107 These are derived largely from a chapter by Fleur Johns, Theorizing the Corporation in International Law, in Anne Orford & Florian Hoffmann (Eds.), *The Oxford Handbook of the Theory of International Law* (2013).
108 *Id.*
109 *Id.*
110 *Id.*
111 See seminally, Joseph Nye, The Changing Nature of World Power, *Political Science Quarterly* (1990).
112 See e.g., Milan Babic, Jan Fichtner & Eelke M. Heemskerk, States versus Corporations: Rethinking the Power of Business in International Politics, *The International Spectator* (2017).
113 Congressional Research Service Report, Department of Defense Contractor and Troop Levels in Afghanistan and Iraq: 2007–2018 (10 May 2019), available at https://fas.org/sgp/crs/natsec/R44116.pdf.
114 John Dewey, The Historic Background of Corporate Legal Personality, *Yale Law Journal* (1926).
115 W Bratton Jr., The 'Nexus of Contracts' Corporation: A Critical Appraisal, *Cornell Law Review* (1989).
116 See e.g., Astrid Kjeldgaard-Pedersen, *The International Legal Personality of the Individual* (2018); Markos Karavias, *Corporate Obligations Under International Law* (2014); Roland Portmann, *Legal Personality in International Law* (2010); Peter Muchlinski, *Multinational Enterprises and the Law* (1995). Important cases in international courts have also grappled with how to situate the corporation as a bearer of rights and duties under international law, e.g., *Reparations for Injuries* at the ICJ (AO in 1949) and, more recently, *Urbaser v. Argentina* (ICSID Award in 2016).
117 M Paparinskis, Analogies and Other Regimes of International Law, in Zachary Douglas, Joost Pauwelyn, and Jorge E. Viñuales (Eds.), *The Foundations of International Investment Law: Bringing Theory into Practice* (2014); A Roberts, Clash of Paradigms, *AJIL* (2013).
118 Markos Karavias, *Corporate Obligations Under International Law* (2014).
119 Joshua Barkan, *Corporate Sovereignty* (2013).
120 See e.g., the Malaysian Law, MACC Act Section 17A, which will enter into force in 2020.

121 Eric W. Orts, *Business Persons: A Legal Theory of the Firm* (2013).
122 See John Dewey, The Historic Background of Corporate Legal Personality, 35 *Yale L. J.* 655 (1925–1926).
123 Arthur Machen, Jr., Corporate Personality, Pt.s I & II, 24 *Harv. L. Rev.* 253, 261 (1910–1911).
124 W. Jethro Brown, The Personality of the Corporation and the State, *L. Q. Rev.* 365, 367, 371 (1905).
125 John Dewey, The Historic Background of Corporate Legal Personality, 35 *Yale L. J.* 655, 671 (1925–1926).
126 Henry Osborn Taylor, *A Treatise on the Law of Private Corporations Having Capital Stock 8* (1884); see also P W Duff, *Personality in Roman Private Law* (1938).
127 Phillip I. Blumberg, The Corporate Entity in an Era of Multinational Corporations, 15 *Del. J. Corp. L.* 283 (1990).
128 *Trustees of Dartmouth College v. Woodward*, 17 US 481 (1819). For a critique, see Arthur Machen, Jr., Corporate Personality, Pts. I & II, 24 *Harv. L. Rev.* 253, 347, 257 (1910–1911).
129 Morton J. Horwitz, Santa Clara Revisited: The Development of Corporate Theory, 88 *W. Va. L. Rev.* 173 (1985).
130 *Burwell v. Hobby Lobby Stores, Inc.*, 134 S. Ct. 2751, 2768 (2014).
131 Adolf Berle & Gardiner Means, *The Modern Corporation and Private Property* (Macmillan 1932).
132 Eric Hilt, When Did Ownership Separate From Control? Corporate Governance in the Early Nineteenth Century, 68 *Journal of Economic History* 645 (2008).
133 See e.g., OECD Corporate Governance, The Role of Institutional Investors in Promoting Good Corporate Governance (2011); see more recently Kedia, Simi and Starks, Laura T. and Wang, Xianjue, *Institutional Investors and Hedge Fund Activism* (March 24, 2020). Available at SSRN: https://ssrn.com/abstract=3560537 (accessed 20 May 2020).
134 See representatively, Barnali Choudhury & Martin Petrin, *Corporate Duties to the Public* (2019); Markos Karavias, *Corporate Obligations under International Law* (2013).
135 E.g., Barnali Choudhury & Martin Petrin, *Corporate Duties to the Public* (2019); *Urbaser S.A. v Argentine Republic* (ICSID Case No. ARB/07/26) Award (8 December 2016).
136 The Alien Tort Statute (ATS) once provided hope for such an avenue of liability circa 1980 but U.S. Supreme Court Cases over the past two decades have dampened that hope. More thorough discussions of the ATS decisions are available in Chapters 2 and 5 of this book.
137 Kevin Crow, *Bandung's Fate*, in Ingo Venzke and Kevin Jon Heller (eds.), *Contingency in the Course of International Law* (forthcoming, OUP 2020). See also Kevin Crow, *'Acceptance': International Law in Post-Colonial Asia, 1955–1995* (book forthcoming, hopefully in late 2022).
138 See e.g., Milton Friedman, The Social Responsibility of Business is to Increase its Profits, *New York Times Magazine* (13 Sept. 1970).
139 ILO, Tripartite Declaration of Principles Concerning Multinational Enterprises and Social Policy (Nov. 1977).
140 OECD, OECD Guidelines for Multinational Enterprises (2011).
141 See generally U.N. Dev. Program, Global Public Goods: International Cooperation in the Twenty-First Century (1999), discussing the existence of global public policy based on the idea of global public goods.
142 ILO, Tripartite Declaration of Principles Concerning Multinational Enterprises and Social Policy (Nov.1977).

Chapter 2

The international corporate person in international law

Judge-made law

I. Preface to the next two chapters

While many international legal texts describe MNEs and ICPs in a manner that suggests an entity closer in form to a para-Statist legal fiction, judge-made law has slowly moved the needle toward (or perhaps split the needle to include) para-Individualism. This chapter and the next one track this process, and as such, they are a bit more technical than the others included in this book. The present chapter sets out the specific cases from which international law's relationship to the international corporate person derives and the next chapter does the same with international agreements and other texts. As noted throughout this book, the picture that emerges is amorphous and at times convoluted, but it is nevertheless necessary to document the status quo to move toward a more cohesive theory if the ICP. Accordingly, these chapters are meant primarily for readers who desire a launchpad for research into the ICP or for those who read other sections of this book and would like greater specificity regarding the cases or texts mentioned in other chapters. For readers who are seeking a broad overview of the theoretical challenges and future trajectories of international corporate personhood, Chapters 2 and 3 may be a bit dry. I therefore advise those readers to skip these chapters on the first read and return to them if the other chapters leave you wanting.

II. The ICP in international tribunals

This section focuses on the role international tribunals played in creating and generating present understandings of the ICP. It tracks the process through which what began as a nominally para-Statist organization in the immediate post-WWII period became increasingly para-Individual over time and across space. While Section III focuses on divergent views on the source of authority for creating new rights or obligations for corporations, this section focuses on judicial decisions that have moved the needle on the ICP's form and function. I argue that, through the category of 'investor', international investment law has enabled a fundamental transition in international legal practice. The 'investor' introduced by bilateral investment treaties (BITs) in the post-WWII period gained substantive rights within BITs throughout the remainder of the millennium. It is a category that is both human and corporation – both natural person and ICP. And because the growing body of international investment law cannot discriminate between investors based merely upon human or non-human status, the distinctions between these two categories have increasingly collapsed. The remaining question is how far this collapse will go and how broadly it will reverberate in other areas of international law.

i. Subjectivity of the corporation

Although earlier discussions exist, virtually any practical analysis of corporate subjectivity should begin with the ICJ's 1949 *Reparations for Injuries* Advisory Opinion.[1] That opinion set out a four-part test for identifying non-State entities that can be considered subject to international law. The entity must have (1) an independent or autonomous existence, (2) the ability to possess international rights or obligations, (3) the actual possession of those rights and obligations, and (4) the ability to petition to have its rights enforced in international venues.

These elements are great starting points, but they assume that non-State entities are static and defined in nature. As we have already seen, this is not the case when it comes to the ICP. Legally and physically, ICPs are amorphous in nature. Do the *Reparations* factors apply to the ICP in its own right or do they apply to the legal and natural persons that compose them? (Here I am speaking of shareholders and directors, not employees.)

In 1970, the *Barcelona Traction* case brought greater clarity to this question. It was the first ICJ case to directly consider the question of corporate subjectivity – albeit on a jurisdictional question – and it found no independent cause of action for shareholders against a State under international law.[2] The ICJ considered whether shareholders who were nationals of one State (Belgium) could bring a claim in against the State in which the ICP's principle assets were held (Spain) when the ICP was headquartered in a third State (Canada), and whether the ICP's arm in Spain could claim diplomatic immunity (as a Canadian). The ICJ rejected Belgium's claims on two principal grounds. First, shareholders could not bring claims against a State when the company itself could bring a claim in its name. Only where the company had ceased to legally exist could shareholders bypass the ICP to petition the State to bring a claim in their own right. Second, Belgium was not the State of incorporation of the company and so could not bring a claim in the company's name; the nationality of the ICP took diplomatic primacy over the nationality of the shareholders. Only Canada as the State of incorporation could bring a claim on the ICP's behalf. The ICJ did suggest, however, that if the ICP's arm in Spain had sufficient Belgian characteristics – such as a central management office located in the State or principal operations in the

State – then perhaps its claim could have been sustained. The ICJ emphasized that the ICP was an institution of domestic law – that is, an institution animated by multiple domestic laws – and was therefore an entity distinct from its shareholders.[3] As such, where a wrong was done to the company, the interest of the shareholders may be affected but it was the ICP alone that had the right to maintain an action in international law. It could not maintain that action, however, without the petition of its home State or without a treaty that created an independent avenue through which the ICP could sue the host State – that is, the precise arrangement that gives rise to international investment law. In doing so, the ICJ articulated a vision of the ICP that veers closer to an individual than to a State insofar as it considered ICP subsidiaries to be 'citizens' of only one State, and one that distinctly reflects the 'veil piercing' doctrines found in common tort law, discussed in Chapter 4.

Unlike at the ICJ, arbitral panels at the International Centre for the Settlement of Investment Disputes (ICSID Tribunal) are tasked with determining whether a State hosting an investment from a national of another State (the 'home' State) has upheld its obligations to the investor under a bilateral or multilateral agreement between the States. However, arbitrators on these Tribunals very often reference doctrines developed in international courts or public international law more generally.[4] Throughout this book, I often substitute the term ICP for 'investor' in these cases to denote the frequent cases in which the 'investor' is in fact a corporate person petitioning for international rights.

Years after the *Barcelona Traction* case, in 1994, an ICSID Tribunal issued a Decision on Jurisdiction in the case of *Vacuum Salt Products v. Ghana.*[5] That case involved an international investment agreement between Ghana and a second State, yet Vacuum Salt was incorporated in Ghana as well as the second State. The foreign State had invested in Vacuum Salt in reliance on a series of contractual agreements dating from 1981 until the complaint was lodged in 1992. These agreements, according to Vacuum Salt, should have allowed the ICP to develop and exploit a mining facility at Ada-Songor Lagoon. The government of Ghana, however, stymied these efforts through a series of encroachments over a period of years before ultimately reneging on the agreement. The big question was, could the ICP (Vacuum Salt) access the international remedy (the IIA) even though it was a national of Ghana? The answer was yes, and again, the reasoning revolved around the issue of control. Among other elements, the ICP must, as a matter of fact rather than form, be controlled from a foreign State.

Note how the waters get murkier in international investment. For example, if nationals of a home State can sue a host State through an ICP-citizen of the host State, can nationals of a home State sue the home State through ICP-citizens of a host State? What if I live in the U.S. and want to sue the U.S. through my ICP's arm in Canada? Apparently, such claims can stick, so long as U.S. nationals control the Canadian firm. In 2004, an ICSID Tribunal in

Tokios Tokeles v. Ukraine found that Ukrainian controlling shareholders of a Lithuanian incorporated company could bring a claim before the ICSID, through the company, against Ukraine under the provisions of the Ukraine-Lithuania BIT.[6] The Tribunal held that a company incorporated in Lithuania, but owned and controlled by Ukrainian nationals (who owned 99% of the shares and comprised two-thirds of the management), was a Lithuanian national for the purposes of Article 25 (2) (b) of the ICSID Convention, which deals with jurisdiction over legal persons for the purposes of that Convention and which contains a control-based test of corporate nationality.[7] The approach of the majority in the *Tokios Tokeles* case is not uniformly followed. However, several more recent cases refer to *Tokios Tokeles* as authoritative where the applicable treaty and the applicable national law refer only to a test of formal incorporation as determining nationality.

There are many cases that refine the contours set out in the previous section, but the basics are clear: subjectivity persists where the ICJ elements are met. The final ICJ element – the ability to access international remedies – depends largely on whether control can be construed internationally. The contours of how international control is determined are unclear, but it appears nevertheless that ICPs can incur direct obligations under international law through two broad means: first, through reference to domestic law defining either ownership or control using terms that can be internationally construed, and second, through reference to *erga omnes* obligations, which will be discussed in more detail in Section III of this chapter.

ii. Substantive rights

In 2007, an ICSID Tribunal in *Archer Daniels & Lyle Ingredients v. Mexico* examined Mexico's argument that the tax measures adopted were a legitimate 'countermeasure' under customary international law in response to a breach by the U.S. government of its obligations under NAFTA Chapter 20.[8] In its discussion of admissibility, the Tribunal took the view that NAFTA's *substantive* investment protections were not individual rights possessed by ICPs, but rather rights possessed by an ICP's home state. The only right directly possessed by an ICP or investor was the *procedural* right to submit a claim to arbitration – a *passive* claim right.

This position evolved slightly in the 2008 ICSID case of *Corn Products International v. Mexico.*[9] Again under NAFTA Chapter 20, the case concerned a U.S. ICP with a wholly owned subsidiary in Mexico engaged in the production of high fructose corn syrup. When Mexico adopted a 2002 tax on high fructose corn syrup, the ICP sued the State alleging that the tax was aimed at protecting Mexico's domestic sugar producers and excluding high fructose corn syrup from the soft drink sweetener market.[10] Crucially, the Tribunal found that 'the NAFTA confers upon [ICPs] substantive rights separate and distinct from those of the State of which they are nationals' and that 'an

[ICP] which brings a claim is seeking to enforce what it asserts are its own rights under the treaty and not exercising a power to enforce rights which are actually those of the State'.[11]

Again, these cases are not exhaustive. And obviously the NAFTA is only one of the many possible agreements to which ICPs can be subject, but the principles set out in these cases reverberated throughout investment arbitration, regardless of the adjudicated treaty or agreement. They are frequently cited as authoritative on similar questions in subsequent ICSID Awards.[12] Most importantly, these cases represent a seminal shift in the ICP's conceptualization. Specifically, in *Archer Daniels*, the ICP sprouts characteristics of a para-State, able only to access certain procedures under certain conditions – not a rights-holder in itself. This was typical of arbitral awards and decisions in international courts dealing with MNEs. But one year later, by *Corn Products*, a positivist para-Individualism breaks through. The ICP can also claim *active* substantive rights independent of the rights authorized by the State – an *active* right to sue and stake claims under international law. Setting aside debates about the 'intrinsicality' of human rights and thinking purely in terms of positive law,[13] this development places the ICP in striking parallel to individuals living within States Parties to the European Convention on Human Rights (ECHR). States Parties have committed themselves to an external cause of action if specific enumerated international rights are breached; individuals have a *passive* procedural right to a claim after exhausting remedies of the State but individuals cannot assert the rights of the State (e.g., the right to regulate, or the right to deference within the margin of appreciation); however, individuals have *active* substantive rights listed in the ECHR as accorded by the State.[14] [As a side note, the European Court of Human Rights (ECtHR), which adjudicates the ECHR, also accords human rights to corporations.][15] The *Archer Daniels* and *Corn Products* cases concerned only economic rights, not political or human ones, but *Corn Products* nevertheless edges closer to the ECHR, and these provisions remain unchanged in the USMCA (also known as 'the updated NAFTA').[16] Thus, while the shift they represent is seminal, the cases themselves are not; they are representative of a wave of cases that split the international legal needle, sprouting new possibilities for substantive rights that reach toward ICP para-Individualism.

iii. Criminal liability of corporations

Ever since the 1948 *IG Farben* trial at Nuremberg following WWII, the international criminal liability of corporations has been a fluctuating concept. Domestically, criminal liability for corporations persists in many states, even if nominally. But internationally, after a surge of enthusiasm that lasted into the 1970s, the idea of corporate criminal liability has largely subsided.[17] In the *IG Farben* case, some directors at IG Farben – a large German chemical conglomerate – incurred criminal liability for furthering goals of the firm that were prohibited under international law, not under domestic law in Nazi Germany. The company had been a major actor in World War II because its development of the Haber-Bosch Process helped Germans replace loss of access to the Chilean nitrate trade with domestically produced synthetic nitrate.[18] Like many corporate actors at the Nuremberg Trials, IG Farben was treated as a legal person capable of violating the Geneva Conventions, just as natural persons could, and those violations were transmuted to the directors of the company who participated with knowledge and intent.[19] Nuremberg's focus on the firm showed that ICPs held direct duties under international law. Without a duty, there could have been no criminal breach. As we shall see in the following section in our discussion of the SCSL's *Charles Taylor* case,[20] the doctrinal waters of enterprise liability have muddied considerably since 1948.

In recent years, domestic courts have also played an increasing role in shaping the international criminality of the ICP. For example, in the 2013 *Amesys Case*, a French appeals court found that a judicial investigation into one corporation's criminal activity could go forward – an acknowledgment that jurisdiction could stick for allegations of corporate criminal behavior if not merits. The as-yet-unresolved case is particularly fascinating because it was brought by two third-party French NGOs seeking accountability for the allegedly criminal behavior of a French company abroad. The allegations claim that Amesys knowingly provided Gaddafi's Libyan government with telecommunications equipment that would enable the government to monitor the communications of their opponents, many of whom were detained and tortured. The company does not dispute that it provided said equipment but denies that the equipment could be used to monitor communications and further contends that it was assisting the government in good faith based on its claims that it wanted to fight terrorism. As of this writing, the judicial investigation is ongoing.[21]

iv. Alien Tort Statute

The developments in France's *Amesys* case parallel those of many an Alien Tort Statute case pre-2013, when the Supreme Court effectively killed corporate liability under the ATS in the *Kiobel* case before sinking the final nails into its coffin in the *Jesner* case. Some of the earlier ATS cases are worth mentioning due to the doctrinal 'normative surplus' they left in their wake.[22] For the narrow aim of this book, I will skip explanations of the facts for the most part and stick to the doctrinal developments that bore influence on the treatment of corporations under international law. Because domestic tort law in common law jurisdictions allows for 'horizontal' claims between individuals within a state, based on rights that are traditionally considered 'vertical', tort law has offered a very flexible rout to frame human rights claims in tort terms.

The ATS is almost as old as the United States. The 1789 drafters included the ATS in the Judiciary Act along with other the provisions establishing the

Supreme and district U.S. courts themselves. The ATS reads: 'The district courts shall have original jurisdiction of any civil action by an alien for a tort only, committed in violation of the law of nations or a treaty of the United States'.[23] Given the legally shaky past and uncertain future of the then-new American experiment, some scholars have suggested that the ATS was included to give foreign governments assurances that customary international law would be respected – that it would be safe to send diplomats to and receive diplomats from the United States.[24] Whatever its original purpose, the ATS was initially uncontroversial and sat largely dormant for about 200 years. But beginning in the early 1970s, coinciding with the era in which MNEs were coming under serious international scrutiny for the first time since their rapid post-War expansion, human and constitutional rights activists saw in the ATS a means through which to hold first individuals and then corporations accountable to customary international law for tortuous behavior abroad. In 1980, the *Filártiga* case became the first to apply U.S. law to a tort that had occurred entirely outside of its borders – a tort whose perpetrator and victim were neither citizens of nor present in the United States when it occurred. The U.S. Second Circuit found that violations of 'the law of nations' fell within its jurisdiction because customary international law was *de facto* 'part of the federal common law'.[25] It found that the defendant knew or should have known that torture was a violation of customary international law on the basis of UN Resolutions, the Universal Declaration of Human Rights (UDHR), bilateral and multilateral prohibitions on torture, and consistent state practice. Thus, *Filártiga* set out a standard of proof by which a 'person' breaches a duty under U.S. tort law if the 'person' knows or should know that a given action is impermissible under international law.

Even though the *Filártiga* case is now specifically inapplicable to ICPs under domestic U.S. law, it nevertheless created a 'normative surplus' with respect to the treatment of ICPs under international law. As recently as late 2016, an ICSID Award citation of *Filártiga* indicated suggested that ICPs could be held liable for *jus cogens* violations against States or individuals in Investor-State Dispute Settlement (ISDS) proceedings – that is, violations of extremely pervasive international norms – even if liability could not be found in the applicable treaty or domestic law.[26]

In 2004, the case of *Sosa v. Alarez-Machain* began what would become a substantial walking back of foreign liability under the ATS.[27] The Court set out two circumstances under which 'purely private actors' could incur ATS liability for violations of international law: (1) when the actions in question impinged upon sovereignty and gave rise to risk of war or substantial diplomatic difficulty or (2) when an ICP or individual is situated 'outside domestic boundaries',[28] presumably meaning not present in any State, that is, in international waters, on an airplane, or in outer space.

Further limitations came in 2009 with *Presbyterian Church of Sudan v. Talisman Energy*.[29] The Court found – erroneously, in my view[30] – that the standard for aiding and abetting liability under international law is 'purpose rather than knowledge alone'. Emphasizing that it was drawing the 'purpose' standard from international law, not domestic law, the Court found that Talisman had not acted with the 'purpose of harming civilians living in southern Sudan'. Given the status quo of corporate law in most States,[31] this conclusion is axiomatic. As in most cases, it was obvious that the corporation did not act with the purpose of harming civilians. But this is due to a sort of corporate legal 'predestination': by definition, a corporation's 'purpose' – its *raison d'être* – is to produce profits for its shareholders and it almost always acts with that purpose in mind; harm to civilian populations is often termed a 'negative externality',[32] to deploy economic terminology exemplary of the discipline's tendency to distance human decision from market forces.

These quibbles aside, the Court's finding is dodgy on at least two grounds. First, the ATS does not call upon the U.S. Supreme Court – an appellate court interpreting law rather than determining fact – or a lower district court to act as an international criminal court of first instance. And second, in deciding upon the standard for 'aiding and abetting' under international law, the Court relied heavily upon the Rome Statute's Article 25, but it only cited *part* of the standard. Article 25(3)(c) requires that an ICP act with 'purpose of facilitating commission' of the crime, but Article 25(3)(d) provides another avenue. An ICP:

> [S]hall be liable . . . if that person . . . *in any other way contributes* to the commission of a crime . . . by a group of persons acting with a common purpose. . . . Such *contribution* shall be intentional and shall *either* [b]e made with the aim of furthering [the crime] *or* [b]e made with the *knowledge* of the intention of the group.[33]

In other words, the Rome Statute provides circumstances for both elements, not just one. Under Article 25(3)(c), the ICP is liable for aiding and abetting if it acts with the 'knowledge' of a crime and with the 'purpose' of assisting in its commission. However, under Article 25(3)(d), an ICP is liable for aiding and abetting if the ICP if it 'contributes' to the commission of the crime with the 'knowledge' that the principal perpetrator intends to commit that crime. These points are reaffirmed by the *Charles Taylor* case discussed earlier, which came down two years after this one but which relied on a line of precedent dating back to almost a decade earlier.

Also in 2009, beginning with the Second Circuit in *Abdullahi v. Pfizer*, federal courts began to chip away at the idea that U.S. Courts had jurisdiction to hear cases from foreign companies – even wholly or majority-owned subsidiaries of U.S. corporations.[34] The *Pfizer* case was twice dismissed on the grounds that Nigeria, where the BigPharma defendant had conducted drug experiments on sick children without consent, was the proper place to bring suit. Although the plaintiffs sought redress in U.S. Courts because they distrusted the Nigerian judiciary, they eventually obtained a judgment and settled before the appeal, after it was exposed that Pfizer attempted to obtain evidence of corruption with which to blackmail the prosecution. (We will briefly discuss how international anti-corruption law and its understanding of corporations facilitates the use of corruption as blackmail later.)

By the time the now-famous *Kiobel v. Royal Dutch Petroleum* saga began in 2010, the ATS was on its last legs. That saga ended in 2013 with a Supreme Court assertion that current international law does not hold corporations responsible for human rights violations generally, and for international crimes. The foundational premise in *Kiobel* – one that is by now obviously misguided – is that the actors in international law are almost exclusively states, therefore private corporations do not have obligations under international law and thus cannot have liability under the ATS. The majority found that the ATS is not suitable for claims against corporations and clearly distinguished between domestic liability and international liability of corporations:

> [I]nternational law has steadfastly rejected the notion of corporate liability for international crimes, and no international tribunal has ever held a corporation liable for a violation of the law of nations.[35]

As we have already seen, this statement is simply false. In fact, corporations have been found liable for violations of the law of nations at least since 1880, when dozens of ships were seized, sanctioned, and auctioned by order of international antislavery courts.[36] In 1948, at Nuremberg, the I.G. Farben conglomerate discussed earlier was found to have violated the 1907 Hague Convention.[37] In 2003, at the ICTR, a Rwandan radio-television company and a newspaper were found to have participated in international crimes.[38] And by 2010, even international investment Tribunals had found that the corrupt acts of private corporate investors had breached customary international law.[39] Similar examples abound. The Court could only have accurately reached the conclusion it reached if it presupposed that the private business corporation acting internationally was something legally distinct from the international legal personality.

Some notion of corporate exceptionalism like the 2010 presupposition runs through the final entry to the *Kiobel* saga, which came down from the U.S. Supreme Court in 2013.[40] That decision set out the 'touch and concern' standard for corporate liability: corporate activity must 'touch and concern' the U.S. with 'sufficient force'. The Court stressed that 'mere corporate presence' does not meet the standard. Finally, the 2018 *Jenser v. Arab Bank* case found that foreign corporations – even if they are subsidiaries of U.S. corporations – cannot be sued in the United States.[41] The only way to reach the corporate parent would be to pierce the corporate veil, a concept discussed at length in the next chapter of this book. The splitting of liability in *Jenser*, as in many

ICP cases, is due to the separation of ownership and control that has become a globally pervasive hallmark of the ICP.

In sum, after *Jenser*, claims under the ATS must demonstrate (1) that the U.S. corporation, not just its foreign subsidiary, violated customary international law; (2) if the claim is for aiding and abetting, that the U.S. corporation had the requisite *mens rea* under international law; and (3) that there was sufficient conduct in the United States to satisfy *Kiobel*'s 'touch and concern' test. Each of these prongs are doctrinally dodgy and likely inconsistent with international law. But what concerns this book's topic the most is the 'normative surplus' that has emerged from forty-some years of ATS litigation and influenced the conceptualization of the corporation under international law more generally. As legal education and services become increasingly globalized, especially in the field of corporate law,[42] the doctrinal developments in the United States have disproportionately bled into international conceptualizations of the ICP. Indeed, most of the lawyers appointed to international arbitral tribunals, for instance, were educated at least partly in the United States or the United Kingdom.[43]

One important element to note from the ATS conceptualization of jurisdiction for the ICP is its heavy reliance on the concept of sovereignty. The Court's presumption against extraterritoriality and the hurdles it sets up to overcome that presumption are based on the primacy of another State's jurisdiction. Put another way, the Court's standards presuppose that corporate torts take place within States. But this is an increasingly inaccurate assumption. Imagine, for instance, an oil company negligently causing a massive spill in international waters, or an ICP utilizing a vast array of shell companies, private individuals, and networks to evade taxes. What happens to ICP liability beyond the State?

v. Human rights

Recent international investment tribunals suggest that, when it comes to human rights, the ICP holds negative obligations toward the state, but no positive obligations toward natural persons. For example, in late 2016, an ICSID Tribunal argued in *Urbaser v. Argentina* that international law cannot 'reject by necessity any idea that a foreign investor company could not be a subject to international law obligations'.[44] *Urbaser* observed that corporations have the capacity to hold rights under IIAs which constitute part of international law, which implies the capacity to hold obligations under international law as well.[45] While *Urbaser* found difficulties in transferring to a corporation the state-tailored obligation to ensure the right to water,[46] it stressed the integrated nature of international investment law and human rights.[47] Perhaps most importantly for the development of the ICP, *Urbaser* was the first IIL case to hear a counterclaim on the basis of an alleged human rights violation.[48] Prior to that, and especially prior to the 2011 *Roussalis v. Romania* Award,[49] the general rule was that States could bring counterclaims against investors only if the investor consented to the counterclaim. Needless to say, this was not a common occurrence. Today, it is still the case that States cannot initiate claims against investors, as it is States that form IIAs allowing indeterminant future investors to initiate claims against either State party. As a colleague and I have noted elsewhere,[50] it is an asymmetry of legal power inherent to the system.

The *Urbaser* case was invoked by the Tribunal in *David Aven v. Costa Rica* in late 2018 to justify a counterclaim not explicitly provided in the IIA. 'This trend is likely to continue', it declared. '[It] shows that investment tribunals are ready to hear counterclaims when dealing with investor wrongdoing'.[51] In this way, the *Aven* Tribunal decided that it had jurisdiction to hear a counterclaim concerning a corporation's alleged damage to the environment. It found that, by contemplating the existence of 'claimants' and 'respondents', investors automatically consented to counterclaims under Article 46 of the ICSID Convention (which allows for counterclaims if they fall 'within the scope of consent' of ascending to the IIA), because there would be no other possible actor capable of bringing a counterclaim.[52] An even more recent report from an expert's commission in the Hague echoed this understanding, finding that in order for a State to sustain a counterclaim against an ICP or other investor, the counterclaim must:

(1) Be within the jurisdiction of the Tribunal and
(2) Arise directly out of the subject matter of the investment.[53]

Even with these elements met, though, the question remains: what can a State counterclaim under an IIA that spells out only State obligations? Here *Aven* affirmed that "it could be argued that [the IIA] contains, at least implicitly, some obligations to investors, especially with respect to the environmental laws of the host State."[54] The Tribunal essentially found that clauses in the IIA that prohibited exceptions to State environmental laws could apply only to investors. Although the clauses implicated Costa Rica's domestic laws, the IIA itself was part of international law subject to the full arsenal of international law interpretive tools. Thus, in this instance, the ICP – the categorical 'investor' – was a direct subject of international law, and the State was the apparatus through which to enforce international law.

Although the Tribunal ultimately gave primacy to the State (because the ICP had violated both domestic and international law), the finding in *Aven* building off of *Urbaser* is an astounding judge-made development in the ICP. As the ICP is neither State nor human, it could be said that the ICP owes negative obligations toward the former and positive obligations toward the latter. That is, the ICP has a negative duty not to interfere with the State's ability to protect human rights and a positive duty to 'the international community', in the words of *Barcelona Traction*.[55] These cases set out two different visions for the future of ICP rights and obligations under international law, one grounding subjectivity for corporations in *jus cogens* norms and the other in *erga omnes* obligations.

These developments are significant for the protection of human rights in their implicit acknowledgment that domestic systems alone – no matter how diligent – are inadequate and unable to protect human rights across ICP supply chains. To monitor the complete supply chains of many ICPs would not only be impractical for each State along that supply chain, but it would also contradict basic notions of State sovereignty and non-interference. A high degree of State cooperation and corporate subjectivity are practical solutions, and States perceive international obligations in different ways. A recent example of such challenges can be found in the 2015 U.S. Federal District case of *Melanie Barber v. Nestle*.[56] There, the plaintiff alleged that Nestle had violated California consumer protection statutes by failing to disclose that some ingredients in their cat food products contained seafood which was sourced from forced labor. But the court found that the relevant domestic law required only disclosure of the measures taken; Nestle was obligated only to disclose its rules to consumers, not to enforce on suppliers. Indeed, as a practical matter, neither States nor ICPs can unilaterally monitor how every element of every product from every participant in their supply chain is produced. I want to suggest that international economic agreements – conceiving like *Aven* of each State as its enforcement – are best equipped for such a task. The primary problem, which judge-made law on the ICP and other measures are slowly tackling, is that international economic law has largely insulated itself from human and environmental concerns. I have included texts that further elucidate that process in the endnotes.[57]

vi. Environment

The *Aven v. Costa Rica* case also illustrates an internationalization of domestic trends concerning corporate obligations to the environment. That Tribunal found that measures adopted by a home state "should be deemed compulsory for everybody under the jurisdiction of the State, particularly the foreign investors."[58] But in the case of environmental measures, this compulsion transcends the State. For the *Aven* Tribunal, although '[i]t is true that the enforcement of environmental law is primarily [the responsibility of] the State . . . it cannot be admitted that a foreign investor could not be subject to international law obligations in this field'.[59] For *Aven*, ICPs can be directly bound to international law 'when it comes to rights and obligations that are the concern of all States'.[60] Through this language, the *Aven* tribunal suggests that the environment is just such a concern. Moreover, as discussed in the previous subsection, the Tribunal extended State *erga omnes* obligations to ICPs and other investors.

While the implications of *Aven* have yet to ripple through newer decisions, the Tribunal's reasoning strongly suggests that ICPs are part of that *omnium* that was previously inhabited only by the State. Some optimists, such as the Costa Rican Association of International Law, have speculated that *Aven* creates the possibility that environmental arguments in and of themselves can become a 'new source of law' binding ICPs and other investors.[61] While it is still too soon to tell, here lies at least one trajectory that recently moved from 'possibility' to 'potentiality'. Even so, there are older international arbitral cases that cut the other way (see e.g., *Bilcon v. Canada*) and similar concerns to those expressed in *Aven* have been raised in domestic courts for decades with mixed results. I will discuss a few of the more recent of these in Chapter 4.

To highlight the need for rethinking ICP obligations in this area, it is worth noting at least one representative domestic example of an attempt to veil-pierce. Consider the aspirations of India's 1990 Supreme Court in the case, *Charan Lal Sahu v. Union of India*. In a now infamous industrial disaster similar to the Rana Plaza building collapse and the Vizag gas leak,[62] roughly 3,000 people died after lethal gas escaped from a pesticide-producing plant in the city of Bhopal.[63] The plant was an Indian subsidiary of an American company.[64] In addition to the 3,000 deaths, thousands more were affected by injuries of various degrees of seriousness, both permanent and temporary, and there was also interruption of business and damage to livestock, property and the environment. After years of litigation, the District of Bhopal found that it had no satisfying remedy in national courts; the American firm 'owned' but did not 'control' the nearly insolvent Indian subsidiary. The corporate veil could not be pierced. Implicitly acknowledging this, the Indian Supreme Court stated in dicta:

> A transnational corporation should be made liable and subservient to the law and liability should not be restricted to an affiliate company only but the parent corporation should also be made liable for any damage caused to the human beings or ecology. The law must require transnational corporations to agree to pay such damages as may be determined by the statutory agencies and forums constituted under it without exposing the victims to long drawn litigation.[65]

In making this plea (which was ultimately ignored), the Indian Supreme Court cited clauses 9 and 13 of the UN Code of Conduct on Transnational Corporations (now also ignored).[66] Clause 9 of the Code states that:

> Transnational corporations shall/should carry on their activities in conformity with the development policies, objectives and priorities set out by the Governments of the countries in which they operate and work seriously towards making a positive contribution to the achievement of

> such goals at the national and, as appropriate, the regional level, within the framework of regional integration programmes. Transnational corporations shall/should co-operate with the Governments of the countries in which they operate with a view to contributing to the development process and shall/should be responsive to requests for consultation in this respect, thereby establishing mutually beneficial relations with these countries.[67]

Clause 13 reads:

> Transnational corporations should/shall respect human rights and fundamental freedoms in the countries in which they operate. In their social and industrial relations, transnational corporations should/shall not discriminate on the basis of race, colour, sex, religion, language, social, national and ethnic origin or political or other opinion. Transnational corporations should/shall conform to government policies designed to extend equality of opportunity and treatment.[68]

The Indian Supreme Court used these clauses to anchor an argument that, because corporate respect for human rights and compliance with development goals were rooted in respect for sovereignty, and the realization of these clauses require adherence to evolving international standards and domestic constitutional principles, ICPs must ensure that 'safety to the environment and ecology to enable the people to lead a healthy and clean life'.[69] The Court hoped to ground this ICP duty in international law, and perhaps could have if the Code of Conduct was not already effectively a dead document.

The example of *Charan Lal Sahu* is a voice in a chorus of calls for less burdensome requirements for transnational veil piercing or direct ICP liability to international law. (Note: within ICP liability, I include both corporate 'parent' and 'child'.) However, it is in many ways representative of the concerns raised particularly by countries that are more often 'host' than 'home'.[70] Cases like these are especially worth remembering in light of recent scholarship that – perhaps due to an amnesic effect brought on by the (pragmatic but legally soft) Ruggie Principles – sees the methodological challenges of an international system as cause to declare that international corporate oversight reinforced by domestic systems are the way forward when it comes global corporate regulation and accountability.[71] Indeed, this scholarship may ring true for human rights issues. But it does not ring true for many tort claims, for environmental concerns, or for transnational issues such as tax evasion and interstate inequality.[72] In *Aven* and the cases that led to it, international judge-made law finally moved toward making India's 1990 aspirations a reality. The methodological and theoretical challenges that face the present are grave. Sadly, domestic systems are just as inadequate today as they were thirty years ago to address legal problems that span multiple jurisdictions and, by virtue of unique properties, transcend inter-jurisdictional or jurisdiction-dependent thinking on international law. The status quo has changed little in the intervening years, but as discussed in Chapter 5, hope through law is possible in jurisdictions both domestic and international.

vii. Intellectual property

International intellectual property enforcement is a strange and powerful mobilizer of international economic instruments. It is strange because it connects novel and non-universal concepts of intellectual property to trade and investment issues. It is powerful because it is a form of property that serves economically powerful ICPs above all other actors. Of the three primary forms of interstate power – economic, militaristic, and 'soft'[73] – intellectual property serves most directly those actors that possess great economic power.

Intellectual property in relation to economic power has taken on new dimensions in international investment law. For example, in the 2017 case of *Eli Lilly v. Canada*, although the Tribunal denied an investor the right to appeal to international arbitration in order to reinterpret domestic intellectual property law, the litigation brought a number of fascinating issues to the fore.[74] The case involved a domestic court's interpretation of patent law that resulted in a revocation of patents for lack of utility. This was a result of the 'promise utility doctrine' under Canadian patent law, which is comprised of three elements: (1) the identification of a 'promise' in the patent disclosure, against which utility is measured; (2) the prohibition on the use of post-filing evidence to prove utility; and (3) the requirement that pre-filing evidence to support a sound prediction of utility must be included in the patent. Essentially, the federal courts of Canada, all the way up to the Supreme Court, denied Eli Lilly the right to sit on chemical compound patents beyond a certain number of years when the company had not demonstrated that the compounds had promise of fulfilling a given utility. The patent specifications did not contain a factually based sound prediction of utility for the chemical compounds. Eli Lilly commenced international investment arbitration against Canada under NAFTA's Investment Chapter – the now defunct-but-replaced 1994 agreement between Canada, the United States, and Mexico. In the arbitral proceedings, Eli Lilly alleged that the revocation of its Zyprexa and Strattera patents (which were filed in 1991 and 1996, respectively) was an unfair und inequitable treatment contrary to NAFTA Article 1105 as well as an expropriation under NAFTA Article 1110. Eli Lilly argued in this respect that the 'promise utility doctrine' was a radical departure from Canada's traditional utility standard and the utility standards applied by Canada's NAFTA partners, the United States and Mexico. It essentially requested that the arbitral tribunal punish Canada's courts for the way in which it had interpreted Canadian law.

The ICSID Tribunal that heard the complaint dismissed Eli Lilly's claim not on jurisdictional grounds, but on a failure to demonstrate the merits. The

Tribunal found that Canada's patent-utility doctrine underwent an 'incremental and evolutionary change', rather than the radical departure Eli Lilly had alleged. This suggests that, had the Tribunal been convinced of the radicality of Canada's judicial innovations, Eli Lilly – the ICP – would have been able to circumvent the Supreme Court of that State and access a judicial remedy not available to non-ICPs, both legal and natural. In other words, an ICP can attack decisions of a country's judiciary about the meaning of its own law even in the absence of a denial of justice. Allowing ICPs to stake jurisdiction on these grounds creates the possibility of an end run around the domestic principle of judicial finality by framing the claim as one of a violation of fair and equitable treatment or (even more shockingly) one of expropriation.

The intellectual property decision in Eli Lilly is the first of its kind but is nevertheless illustrative in the extreme of the ways in which fairly 'vanilla' investor's rights such as 'FET', 'Expropriation', and 'Full Protection and Security' in reality can accord whole new sets of judge-made rights to ICPs and other investors that are not accorded to any entity except for ICPs and other investors.

viii. Clean hands and corruption

When an ICP becomes intertwined with financial misgivings in securing investment opportunities, a series of arbitral awards have set out what might be called an international obligation but have ensured that this obligation is temporally bound. I am referring here to what has become known as the 'legality principle' or the 'clean-hands doctrine'. These terms refer most fundamentally to the notion that an ICP or foreign investor should not gain access to the rights accorded to them by international investment law if the investor was only able to make the investment because of an unlawful or 'corrupt' act. As a legal doctrine, 'clean hands' first clearly emerged in cases that involved blatantly illegal behavior on the part of ICPs.[75] In cases like *World Duty Free v. Kenya*, Tribunals created an 'international public policy . . . or . . . transnational public policy' in the form of retroactive prohibitions on 'personal donations' to government officials if it is shown that the investment would not have gone forward *but for* the personal donation.[76] (This was essentially an *ex post facto* global ban on bribery, created by three arbitrators.) As elucidated in the 'corruption' section in the next chapter, 'bribery' is far too complex an international concept to be dealt with in this fashion. A better formulation can be found in the seminal 2008 ICSID Tribunal case of *Plama v. Bulgaria*:

> [I]n imposing obligations on States to treat investors in a fair and transparent fashion, investment treaties seek to encourage legal and bona fide investments. An investor who has obtained an investment in the host State only by acting in bad faith or in violation of the laws of the host state, has brought itself within the scope of application of the ECT

> through wrongful acts. Such an investor should not be allowed to benefit from the Treaty.[77]

This language steps away from appeals to the notion of 'transnational public policy' by hinging the clean hands doctrine on 'bad faith' rather than 'public good'. While there is no set definition of 'bad faith' in international law, virtually any definition requires 'double mindedness', intent to deceive, or intentional failure to correct a misconception.[78] This standard was referenced and refined in a 2014 Permanent Court of Arbitration (PCA) Tribunal Award, *Yukos v. Russia*, which found that a treaty need not explicitly include a legality clause in order for an investor to be held to 'good faith' or 'clean hands' standards under general international law. In that case, however, the PCA found that 'good faith' vis-à-vis an investment is temporally bound – 'good faith' only obliges an investor to make its investment 'in accordance with the law' of the host State and does not extend to post-investment conduct.

Thus, ICPs can engage in behavior intended to deceive actors in foreign or domestic markets so long as the ICP did not obtain the initial investment opportunity via deceptive or domestically illicit action. Subsequent behavior may run afoul of domestic law in the jurisdictions in which it operates, but that behavior will not deprive the ICP of its right to access remedies against States under international law. Note that fiscal remedies under these agreements are calculated based on an understanding that a State has committed a legal wrong – a clear cut black and white judgment – and that the State is therefore responsible to compensate the investor based on the 'fair market value' of the investment *but for* the State's actions. Because the idea is that the State is obligated to 'wipe out' the harm caused by its action,[79] compensation is not limited to fiscal harm incurred within the host State. Rather, the State must compensate for all harm caused by its actions, regardless of where the harm occurred or whether it was foreseeable.[80] Needless to say, this standard casts an extremely wide potential net of liability. Thus, where ICPs enjoy the temporal limits of 'bad faith' and access to extra-domestic definitions of corruption, States are potentially liable for harm to the ICP incurred in any jurisdiction at any time so long as an arbitrator finds it was caused by a State's illicit act.

ix. Importing rights through the New York Convention

The first and most widely ratified instrument for modern international arbitration is the New York Convention on the Recognition and Enforcement of Foreign Arbitral Awards (New York Convention). Drafted in 1958 and first effective in 1959, the New York Convention requires the domestic courts of its Parties to recognize private contractual agreements across State borders and to enforce arbitral Awards made in or against the territories of its Parties.[81] It is a document originally aimed toward the enforcement of private international law that today blurs the lines between the private and the public. Importantly, with both the New York and ICSID Conventions, States often enforce Awards and courts import arbitral decisions as a matter of self-interest. As José Alvarez once put it:

> Among the most effective [enforcement tool] is the market for capital. Commercial risk insurers and global suppliers of capital – from the [IMF] to regional development banks to other foreign investors contemplating entry – are likely to extract a serious economic penalty over time on states that renege on their treaty commitments to comply with arbitral awards.[82]

The climate created through the combination of the New York Convention and State eagerness to enforce Awards gives rise to a particularly salient facilitator of the ICP's creation: the willingness of arbitrators to treat both international law and the domestic law of multiple jurisdictions as applicable to a dispute so long as the domestic or international law can attach to some party to the dispute (State, human, ICP, or third party). Once an investment operation has been identified in the territory of the host State, each additional right that the investment acquires is not subjected to an additional assessment of a territorial link.[83] Indeed, the rights arising from international instruments and from home State or third-party domestic legal systems have been protected under investment treaties as much as those arising from the law of the host State.

An instructive example can be found in the 2010 ICSID case of *ATA v. Jordan*.[84] There, Jordan was found to have breached an investor's right to arbitration in contravention of limits imposed by the New York Convention. Although the arbitration agreement between the parties was governed by Jordanian law, the *scope* of the investor's right to arbitrate and even the existence of *a right* to arbitrate was determined by reference to Jordan's obligations under the New York Convention, not by reference to a domestic law. As the Tribunal put it:

> After the annulment by the Jordanian courts, ATA should have been able to invoke the Arbitration Agreement in the Contract; Jordanian courts, in accordance with Article II of the New York Convention, should then have respected ATA's right and refrained from exercising their own jurisdiction on the substance of the dispute. In the Tribunal's view, the relevant issue on which to focus relates to the extinguishment by operation of Jordanian law of the Arbitration Agreement upon the annulment of the Final Award.[85]

This conclusion finds support in cases that have considered whether rights stemming from commercial arbitral awards issued in third States can qualify as part of an investment for the purposes of investment treaty protection. For example, in the 2011 UNCITRAL Award for *White Industries v. India*, the tribunal found that a foreign commercial arbitral award rendered in France created rights that constituted a continuation of the relevant investment in India, the host State.[86] There was no question as to whether there was the need for a territorial nexus between the award and the host State. The issue did not arise as relevant for determination. Instead, the tribunal held that the French arbitral award fell within the definition of 'investment' in the relevant BIT,[87] as part of the claimant's original investment in India:

> [T]he Tribunal concludes that rights under the Award constitute part of White's original investment (i.e., being a crystalisation of its rights under the Contract) and, as such, are subject to such protection as is afforded to investments by the BIT.[88]

The tribunal in *Frontier Petroleum Services Ltd. v. Czech Republic* similarly found that arbitral Awards were 'investments', potentially enforceable in States that were neither party to the original dispute nor subject to the domestic or legal systems that governed the original dispute.[89] This reasoning adds to a class of rights that are only available to ICPs and a small number of natural person investors: the right to enforce a law in a jurisdiction not bound by the law itself but bound by contract to honor it. Once again, through ISDS, international law creates a situation in which a court of 'fourth instance' is available only to investors;[90] a fortified right to due process available only to 'foreign investors', not to other natural or legal persons. Indeed, an arbitral tribunal can review a domestic court's application of compliance with a State's obligations under international law. It can find that, even contrary to a given domestic supreme court's decision, a State has a substantive obligation under the terms of an investment agreement.

III. Conceptualizing judge-made ICP obligations: *erga omnes* v. *jus cogens*

The caselaw presented here indicates that two specific categories of international obligations are emerging, some of which apply only to 'investors', meaning in the vast majority of cases, to ICPs. These categories of obligations are carved out by arbitral tribunals through reference to their source. In *Urbaser* these were *jus cogens* obligations, which references 'hyper norms' in language appealing to tort litigation. In *Aven* these were *erga omnes* obligations, which aligned with *Barcelona Traction*'s acceptance of the notion that some obligations are owed by all toward all, that is, toward the *ominum*. Once that notion is accepted, the question becomes, which legal personalities fit within the *omnium*? The latter category – *erga omnes* – defines international obligations from the top down: a given practice is either so impactful or so important that all individuals or States incur an obligation to uphold it (a). The former category – jus cogens – defines international obligations from the bottom up: individuals or States engage in a practice that becomes so pervasive that all States assume a degree of reliance on its continuation (b). So far, neither type of obligation has been applied directly to ICPs. In both cases mentioned, the ICP's international obligations were drawn from State obligations under international law and were characterized in the negative. That is, the ICP was understood to have an obligation *not to interfere* with the State's positive obligations under international law.

a. Erga omnes

In *Barcelona Traction*,[91] when the ICJ addressed the question of whether losses suffered by Belgian shareholders were the consequence 'of the violation of obligations in which they were the beneficiaries',[92] it was quick to frame its reasoning in terms of State obligations. In other words, the question of the rights of Belgian shareholders was actually a question of rights of Belgium. The then found that, because rights and obligations of corporate entities are merely a matter of domestic law, Belgium did not have a right recognized by international law. However, the ICJ stated in dicta that it would have been different for Belgium if it had represented not rights arising vis-à-vis another State in the field of diplomatic protection, but rather an obligation toward the international community as a whole.[93] The latter are obligations *erga omnes*: they are the concern of all States, all States have a legal interest in their protection,[94] and it is an *international* legal interest. Thus, in theory Belgium would have had title to espouse the claim of its nationals had they suffered a violation to the basic rights of their human person, examples set by the ICJ are slavery and racial discrimination, *i.a.*[95] However, even *erga omnes* rights can only be protected by States when victims are nationals,[96] which in *Barcelona Traction* was questioned given the Canadian nationality of the corporate vehicle the Belgian nationals had invested in.

To conclude, *Barcelona Traction* does not find an independent cause of action under international law for companies or shareholders against a State, in the absence of a specific treaty. Such cause of action belongs to the State alone. Because the grievance suffered by the Belgian nationals did not amount to an *erga omnes* violation, it did not find that Belgium had capacity to represent them; but even considering denial of justice as a violation of an *erga omnes* obligation, it was the nationality of the corporate vehicle that was predominant for the purpose of Belgium's claim, not that of its shareholders. In the 50-plus years since *Barcelona Traction*, its outline of investor rights and obligations is faithfully reflected in the history of international litigation brought by investors and against them.

This does not mean that international efforts are not under way to regulate the transnational company under international law. Indeed, these efforts started as early as the 1970s at the United Nations,[97] and have recently rekindled with the 'Zero Draft' treaty of 2018,[98] a revised draft of which was published in July 2019.[99] The debate at the United Nations, though, does not escape the fundamental challenge acknowledged by *Barcelona Traction*, to the extent even the revised draft addresses business accountability and liability through the lens of domestic legislation, albeit made compulsory by the draft.[100] While the revised draft has made substantial improvements to the Zero Draft,[101] it does not appear to tackle the issue of international law obligations for corporate entities. In other words, domestic litigation would still be the venue to litigate corporate entities' obligations even under a binding treaty such as the one currently being discussed.

b. Jus cogens

The notion of *jus cogens* is codified in Article 53 of the Vienna Convention on the Law of Treaties of 1969, as a peremptory norm of general international law. Any treaty conflicting with such a norm at the time of its conclusion is void, and peremptory norms are defined as:

> [A] norm accepted and recognized by the international community of States as a whole as a norm from which no derogation is permitted and which can be modified only by a subsequent norm of general international law having the same character.

While the International Law Commission has identified certain *jus cogens* norms,[102] judicial bodies have extended the list of norms with peremptory status in a systematic pattern of absence of references to state practice and *opinio juris* to support the conclusion that a given norm is *jus cogens*, even adopting a natural law approach to the issue.[103] The threshold for the recognition of customary law is thus lower than that of *jus cogens*, which makes focusing on customary law more effective than invoking *jus cogens* in international courts.

In domestic courts, the notion of *jus cogens* has been increasingly used with reference to corporate duties to States or shareholders. Hence, *jus cogens* has made what some have called a 'retreat to domestic law',[104] especially when it comes to human rights violations by companies. These domestic cases take on transnational claims of three general types: transnational tort claims, misrepresentation cases and director and officer liability and shareholder class actions.[105]

We have already discussed one thread of transnational tort claim at length in the ATS section. Apart from the ATS cases, one of the most relevant for our discussion is the Nevsun case, currently on appeal in Canada.[106] In that case, Claimants seek to apply public international law directly against an ICP in a national court, making public international law enforceable through civil sanctions under Canadian law. The trial court found that, because corporations are not direct subjects of international law, they cannot be held accountable to norms of customary international law, *jus cogens* or otherwise. The British Columbia Court of Appeal disagreed:

> We have seen that international law is 'in flux' and that transnational law, which regulates 'actions or events that transcend national frontiers' is developing, especially in connection with human rights violations that are not effectively addressed by traditional 'international mechanisms . . . Other jurisdictions have been willing to hold corporate actors accountable for violations of *jus cogens*.'[107]

Here, the Court refers to the fact that domestic courts citing international *jus cogens* obligations have found breaches of fiduciary-based international duties: ICPs have been held liable for misrepresenting their human rights practices;[108] and shareholder class actions address director breach of duty of loyalty when human rights practices and representations are misrepresented or neglected.[109] These decisions are remarkable in that they broaden fiduciary duties to include corporate adherence to public international law. Nevertheless, these decisions hinge corporate liability for breach of public international law on a domestic statute or law that connects the international breach with a domestic one, making it enforceable upon the corporate entity.

What these cases underscore, therefore, is not a direct link between international law and corporate behavior but, rather, that corporate behavior can breach international law. Even if the State is needed to create and enforce the remedy, ICPs have the capacity to breach international law. And while breaches of *jus cogens* are not collective in nature, an obligation *erga omnes* – per *Barcelona Traction* – is owed to the international community as a whole.

Notes

1 *Reparation of Injuries suffered in the service of the United Nations*, Advisory Opinion, 1949 I.C.J. 174, 179 (Apr. 11, 1949).
2 *Barcelona Traction, Light and Power Company, Ltd. (Belgium v. Spain); Preliminary Objections*, International Court of Justice, I.C.J. Reports 1964 (1964).
3 *Id.*
4 José Alvarez, 'Beware: Boundary Crossings' – A Critical Appraisal of Public Law Approaches to International Investment Law, *Journal of World Investment & Trade* (2016).
5 *Vacuum Salt Products v. Ghana*, Award, ICSID Case No. ARB/92/1 (1994).
6 *Tokios Tokeles v. Ukraine*, Award, ICSID Case No. ARB/02/18 (2007).
7 Convention on the Settlement of Investment Disputes Between States and Nationals of Other States [International Centre for the Settlement of Investment Disputes (ICSID)], 575 *UNTS* 159 (1964).
8 *Archer Daniels & Lyle Ingredients v. Mexico*, Award, ICSID Case No. ARB(AF)/04/05 (2004); see also North American Free Trade Agreement, 32 I.L.M. 289 and 605 (1993).
9 *Corn Products International v. Mexico*, Award ICSID Case No. ARB(AF)/04/1 (2004).

10 *Id.*
11 *Id.*
12 For an overview on the 'precedent-like' process through which multilateral judgments in one treaty regime bleed into the reasoning of arbitrators reviewing other treaty regimes, see José Alvarez, 'Beware: Boundary Crossings' – A Critical Appraisal of Public Law Approaches to International Investment Law, *Journal of World Investment & Trade* (2016). See also Chapter 4 of this book.
13 *Corn Products International v. Mexico*, Award ICSID Case No. ARB(AF)/04/1 (2004).
14 See generally Council of Europe, European Convention on Human Rights (ECHR) (1953).
15 See e.g., Vanessa Wilcox, Corporate Rights Under the ECHR, in *A Company's Right to Damages for Non-Pecuniary Loss* (2016).
16 Agreement between the United States of America, the United Mexican States, and Canada 12/13/19 Text (USMCA), available at https://ustr.gov/trade-agreements/free-trade-agreements/united-states-mexico-canada-agreement/agreement-between (accessed 20 May 2020). The agreement is meant to replace NAFTA, but as of this writing has not yet entered into force.
17 See United Nations War Crimes Commission, *IG Farben and Krupp Trials*, Law Reports Vol. X (1949).
18 *Id.*
19 *Id.*
20 *Prosecutor v. Charles Ghankay Taylor (Judgement Summary)*, SCSL-03–1-T (26 April 2012).
21 International Federation for Human Rights, *Amesys Case: The Investigation Chamber green lights the investigative proceedings on the sale of surveillance equipment by Amesys to the Khadafi regime* (17 January 2013).
22 On the concept of 'normative surplus', see e.g., Ingo Venzke, Possibilities of the Past: Histories of the NIEO and the Travails of Critique, 29 *Journal of the History of International Law* (2019); Kevin Crow, Bandung's Fate, in Ingo Venzke and Kevin Jon Heller (Eds.), *Contingency in the Course of International Law* (2020).
23 28 USC Section 1350.
24 E.g., Beth Stephens, The Curious History of the Alien Tort Statute, *Notre Dame L. Rev.* (2014).
25 *Filártiga v. Peña-Irala*, 630 F.2d 876 (2d Cir. 1980).
26 This refers to the ICSID Award of *Urbaser v. Argentina*, described in some detail in a following section and cited earlier. The case does not directly assert the conclusions I offer, but it implies these conclusions *a contrario* through its reference to *Filártega* in a footnote.
27 *Sosa v. Alarez-Machain*, 542 US 692 (2004).
28 *Id.*
29 *Presbyterian Church of Sudan v. Talisman Energy*, 582 F.3d 244 (2nd Cir. 2009).
30 Kevin Crow, International Law and Corporate Participation in Times of Armed Conflict, *Berkeley J. Int'l L.* (2019).
31 The typical statement in the 'purpose' section, which is typically required in articles of incorporation or articles of organization that found ICPs and other company forms, is 'to engage in any lawful business activity' – so long as the business act is lawful the *mens rea* of the business transaction or the broader purpose of the act is not generally questioned.
32 See e.g., Kevin Crow, International Corporate Constituency as a Human Problem, *Transnational Legal Theory* (forthcoming, 2021).
33 UN General Assembly, *Rome Statute of the International Criminal Court (last amended 2010), 17 July 1998* (2002).
34 *Abdullahi v. Pfizer*, 562 F.3d 163 (2nd Cir. 2009).
35 *Kiobel v. Royal Dutch Petroluem*, 569 US 108 (2013).
36 See e.g., Jenny S. Martinez, Antislavery Courts and the Dawn of International Human Rights Law, 117 *Yale Law Journal* 550 (2008).

37 United Nations War Crimes Commission, *IG Farben and Krupp Trials*, Law Reports Vol. X (1949).
38 *Prosecutor v. Nahimana, Barayagwiza and Ngeze*, Case No. ICTR-99–52-T (2003).
39 See e.g., Paul D. Carrington, Essay, Enforcing International Corrupt Practices Law, 32 *Mich. J. Int'l L.* 129, 160–64 (2010).
40 *Kiobel v. Royal Dutch Petroleum*, 569 US 108 (2013).
41 *Jesner v. Arab Bank*, No. 16–499, 584 US ___ (2018).
42 See e.g., Franklin A. Gevurtz, The Globalization of Corporate Law: The End of History or a Never-Ending Story?, *Washington L. Rev.* (2011).
43 Anthea Roberts, *Is International Law International?* (2017).
44 *Urbaser S.A. v Argentine Republic* (ICSID Case No. ARB/07/26) Award (8 December 2016).
45 *Id.*
46 See Kevin Crow & Lina Lorenzoni Escobar, International Corporate Obligations, Human Rights, and the Urbaser Standard: Breaking New Ground?, *Boston University Int'l L J. (2018).*
47 See Andreea Nica, *Daven Aven v. Costa Rica: An Aftershock of Urbaser v. Argentina?* Kluwer Arbitration Blog (12 Dec 2018), available at http://arbitrationblog.kluwerarbitration.com/2018/12/12/david-aven-v-costa-rica-an-aftershock-of-urbaser-v-argentina/ (accessed 20 May 2020).
48 See Christian Tietje & Kevin Crow, The Reform of Investment Protection Rules in CETA, TTIP, and Other Recent EU-FTAs: Convincing?, in Stefan Griller, Walter Obwexer & Erich Vranes (Eds.), *Mega-Regional Agreements: TTIP, CETA, TiSA. New Orientations for EU External Economic Relations* (2017).
49 A colleague and I analyze the evolution of this doctrine in great detail in a forthcoming paper: see, eventually, Kevin Crow & Lina Lorenzoni-Escobar, *From Traction to Treaty-Bound:* Erga Omens, *Multinationals, and the Arbitral Use of Judge-Made Law* (forthcoming, 2020–2021).
50 See Tie Christian Tietje & Kevin Crow, The Reform of Investment Protection Rules in CETA, TTIP, and Other Recent EU-FTAs: Convincing?, in Stefan Griller, Walter Obwexer & Erich Vranes (Eds.), *Mega-Regional Agreements: TTIP, CETA, TiSA. New Orientations for EU External Economic Relations* (2017), Crow chapter.
51 *David R. Aven and others v. Republic of Costa Rica*, ICSID Case No. UNCT/15/3, Award dated 18 September 2018 (David Aven v. Costa Rica), Paragraph 697. In its argument, Respondent affirms that because Claimant had caused environmental damage, and because wrongful acts involve responsibility under international law, then Respondent is under an obligation to make reparation, 'as recognized in Article 1 of the ILC Articles on the Responsibility of States for Internationally Wrongful Acts (2001)' (paragraph 709). Respondent here quotes the articles on state responsibility to extend their application to the investor, which is yet another manifestation of a trend to extend some kind of responsibility to foreign investors, without any kind of in-depth reasoning on how this responsibility should be allocated.
52 *David R. Aven and others v. Republic of Costa Rica*, Award, ICSID Case No. UNCT/15/3 (2018).
53 Institution de Droit de International, 18th Commission, Equality of Parties Before International Investment Tribunals, Campell McLachan (31 August 2019), Article 6, available at www.idi-iil.org/app/uploads/2019/09/18-RES-EN.pdf (accessed 20 May 2020).
54 *David Aven v. Costa Rica*, Award, ICSID Case No. UNCT/15/3 (2018).
55 *Barcelona Traction, Light and Power Company, Ltd. (Belgium v. Spain); Preliminary Objections*, International Court of Justice, I.C.J. Reports 1964 (1964).
56 *Melanie Barber v. Nestle USA, Inc.*, No. 16–55041 (9th Cir. 2018).
57 See especially Quinn Slobodian, *Globalists: The End of Empire and the Birth of Neoliberalism* (2018); Ingo Venzke, International Law and the Spectre of Inequality [2019]

Inaugural Lecture No. 607, University of Amsterdam, available at http://cf.bc.uva.nl/download/oraties/oraties_2019/Venzke_Ingo.pdf (accessed 12 October 2019).

58 *David Aven v. Costa Rica*, Award, ICSID Case No. UNCT/15/3 (2018).

59 *Id.*

60 *Id.* 'It [investor subjectivity] is particularly convincing when it comes to rights and obligations that are of the concern of all States, as it happens in the protection of the environment'. Aven carries out this reasoning by quoting the ICJ's *Barcelona Traction* case. *Barcelona Traction, Light and Power Company, Ltd. (Belgium v. Spain); Preliminary Objections*, International Court of Justice, I.C.J. Reports 1964 (1964).

61 Mario Peña Chacón, Lecciones Ambienntales del Laudo Aven y otros contra Costa Rica, ACODI (25 Oct 2018), available at www.acodicr.org/single-post/2018/10/25/LECCIONES-AMBIENTALES-DEL-LAUDO-AVEN-Y-OTROS-CONTRA-COSTA-RICA?fb_comment_id=1401350216576187_1402409089803633 (accessed 20 May 2020).

62 ILO, The Rana Plaza Accident and its Aftermath, Bangladesh Move Towards Employment Injury Insurance: The Legacy of Rana Plaza (13 June 2018), available at www.ilo.org/global/topics/geip/publications/WCMS_632364/lang-en/index.htm (accessed 20 May 2020).

63 See e.g., Siva G., 11 Killed in Pre-Dawn Disaster as Gas Leaks at Vizag Plant, *The Times of India* (8 May 2020).

64 The American firm was the Union Carbide Corporation; its wholly owned Indian subsidiary was Union Carbide Limited. See *Charan Lal Sahu v. Union of India*, India (Supreme Court), in Elihu Lauterpacht et al (eds.), 118 *International Law Reports* 509 (2001) (recapping the case from 1990).

65 *Charan Lal Sahu v. Union of India*, India (Supreme Court), in E. Lauchterpacht et al (Eds.), 118 *International Law Reports* 509 (2001), recapping the case from 1990.

66 For a recap of the Code of Conduct's fate (also discussed in the next chapter), see Karl P. Sauvant, *Negotiations of the United Nations Code of Conduct on Transnational Corporations: Experience and Lessons Learned*, 16 *J. of World Investment & Trade* 11 (2015).

67 Draft United Nations Code of Conduct on Transnational Corporations [1983 Version], clause 9, available at https://investmentpolicy.unctad.org/international-investment-agreements/treaty-files/2891/download (accessed 10 May 2020).

68 *Id.* at Clause 13.

69 *Charan Lal Sahu v. Union of India*, India (Supreme Court), in E. Lauchterpacht et al (Eds.), 118 *International Law Reports* 509 (2001).

70 See seminally Antony Anghie, *Imperialism, Sovereignty, and the Making of International Law* (2005); see also L Eslava & S Pahuja, The State and International Law: A Reading from the Global South, *Humanity Journal* (2020).

71 Markus Krajewski, A Nightmare or a Noble Dream? Establishing Investor Obligations Through Treaty-Making and Treaty-Application, *Business and Human Rights Journal* (2020).

72 See Chapters 3 and 4 of this book.

73 At least similar to L Eslava & S Pahuja, The State and International Law: A Reading from the Global South, *Humanity Journal* (2020).

74 *Eli Lilly and Company v. The Government of Canada*, Award, UNCITRAL, ICSID Case No. UNCT/14/2 (2017).

75 See e.g., *Inceysa Vallisoletana v. El Salvador* (2006).

76 *World Duty Free Co. v. Kenya* (2006).

77 *Plama Consortium Limited v. Republic of Bulgaria*, ICSID Case No. ARB/03/24 (2008).

78 E.g., an old source but a good one, *Black's Law Dictionary*.

79 *Metalclad Corporation v. Mexico*, Award, ICSID Case No. ARB(AF)/97/1 (2000).

80 *S.D. Meyers v. Canada*, UNCITRAL Award (30 Dec 2002).

81 UN Secretary General, Convention on the Recognition and Enforcement of Foreign Arbitral Awards (1958).

82 José Alvarez, Are Corporations "Subjects" of International Law?, fn. 94, 9 *Santa Clara J. Int'l L.* 21 (2011).

83 The Honorable High Court seemed to suggest that the requirement of a territorial link also meant that each right arising in connection with an investment must bear a territorial link with the host State for it to be cognizable. [GD, pars. 202–203 (CB Vol I, pp. 8–183).]

84 *ATA Construction, Industrial and Trading Company v. The Hashemite Kingdom of Jordan*, ICSID Case No. ARB/08/2, Award, 18 May 2010 (*ATA v. Jordan*).

85 *ATA v. Jordan*. The tribunal further identified the New York Convention as the source of the protected right to arbitrate in p. 128: 'By virtue of Article II of the New York Convention, Jordan's State courts are required to "recognize an agreement in writing under which the parties undertake to submit to arbitration", and in such circumstances to "refer the parties to arbitration, unless it finds that the said agreement is null and void, inoperative or incapable of being performed"'.

86 *White Industries v. India*, UNCITRAL (30 Nov 2011).

87 The tribunal was seated in Paris; hearings were held in London. *White Industries Australia Limited v. Republic of India*, UNCITRAL Final Award (30 November 2011) (*White Industries*).

88 *White Industries*. See also *Saipem S.p.A. v. The People's Republic of Bangladesh*, ICSID Case No. ARB/05/07, Decision on Jurisdiction and Recommendation on Provisional Measures (21 March 2007), p. 127 ('[T]he rights embodied in the ICC Award were not created by the Award, but arise out of the Contract. The ICC Award crystallized the parties' rights and obligations under the original contract. It can thus be left open whether the Award itself qualifies as an investment, since the contract rights which are crystallized by the Award constitute an investment within Article 1(1)(c) of the BIT'.).

89 See e.g., *Frontier Petroleum Services Ltd. v. The Czech Republic*, Final Award (12 November 2010) (arbitral award in Sweden; investment in Czech Republic).

90 That is, one step beyond the typical judicial structure: trial in the first instance, appeal in the second, and (rarely) contentious constitutional questions of law in the third. The arbitral tribunal can be thought of as a 'fourth instance' beyond these three.

91 *Barcelona Traction, Light and Power Company, Ltd. (Belgium v. Spain); Preliminary Objections*, International Court of Justice, I.C.J. Reports 1964 (1964).

92 *Id.* at par. 35

93 *Id.* at par. 33

94 *Id.* at par. 33

95 *Id.* at par. 34

96 *Id.* at par. 91

97 UN ECOSOC, Multinational Corporations in World Development (1974), and OECD, International Trade, and its Social and Economic Affects (1973). As of mid-May 1975, the OECD was engaged in an intensive effort to draft a code of conduct for TNCs and related documents. See Report Prepared for the AFL-CIO Maritime Trades Department Executive Board Meeting in Hearings; Testimony of Paul Jennings, Pres., Int'l Union of Electrical Radio and Machine Workers, in *Hearings on a Foreign Economic Policy for the 70's Before the Subcomm. on Foreign Economic Policy of the Joint Economic Comm.*, 91st Cong., 2d Sess. (1970); Testimony of I. W. Abel, Pres., Int'l Steelworkers Union, in *Hearings on the Trade Reform Act of 1973 Before the House Ways & Means Comm.*, 93rd Cong., 1st Sess. (1973).

98 Open-Ended Intergovernmental Working Group on Transnational Corporations and other Business Enterprises With Respect to Human Rights (2018). Zero draft of a legally binding instrument to regulate, in international human rights law, the activities of transnational corporations and other business enterprises.

99 Open-Ended Intergovernmental Working Group on Transnational Corporations and other Business Enterprises With Respect to Human Rights (2019). Revised draft of a legally binding instrument to regulate, in international human rights law, the activities

of transnational corporations and other business enterprises. Available at www.ohchr.org/Documents/HRBodies/HRCouncil/WGTransCorp/OEIGWG_RevisedDraft_LBI.pdf.

100 State Parties are the subject of most provisions of the revised draft. The only exception is the reference to the UN Guiding principles on Business and Human Rights in the preamble of the draft, and the reproduction of its causation language in one of the recitals: 'Underlining that all business enterprises, regardless of their size, sector, operational context, ownership and structure have the responsibility to respect all human rights, including by avoiding causing or contributing to adverse human rights impacts through their own activities and addressing such impact when they occur, as well as by preventing or mitigating adverse human rights impacts that are directly linked to their operations, products or services by their business relationships'.

101 Carlos López, The Revised Draft of a Treaty on Business and Human Rights: Ground-Breaking Improvements and Brighter Prospect, 4 (10) *Investment Treaty News* 721–28 (October 2019) 11–14. Available at www.iisd.org/sites/default/files/publications/iisd-itn-october-2019-english.pdf.

102 *Op. cit.*

103 Erika de Wet, Jus Cogens and Obligations Erga Omnes, in Dinah Shelton (Ed.), *The Oxford Handbook of International Human Rights Law* (2013).

104 Michael P. Van Alstine, Dynamic Treaty Interpretation, 146 *U. Pa. L. Rev.* 687 (1997–1998).

105 Yousuf Aftab & Audrey Mocle, *Business and Human Rights as Law: Towards Justiciability of Rights, Involvement, and Remedy* (2019).

106 *Nevsun Resources Ltd. v. Araya*, 2020 SCC 5 (21 March 2020).

107 Yousuf Aftab & Audrey Mocle, *Business and Human Rights as Law: Towards Justiciability of Rights, Involvement, and Remedy* (2019).

108 *Id.*

109 *Id.*

Chapter 3

The international corporate person in international law

Texts and practices

I. Exclusivity and the text

This chapter builds on the last by identifying rights and privileges accorded to the ICP through international legal texts and practices. Whereas texts can (and do) create explicit or implicit rights and differences, texts and the absence of texts can also create practices which become 'rules' solidified by inertia more than deliberate intention. For example, there is no text creating the 'tax haven', but rather a collection of domestic systems facilitate the corporate practice of using them. International law did not create this right, nor did it create the ability of multinationals to move assets and liabilities through multiple types of corporations in different jurisdictions, but it omitted taking meaningful action to halt the practice. International law is not so much responsible for as it is complicit in the near-exclusive corporate use of these privileges, some of which by their very nature can attach only to the corporate form. Since natural persons cannot be in more than one place at the same time, they cannot so easily obtain citizenship or residence simultaneously in multiple jurisdictions. And since most gainful employment attaches payment to an individual employee rather than an entity wholly owned or controlled by an individual, natural persons cannot casually access many of the benefits provided by 'offshores'. Moreover, while international legal texts are often the product of belabored diplomatic negotiations and lengthy consultations involving experts and various stakeholders, the texts that most affect ICPs are also heavily influenced by them, which I discuss in Section III. Indeed, while this theme will play a more dominant role in the next chapter, even notions such as 'sovereignty' so dear and foundational to public international lawyers are increasingly weaponized and shaped by the interests of private capital.[1] In order to arrive at these foundational critiques, this chapter builds on the last through two contributions. First, it analyzes exclusive rights and privileges accorded to the ICP in the five areas of international law most relevant to ICPs (**II**). And second, rather than exploring international law's influence on the form and function of the multinational enterprise as many books have done,[2] I explore how multinationals and other private entities have influenced the form and function of international law (**III**). The upshot is that, despite lawyerly tendencies to analogize the ICP to the State, individual, or intergovernmental organization, the ICP is not realistically analogous to any existing legal form (**IV**).

II. The ICP in international legal texts and practices

The following subsections track rights and practices codified in or facilitated by international texts that are exclusively available to ICPs in the five areas of international law most relevant to the ICP: Business and Human Rights (a), international criminal law (b), international corruption texts and associated practices (c), international environmental law (d), and international economic law (e). A short discussion contextualizing the OECD Guidelines for Multinational Enterprises is also included (f). Although labor is an important concern of ICPs and although the ILO Tripartite Declaration is referenced throughout this book, it is not an area of law with sufficient international 'teeth' to be included here. Domestic labor regulations are more likely to change through the coercive economic power of regional trade agreements than ILO Declarations;[3] but the ILO serves other important functions.[4] Moreover, since I discuss the WTO at length in Section III of this chapter, I have left WTO law out of the 'economic law' subsection of this chapter.

a. Business and Human Rights

i. The European Convention on Human Rights and the European Court of Human Rights

The ECtHR is the only international tribunal authorized to interpret human rights law that has explicitly protected ICP rights. For our purposes, it is useful to compare the development of corporate rights under the ECHR with the development of corporate rights under international investment law. Although the ECtHR does have some textual basis in the ECHR for protecting corporate rights, that textual guidance is not quite as clear or as detailed as that typically found in international investment treaties.[5] For this reason, judicial interpretations have proven to be key in the development of corporate rights under the ECHR.

The substantive provisions of the ECHR do not specifically refer to legal or natural persons; only Protocol 1 to the Convention makes that distinction. Rather, they refer either to 'persons' or simply to 'everyone'. For instance, Article 2 holds that '[e]veryone's right to life shall be protected by law'. Protections are also phrased in the negative. For example, Article 3 states that '[n]o one shall be subjected to torture or to inhuman or degrading treatment or punishment'. Still other provisions are phrased without any specific object of protection. There are, however, two provisions that support the notion that rights enshrined in the ECHR extend to ICPs. Article 10 states that 'everyone has the right to freedom of expression', but that this right does not prevent States from licensing 'broadcasting, television or cinema enterprises'. And Article 25, which grants the European Commission (and later the Court in amended Article 34) the right to receive petitions from 'from any person, non-governmental organization or group of individuals claiming to be the victim of a violation by one of the High Contracting Parties of the rights set forth in this Convention'. The reference to media enterprises in the former Article and NGOs and groups in the latter provide the textual basis. Moreover, Protocol 1 states that '[e]very natural or legal person is entitled to the peaceful enjoyment of his possessions. No one shall be deprived of his possessions except in the public interest and subject to the conditions provided for by law and by the general principles of international law'. It is only in this provision, where property is the focus, that legal persons make any explicit appearance in the Convention.

Nevertheless, the ECtHR has not been shy about extending ECHR protections to ICPs. However, it has been shy on reasoning. For instance, in the 1985 decision *A v. Austria*,[6] the Court noted simply that the 'freedom of assembly under Art. 11 . . . can be exercised [ ] by the organizer of a meeting, even it if should be a legal person'. This analysis was apparently uncontested within the Court, even though Article 11 does not make any specific reference to legal entities or legal persons. Similarly, in 1990 case of *Autronic AG v. Switzerland*, the Court found:

> [N]either Autronic AG's legal status as a limited company nor the fact that its activities were commercial nor the intrinsic nature of freedom of expression can deprive Autronic AG of the protection of Article 10. The Article applies to 'everyone', whether natural or legal persons.[7]

The Court went on to note that it had allowed similar claims by companies under Article 10 before without controversy, or even discussion. Indeed, the idea that companies and other entities qualify for protection under the ECHR has been so accepted within the ECtHR's jurisprudence that there is literally no discussion on the question in court opinions. Even a leading commentator notes that the Court has 'not developed a corporate theory for the ECHR'. The ECtHR has, however, refused on several occasions to allow shareholders to sue on a corporation's behalf, presenting themselves rather than the corporation as the 'victim' for purposes of Article 34 ECHR.[8]

ii. The protect, respect, and remedy framework

The UNGPs are discussed in greater detail in other Sections of this book; my sketch depicting a 'liability' or 'responsibility' map of the UNGP Framework can be found at the end of this chapter. The product of more than half a decade of research and deliberation with (some) interested 'stakeholders', the

'Protect, Respect and Remedy Framework' was submitted as a report to the UN Human Rights Council in 2008 by then-Special Representative John Ruggie (the 'Ruggie Framework' or the 'Guiding Principles').[9] The literature on Ruggie's Framework is vast and I would encourage any interested reader to embark on an independent investigation that involves the drafting history as well as the current application. This book is interested in the Principles mostly with respect to how they understand the form, function, and responsibility of the ICP vis-à-vis the State. Nevertheless, a brief overview of the basics of the Framework is warranted.

The Framework sets out 31 principles intended to articulate business responsibilities with respect to 'human rights' as envisaged by existing human rights instruments in public international law, each accompanied by extensive commentary.[10] The principles are divided into three categories (protect, respect, and remedy), only one of which is addressed to corporations (respect). One of the categories (protect) is primarily addressed to States, setting out what may be characterized as a 'best practices' model to 'enable' corporations to 'avoid' human rights violations, and the final category (remedy) is something of a hybrid 'best practices' model that encourages both States and corporations to have processes and means available to address harms to victims of human rights violations. Moreover, an analysis of these principles reveals a clear understanding of the corporation as something that veers closer to a para-State than to a para-Individual insofar as it sees ICPs as private entities that have acquired or can acquire public functions. But the Framework also explicitly views the State as the legal personality responsible to international law for the (in)actions of ICPs through appropriate regulation and enforcement. The 'protect' part articulates clear legal liability, whereas the 'respect' and 'remedy' parts focus on the softer responsibilities of private businesses and governments.[11] As the principles put it, an ICP 'must consider the needs not only of internal stakeholders, such as the shareholders, managers and employees, but also the external stakeholders, such as customers, suppliers, competitors, and other special interest groups'.[12]

Under this governance-focused account of ICP responsibility, the language indicates that responsibility vests directly in ICPs themselves, and not to States as enforcers. It also seems that, to move forward with a theory of the ICP, Ruggie's work suggests that one should take a para-Statist view toward the ICP as a parallel to government: an institution with internal rules affected the actors that compose it. Although many international lawyers and human rights activists wish to see States seize greater 'control' over ICPs, Ruggie's Framework joins the ranks of CSR and other 'softer' bounded forms of responsibility attrition in suggesting that ICP responsibility – while 'good' and 'right' and 'ethical' – is voluntarist in nature. In sum, at the same time as the seminal UN Framework views a corporation primarily as analogous to the State, it views its international obligations as 'soft', voluntary, a result of good management and 'best practices' and views the State as ultimately responsible for providing regulatory frameworks that encourage corporate compliance with the State's 'hard' obligations. For Ruggie, it seems at least, these 'soft' obligations are akin to a call to ICPs to appropriate the discussion on corporate subjectivity to international law: 'What I've said to the companies is . . . *take the game over* and stop being reactive, and become proactive, and drive the agenda'.[13] As Fleur Johns has noted, the business executive in this view becomes the classical 'prince' – the embodiment of political and economic power – and international law becomes 'counsel' or 'guidance' to the corporate executives effectively 'ruling' a set of constituents.[14] My attempt to sketch the ring of binding and non-binding responsibilities set out in the Framework can be found at the end of this chapter.

iii. The OEIGWG draft binding instrument

After the UN Human Rights Council (HRC) unanimously endorsed the Ruggie Framework in 2011, christened the Guiding Principles, it set up the open-ended intergovernmental working group on transnational corporations and other business enterprises with respect to human rights (OEIGWG). The OEIGWG then quickly set about devising a binding instrument that could supplement the UNGPs. In initial discussions, one question was whether the instrument should be binding directly on ICPs – that is, with ICPs as signatories – but difficulties with that level of para-Statism soon became too vast. For example, if ICPs were to directly bind themselves to an instrument, should they then be more directly involved in drafting the instrument? Would the instrument bind only those ICPs that signed it, or would it also bind subsidiaries, corporate parents, controlling institutional shareholders, and other actors within the varied legal constellations of corporate groups? To bind only the legal signatory seemed too narrow – any company could easily create a subsidiary and transfer assets or control when treaty obligations seemed too burdensome; but to bind all actors within a corporate constellation seemed too broad, with no principled cut off for legal liability. Thus, where the UNGPs almost presuppose a para-Statist understanding of the ICP through provisions acknowledging its responsibility for traditionally State functions, the OEIGWG's work building on the UNGPs has moved toward a para-Individual understanding of the ICP, at least insofar as international law can attach to the ICP. That is, just as natural persons do not individually accede to an international treaty but incur both rights and obligations to them through the proxy of the State, the OEIGWG's 2018 'Zero Draft' and 2019 'Revised Draft' would not require individual accession of ICPs but would assign rights and obligations to them through participating States in which they operate.[15]

The OEIGWG's work is ongoing; it is likely to publish another revised version of the text before this book even hits the press. If a binding instrument emerges from its work, it is likely to be many years in the future and likely to be substantially different than the two existing drafts. However, the draft binding instruments are useful for our purposes in at least two ways. First, they provide an example: they are emblematic of many of the theoretical difficulties associated with the ICP, which are discussed further in the next chapter.

Second, they provide a window into the ways in which experts, NGOs, and interest groups are already conceptualizing the ICP and its relationship to international law, even without explicitly articulating a theory of the ICP or corporate subjectivity. For example, the provisions on jurisdiction in Article 7 are vast and have profound implications for anyone concerned about extraterritoriality. While the instrument is set up as an agreement between States to adopt regulations guaranteeing that victims of human rights abuses will have means to investigate and bring claims against ICPs for their role in facilitating abuses, Article 7 vests the right to adjudicate such claims in

> [T]he courts of the State where: (a) [the alleged] acts or omissions occurred; or (b) the victims are domiciled; or (c) the natural or legal persons alleged to have committed such acts or omissions in the context of business activities, including those of a transnational character, are domiciled.[16]

Article 7 goes on to clarify this last category, noting that natural and legal persons engaged in transnational business activities, including contracts, are domiciled 'where it has its: (a) place of incorporation; or (b) statutory seat; or (c) central administration; or (d) substantial business interests'. This final category is potentially broad, and if the experience of domestic courts dealing with similar language can be considered prologue,[17] 'substantial business interests' would likely take the form of a minimal thresholds on asset ownership, transactions, or personnel present in a jurisdiction. Thus, Article 7's jurisdictional provisions provides the possibility of bringing a claim against an ICP in a jurisdiction where the ICP is not headquartered, where the alleged violation did not occur, and where the Claimant has never set foot. The signatory State would apply domestic law in domestic courts 'in accordance with' the instrument's provisions. Combined with the 'mutual legal assistance' provisions in Article 10 and the 'international cooperation' provisions of Article 11, and skipping over details for now, a broad picture emerges in which the dominant prosecuting States are likely to be those with the most resources devoted to judicial and law enforcement mechanisms, that is, the richest States. In this context, it is difficult not to see the irony in Article 12, 'Consistency with International Law'. Paragraph 1 calls for States to carry out their obligations 'in a manner consistent with the principles of sovereign equality and territorial integrity of States and that of non-intervention in the domestic affairs of other States'. Paragraph 3 then essentially stipulates that the interests of human rights and remedy for victims will decide which law applies in the case of domestic, regional, and international conflict of law.

Not only are Article 12(3)'s provisions not themselves consistent with international law, Article 12(2)'s provisions directly clash with the broad jurisdiction set out in Article 7.

In order to determine how such provisions inform our understanding of the ways in which human rights experts, NGOs, 'consultants', and governments are conceptualizing the ICP, we can utilize what Koskeneimmi has called 'the transcendental approach'. Namely, we will not ask whether these provisions are reasonable (they likely are not); we will ask rather what the drafters would need to believe about the ICP in order to believe that these provisions are reasonable. The provisions reveal a picture of the ICP as an actor that is static and definable, not fluid and flexible, and whose actions occur in isolation from its ownership and from States themselves. For example, in this instrument, the drafters treat ICP jurisdiction between States in a manner remarkably akin to the U.S.'s 'diversity jurisdiction' in the Federal Rules of Civil Procedure.[18] Diversity jurisdiction determines a federal court's ability to hear a claim between residents of different state territories within the United States but it does so within the context of a unified federal system. In that context, provisions referencing 'substantial activity' or 'central administration' evoke bodies of law that will apply equally no matter which court in the federal system hears the claim. Corporate restructuring, forum shopping, shell companies, all of these are lesser concerns (though existing) within a single federal system, and this suggests an understanding of the ICP that is as static and definable as it can be within a single system. This apparent presumption of homogeneity is affirmed by the composition of Parties that attend the OEIGWG's sessions.[19] Certainly there was representation from the Global South, but the discussion was predominantly driven by European actors. American interests were represented not through diplomatic participation but in the form of trade groups with 'consultant' status, which I discuss at length in the 'lobbying' section that follows.

Finally, and most inaccurately, the provisions assume that States will cooperate with mutual goals and with shared relationships toward ICPs. To adopt the provisions in Articles 10 and 11, one would need to believe that States shared some unity of purpose in regulating ICPs and protecting the UN's understanding of human rights. One would also need to presuppose a unified understanding of which types of provisions are 'more conducive to the respect, promotion, protection and fulfilment of human rights in the context of business activities' when domestic and international law collide, as Article 12 requires.

The Draft Binding Instrument undertakes a massive challenge, and it is still in its beginning phases. The criticisms I have raised are not intended to suggest that the project is not worthwhile; they are intended to demonstrate the complexity involved in thinking about ICP regulation in a transnational and internationally harmonious way. The draft binding instrument also provides a great reference point in Article 6, 'Legal Liability'. There, it amasses the existing international legal agreements it views as potentially applying to ICPs. It consists mostly of those international human rights instruments – apart from the Covenants – that are binding on States: the UN Convention Against Torture and Other Cruel, Inhumane, or Degrading Punishment; the International Convention for the Protection of All Persons from Enforced Disappearance; the Principles on the Effective Prevention and Investigation of Extra-Legal, Arbitrary and Summary Executions; the ILO Forced Labour Convention; the Abolition of Forced Labour Convention; the Convention on the Prohibition and Immediate Action for the Elimination of the Worst Forms of Child Labour; the Basic Principles and Guidelines on Development; and the Rome Statute for the International Criminal Court. The next section deals with the last of these in greater detail, but first, let us turn our attention another non-binding set of rules recently published to give guidance to arbitrators specifically in international investment tribunals.

iv. The Hague Rules on Business and Human Rights arbitration

The Hague Rules, published in December 2019, are an initiative from the Dutch Government-sponsored Center for International Legal Cooperation in the Hague, but the rules themselves were devised and drafted by an all-star cast of international lawyers and legal academics. They are based on and bear a strong resemblance to the UNCITRAL Rules. The Hague Rules differ in that they use Business and Human Rights (BHR) terms as they are understood in Ruggie's UNGPs, but like the UNCITRAL Rules, the Hague Rules emphasize their procedural rather than substantive nature. While some of the text indicates that its drafters intended it for use in business-to-business disputes where human rights violations are involved, the introductory note to the Rules makes clear:

> As with the UNCITRAL Rules, the scope of the Hague Rules is not limited by the type of claimant(s) or respondent(s) or the subject-matter of the dispute and extends to any disputes that the parties to an arbitration agreement have agreed to resolve by arbitration under the Hague Rules. Parties could thus include business entities, individuals, labor unions . . . States . . . as well as any other parties of any kind.[20]

Legal persons are mentioned twice in the Hague Rules. The first instance carves out an exception for disputes exclusively involving ICPs for disclosure and transparency in arbitration. The language of Article 38 Hague Rules – '[i]f all parties are legal persons of a commercial character and the arbitral tribunal determines that there is no public interest involved' – mirrors Article 1 of the UNCITRAL Transparency Rules except that it expands the scope of arbitral discretion in determining 'public interest' to include 'safety, privacy and confidentiality concerns' of all interested parties (Art. 38(2)(c)) and 'potential for aggravating conflicts between and among relevant stakeholders' (Art. 38(2)(d)).[21]

The second instance is in the commentary notes that accompany the actual Rules. Article 11 sets out eligibility requirements for the appointment of arbitrators, and one subparagraph states that '[t]he presiding or sole arbitrator shall not be a national of States whose nationals are parties or of any State that is a party. The nationality of a party shall be understood to include those of its controlling shareholders or interests.' The commentary clarifies that this is an effort to eliminate biases which need not arise from a legal person's State of incorporation, and emphasizes that General Standard 6(b) of the IBA Guidelines on Conflicts of Interest in International Arbitration takes a similar approach.[22] In this conception of procedural law on human rights issues, then, ICPs can potentially hold multiple nationalities at the same time. An ICP could be headquartered in one State, have operations in a second, and have controlling shareholders with multiple citizenships and residences in many other States. The Rules do not seem to anticipate, however, that an ICP's nationalities can be in a State of constant flux.

Perhaps what is most interesting about the Hague Rules for our purposes is the process through which they came into existence. Shortly after the inaugural UN Annual Forum on Business and Human Rights, three senior lawyers – two of whom were European and had long careers in private practice but no theoretical training and one of whom was American professor of business law – formed a working group to discuss the creation of the Rules (initially with the aim of creating a separate tribunal). They obtained funding from the City of the Hague and the Dutch Ministry of Foreign Affairs and recruited a diverse all-star cast of international legal experts to their Drafting Team, all of whom are affiliated with American or European institutions. Over the course of four meetings and several years, these experts honed the language and the commentaries and then released the resulting Rules to the world. The Rules can now govern the engagement of those States, ICPs or other actors that choose, bilaterally, to abide by them. The point is, the Rules represent how a largely entrepreneurial effort – through the authority of pedigree and private sector experience alone – has the potential to become not only part of international law, but the legal apparatus through which ICPs engage with and are subject to a certain branch of international law, that is, human rights.

I am not chiming in on the desirability of developments such as the Hague Rules. In this vein, however, the following subsections will elucidate in greater detail processes through which instruments and declarations similar to the Rules can emerge as enablers of 'boundary crossing' processes in international law, even though they are often expert or entrepreneurial efforts. International judges and arbitrators are often required to face difficult problems in legally uncharted waters; they need justification for applying familiar legal tools from other domestic and international tribunals and agreements to problems for which those tools were not made. It is a pragmatic legalism without which adversarial forms of dispute settlement would often be impossible, especially on the international stage. Perhaps in systems of global governance that lack direct access to the consent of the actors they affect, this process is both necessary and desirable. But if this is so, let it never be said that international law cannot treat ICPs as subjects because they do not accede to it. Of course it can. International law is made; we can make it do as we please, so long as we can provide justification.[23] Neither you nor I ever acceded to any international agreement, yet we are subject to many of their provisions, directly and indirectly. We made the international system so and so it is so, so long as we remain collectively convinced by the reasons given for it being so.

b. International criminal law

Some commentators believe that international legal texts can be interpreted to accord ICPs international criminal liability. The following subsections explore the application of two primary theories of liability that could attach to the ICP by incorporating ICL doctrines into IIL (i) and explore one novel interpretation – a new trajectory regarding criminal liability for environmental harm – which has captured the imagination of some international lawyers (ii).

i. The joint criminal enterprise and aiding and abetting

There is a rich and vibrant debate amongst international criminal lawyers regarding whether and how international corporations and the individuals who run them could be held criminally liable for their contributions to crimes against humanity (CAHs),[24] but recapping a full review of that literature is beyond the scope of this subsection. However, at the risk of oversimplification, and in the context of criminality, there appears to be an emerging consensus among international criminal lawyers that if a corporation possesses 'control over a crime' – an adaptation from German criminal law[25] – then corporate criminal liability is possible.[26] International Criminal Law (ICL) would then pursue the individuals behind the 'control', where the Rome Statute requires alternately 'knowledge' or 'purpose' to incur individual liability. There is no international legal standard by which to demonstrate the 'purpose' of a corporate entity, but in theory, an IIL Tribunal could borrow from ICL's Joint Criminal Enterprise (JCE) doctrines.[27] The goal of general JCE, initially spawned by the Nuremberg Tribunals, was to bypass the justifications of sovereign immunity or superior responsibility when it came to assigning responsibility to individuals for the commission of mass atrocities.[28] In parsing out a corporate *mens rea* standard for an IIL case, therefore, JCE's utility does not lie in transposing the *mens rea* element from a corporation to an individual. Rather, JCE, particularly JCE III, is useful because it employs a standard by which to determine the mental state of a legal person – an 'enterprise' in JCE but a 'corporation' for our purposes here – without attaching any requirement for individual *mens rea*.[29] The corporate standard, first articulated by the International Criminal Tribunal for the former Yugoslavia (ICTY), is that the legal person have a 'common plan or purpose', which can be demonstrated through the results of the legal person's actions.[30] Before delving too deeply into its potential, however, it should be noted that JCE III is an extremely controversial doctrine amongst international criminal lawyers – the harshest criticisms suggest that it accords liability to whatever leaders were in charge when a CAH occurred regardless of whether they had anything to do with the CAH. (Some lawyers joke that JCE stands for 'just convict everyone'.)

Rather than focus on director or shareholder liability beyond ICP liability, in this section I want to suggest that for a corporation to incur financial liability for a human rights violation, a determination that the corporation itself is liable is sufficient. If the corporate criminality literature is to inform an IIL tribunal's analysis, it must be mitigated to the degree that the standard emerges from ICL's mission to determine which actors are 'most responsible' for CAHs, and to shield those actors which were merely following orders or unwittingly producing materials that would later be used in the commission of a CAH. In the criminal context, specific knowledge requirements shield Lockheed & Martin (the United States' largest weapons manufacturer),[31] Boeing (which produces drones),[32] General Electric (which won the largest U.S. government contracts for military technology),[33] Northrop Grumman (which produces various drone-related technologies),[34] and many other companies. And this might be ethically palatable to most in a criminal context, but the fact that the products produced by private companies often exacerbate damage to civilians in times of armed conflict renders the status quo unviable in a civil-financial liability context.

What can IIL take from ICL in evaluating the subjectivity of corporations to international law, and how might ICL converge with cases like *Urbaser* to determine which corporate action should incur financial, rather than criminal, liability? There appears to be an expanse of grey area regarding the international legal status of corporate liability that rests between the extremes of Degesch (which designed the pesticide later used in Holocaust gas chambers long before Hitler took power and continued to produce it under government direction)[35] and the doctrine of 'control over the crime'. On one end, there is an inefficacy of inaction, and on the other, an inefficacy of stringency: 'control over the crime' has yet to be successfully applied to any corporate act or actor on the international stage.[36] Thus, I have previously suggested a possible 'third way', in which lowered *mens rea* standards in JCE and aiding and abetting liability might apply to corporate actors in an ISDS context.[37]

Article 25 of the Rome Statute paragraphs 3(c) and 3(d) set out the ICC's requirements for individuals to incur aiding and abetting liability. In order to incur such liability, paragraph 3(c) indicates that a legal person facilitates the commission of a CAH with the purpose that the CAH be committed.

However, paragraph 3d indicates a second, debatably lower standard. Article 25(3) states:

> [A] person shall be criminally responsible and liable for punishment for a crime within the jurisdiction of the Court if that person: . . .
>
> (c) For the *purpose of facilitating the commission* of such a crime, aids, abets or otherwise assists in its commission or its attempted commission, including providing the means for its commission;
>
> (d) *In any other way contributes to the commission* or attempted commission of such a crime by a group of persons acting with a common purpose. Such contribution shall be *intentional* and shall either:
>
> Be made *with the aim of furthering the criminal activity* or criminal purpose of the group, where such activity or purpose involves the commission of a crime within the jurisdiction of the Court; *or*
>
> Be made in the *knowledge of the intention of the group* to commit the crime.[38]

Article 25(3)(d)(i) and (ii) set out a choice between standards. The first sets out a *mens rea* similar to *Urbaser*'s first standard – an obligation not to engage in activity with the *aim* of destroying human rights. The second, however, opens the window to a lower *mens rea* standard of knowledge of intention, which for practical purposes under public international law, requires knowledge of the likelihood that an international law violation will occur as a result of the 'contribution'.[39] The ICTY Trial Chamber also articulated a similar standard in *Tadić*, though more recent Appeals decisions from that Tribunal may require a more stringent interpretation of the aiding and abetting provisions of the ICTY statute.[40] The Trial Chamber in *Tadić* found that 'there is a requirement of intent, which involves *awareness* of the act of participation coupled with a conscious decision to participate by planning, instigating, ordering, committing, or otherwise aiding and abetting in the commission of a crime'.[41] Various other ICL Tribunals, including Appeals Chambers at the ICTY and the Special Court for Sierra Leone (SCSL), agree that the appropriate interpretation of the 'knowledge' requirement is 'knowledge of the likelihood that a crime would occur', or indifference to whether a crime would occur.[42] This standard is all the more necessary when it comes to the liability of corporate persons. For as an ICJ Expert Panel on Corporate Complicity in International Crimes stated in its 2008 Report,[43] to require the elevated standard of 'purpose', and not merely knowledge, would render the notion of aiding and abetting almost wholly inapplicable to corporate persons, since corporate persons are almost always motivated by the purpose of profit.[44] Thus, in order for a corporate person to incur aiding and abetting liability, the Rome Statute standard, informed by general international law, should apply. It is not necessary that the corporation intend that the actual crime occur, or even that it have 'control over the crime' as is the consensus for choate liability. A corporation should incur inchoate liability if its primary intent is, for example, to increase profits for its shareholders, so long as it acts with the knowledge that increasing profits in a particular way has a likelihood of aiding or abetting a CAH.

Moreover, under the 'attempt' doctrines codified in the ICC statute and other ICL statutes,[45] it is not necessary that the CAH actually occur. Instead, all that is required is that the primary actor intend to commit the CAH and attempt to do so (although the line between attempt and mere preparation is far from settled).[46] Thus, a corporate actor could theoretically incur inchoate liability for assisting another party in preparation for a CAH that is likely to occur, even if the CAH never actually occurs.

In the event that a CAH does actually occur, perhaps the best illustration of a transferable standard for investor liability from ICL is the aiding and abetting standard applied by the SCSL in *Prosecutor v. Charles Ghankay Taylor*.[47] In that case, the Court rejected the prosecutor's claims that Taylor's role in facilitating diamond mining to fund the Revolutionary United Front was sufficient to place him at the helm of a JCE.[48] Instead, the Court found that Taylor had 'aid[ed] and abett[ed]' a JCE in a role the Court described in terms remarkably similar to a business financier or investor.[49] The Court found that, for a determination of aiding and abetting, the offender's acts 'must provide substantial assistance to the commission of a crime with knowledge that such acts would assist the commission of the crimes or with awareness as to the likelihood that such acts would render assistance'.[50] In the case of Charles Taylor, the nature of the Revolutionary United Front's criminal conduct was so well-known that Taylor's willingness to work with the group left little question as to whether the standard was met, but that does not preclude potential liability for working with less extreme groups, especially if IIL were to draw on SCSL jurisprudence to articulate a standard for corporate financial liability. In virtually all the world's democracies, the burden of proof for civil financial claims is lower than that for criminal claims;[51] one might presume that in IIL, a preponderance of the evidence would be sufficient to determine that a corporation's leadership was aware of a likelihood that atrocities would occur as a result of the corporation's assistance or would be perpetrated by the organization the corporation assisted.

ii. Environmental harm as a crime against humanity

Some international criminal lawyers have been sympathetic to the idea that certain types of intentional environmental harm can be considered CAHs as defined in the Rome Statute.[52] Here I build on this discussion suggesting that JCE theories, while controversial, enable the ICP to be conceptualized as a perpetrator. The application of the Rome Statute's provisions thus far fortifies assumptions regarding its scope, conceptualizing perpetrators as political actors motivated by non-economic interests, even foreclosing other possibilities. However, the Rome Statute contains many phrases that do not necessitate state or political action with respect to perpetrators in its descriptions of crimes. It almost always couples references to 'policy' with an interchangeable 'plan', and references to 'States' as potential perpetrators with categorically interchangeable 'organizations'. Accordingly, this section seeks to highlight what is possible given the language of the Statute regardless of status quo application. It demonstrates that 'purpose' can be broader than 'profit' when it comes to ICPs.

What the Rome Statute terms 'crimes against humanity' are specific atrocities 'committed as part of a widespread or systematic attack directed against any civilian population'. The perpetrator must also have 'knowledge of the attack', which can be met by demonstrating an awareness of consequences of an act 'in the ordinary course of events'.[53] The definition of 'widespread and systematic attack against civilians' is, according to the Statute, 'a course of conduct involving the multiple commission of acts . . . pursuant to or in furtherance of a State or organizational policy to commit such an attack'.[54]

The Rome Statute enumerates several horrific (non-environmental) crimes that ICPs are incapable of directly committing. But at least three provisions could apply to an ICP's interactions with the environment: (1) extermination, defined as 'the intentional infliction of conditions of life, inter alia the deprivation of access to food and medicine, calculated to bring about the destruction of part of a population'; (2) deportation or forceable transfer of a population, defined as 'forced displacement of persons concerned by expulsion or other coercive acts from the area in which they are lawfully present'; and (3) the so-called 'catch all' provision: 'Other inhumane acts of a similar character intentionally causing great suffering, or serious injury to body or to mental or physical health'.[55] Part of the nature of criminal law is that victims must be human, so environmental harm in each of these provisions must link to human harm. This makes demonstrating *mens rea* elements difficult in the case of ICPs. Often, an ICP might be aware of the human cost of its actions, but it does not partake in the action with the purpose of causing that human cost. However, the 'knowledge' standard at the ICP might open a window to liability: the primary purpose of an ICP's act may be economic gain but if it engages in an act that, in the ordinary course of events, will produce severe conditions of life, will make a certain area of the planet uninhabitable, or are similarly inhuman, one can imagine reasonable arguments through which judges might apply a doctrinal development akin to 'transferred intent'.

Another problem that would arise would be accurate attribution of responsibility. There may be cases in which environmental damage occurs as the result of a single ICP, but more often it occurs as the cumulative result of many. In such situations, judges might borrow from a somewhat obscure tort law concept called 'market share liability' wherein, when exact attribution of damages are impossible to determine, each tortfeasor in a class action is responsible for a percentage of the entire harm that corresponds to their share of the market for the product that caused the harm. For example, in asbestos tort cases, the company producing an asbestos product that controlled 40% of the market for that product would be responsible for 40% of the damages in a given class action judgment.[56] Likewise, liability for environmental damage caused by a particular ICP behavior could be attributed according to the share of the market for that particular behavior that each ICP controls.

It is clear that there is no direct *de facto* parallel between corporate and natural persons, and no *de facto* parallel between crimes against humanity and environmental harms. Nevertheless, many scholars believe that the lack of charges against ICPs for environmental harm is not due to issues surrounding responsibility attribution or even organizational responsibility.[57] Rather, it is due largely to perceived difficulties in determining corporate *mens rea*. The assumption is always that a corporation's legally predetermined intent, or in other words *mens rea*, is to increase profits for shareholders. Indeed, perhaps one lesson here is the cruciality of legally defined 'purpose'. If ICPs are to be held financially or criminally liable for participation in mass atrocities, CAHs, or environmental damage, more attention should be focused on reforms that seek to redefine corporate purpose.

c. International anti-corruption texts and practices

International anti-corruption law overwhelmingly is focused on the act of bribery by public officials and on the State's responsibility to prevent bribery and similar acts. While it was not conceived this way during initial UN discussions,[58] the international law of corruption today is obsessed with the criminalization of the individual acts of natural persons. While many of the relevant instruments discuss legal persons, none of them require States to criminalize ICP behavior. Moreover, the UN and OECD instruments which dominate the international framework conceive of corruption as something that can be eliminated through domestic regulation – the assume a 'correct' approach to transactions and financial dealings within States and do little to nothing to address problems that can truly be characterized as 'international'. Rather than focus on the harm caused to State through revenue through misappropriation of public funds through international transactional systems – which is presumably the reason why morality and criminality are attached to the act of bribery – the primary instruments focus on State-level requirements that assume natural persons and moral failure as the loci of causation (i). Yet the primary financial harm caused to States through the misappropriation of public funds can just as easily be characterized as systemic, even required, through legal technologies such as transfer pricing (ii) and tax havens (iii). This is not to say that the moral failures of natural persons do not create significant harms to State revenues – they do. The critique in the following subsections is that States do not need international law to address those failures; that international law is better suited to address systemic harms facilitated by corporate groups and networks; and that OECD instrument and other international instruments in fact hinder the development of State-level systems to address corruption through the dual legal technologies of criminalization and DPAs (iv).

i. Explicit international anti-corruption instruments

The U.S.'s 1974 Foreign Corrupt Practices Act (FCPA) set the tone for international anti-corruption instruments (IACIs). Its characterization of corruption as a criminal act for which individuals are morally culpable is a political artefact; it could have just as easily characterized individual corruption in amoral terms. Indeed, prior UN anti-corruption discussions never mentioned individual criminalization,[59] and the U.S. Congress initially framed transnational bribery as an issue of 'foreign policy', not as an issue of 'right and wrong'.[60] The U.S. SEC chose to regulate corruption on the grounds that transnational bribes inhibited the SEC's ability to honestly report financial transactions and expenditures in financial statements. When the SEC's initial investigation found that illicit payments were commonplace, the U.S. Congress (politically) located causation not in the global structure of capital markets but in individual morality: human greed causes corruption, not systems or institutions or markets. In this way, the way in which corruption is moralized in international instruments is based upon a political decision, not upon any solid theoretical foundation.

The understanding that was politically codified in the FCPA was exported to the OECD instruments and beyond. This is not to say that international instruments would not have moralized corruption in other ways, but the specific ways in which it was moralized – an emphasis on individual culpability for direct acquisitions of benefits appropriated through public office – imposed arbitrary limits. Indeed, virtually all IACIs require that States criminalize a specific set of financial transactions perpetuated by individuals in public office. For example, the 1996 Inter-American Convention required Parties to 'establish as criminal offenses under their domestic law all acts of corruption';[61] the 1997 OECD Convention was in part aimed at realizing 'the prompt criminalization of . . . bribery in an effective and coordinated manner'[62] and required Members to sanction 'bribery of a foreign public official shall be punishable [with] effective, proportionate and dissuasive criminal penalties';[63] the 1999 GRECO Criminal Law Convention requires sweeping criminalization for both active and passive bribery in both the private and public sectors;[64] and the 2003 UN Convention 'calls for preventive measures and the criminalization of the most prevalent forms of corruption in both public and private sectors'.[65] Notably, breaking with the dominant UN and OECD locations of corruption's criminality, the 2003 African Union Convention requires only that Parties criminalize the laundering of the proceeds of corruption, not specific acts of corruption.[66]

The internationalization of the 'moralization' of anti-corruption law is driven not by a direct effort to internationalize domestic understandings of virtue morality so much as it was driven by a comparative disadvantage that resulted from the domestic understanding when U.S. corporations pursued their interests on the international stage. I want to suggest that much of this occurred because of a lack of clear ICP contours under international law. The FCPA attaches criminality only to natural persons but imposes harsh civil penalties on corporations that bribe or otherwise unduly influence foreign public officials.[67] At first, in the 1970s, by expressing this morality through domestic law, the United States placed its multinational corporations at a disadvantage compared to multinationals headquartered in other parts of the world.[68] However, that scenario soon changed as subsequent efforts through which private lobbyists and public officials pushed to internationalize the U.S. rules[69] – the motive being to 'level the legal playing field' between U.S. multinationals and their peers,[70] even though the actual leveling had taken place before the lobbying, if conventional economic metrics are to be trusted. Thus, given the powerful interests behind the effort and given the ideological similarities between the United States and most of the OECD countries, it is perhaps unsurprising that the FCPA was very nearly 'copy-pasted' as the Organization's first internationalized anti-bribery effort.[71] Fast forward through a number of other commendable but linguistically deferential efforts by other international organizations,[72] and we arrive here at the present status quo: internationalized virtue morality rather than consequentialism driving the logic of the sanction, evident through criminal penalties required only for natural persons.

Criminalization warrants critical examination in these texts precisely because it is a statement of morality. Conventionally, punishing an actor through State-endorsed deprivation of liberty is considered justified only when the act is *mala in se*, not *mala prohibita*.[73] Indeed, while criminal convictions are often accompanied by economic sanctions, the distinguishing feature of criminalization is often state deprivation of physical or intellectual freedom. Ironically, in the United States – on whose legislation and jurisprudence international anti-corruption law is now based[74] – natural persons can be physically imprisoned even when they pose no physical danger to society, as is the case with those convicted of drug possession or severe financial crimes. By contrast, when it comes to legal persons which cannot be imprisoned, DOJ prosecutors are required to assess whether criminal charges would result in benefit or harm society (the DOJ Memo suggests these terms encompass only *economic* benefit or harm),[75] as the corporate person was initially conceived as a public good in the United States.[76]

The point is there is no good reason why moral judgment in the legal sense should attach only to natural persons or should attach to natural persons at all. Although differential treatment can be justified through consequentialist reasoning – that is, let the result of action upon a subject determine what is 'correct' – there is no consistent moral explanation for this specific type of differential treatment unless we assume Abrahamic concepts of reciprocity, debt, and salvation. Moreover, while the instruments purport to criminalize individual acts, the fact that criminality attaches only to individuals undermines the assumption that the act itself is immoral – that corruption is 'an insidious plague' or an 'evil phenomenon', as the late Kofi Annan declared.[77] Rather, it seems that criminalization requirements are misplaced outliers within the broader utilitarian consequentialism that drives the logic of many anti-corruption treaty provisions.

If anti-corruption policy is based upon a market logic that seeks to punish those actors that facilitate the greatest loss of revenue to a State through virtue of their special legal status within the State, then the opposite arrangement of the status quo should be the reality: only legal persons should be criminalized. At the very least, legal fictions should be the primary focus of IACIs rather than natural persons. While the 'corruption' of State officials in a given state is virtually always measured as a matter of 'perception',[78] it has been empirically demonstrated that international legal technologies such as tax havens, transfer pricing, and to a lesser extent, special law firm accounts, eclipse the losses of revenue to States that are caused by crimes that can attach to single individuals, most notably the bribe.[79]

One prominent account of the bribe's evolution was provided in 1984 by John T. Noonan, a late U.S. Federal Circuit Court Judge and Berkeley law professor. In his thorough genealogy of moral judgment upon the bribe, Noonan traced the concept in Western legal traditions to pre-Roman Jewish readings of the Torah.[80] He found that attaching morality to the concept of favor-seeking gift-giving broke with older, pre-state understandings in which gifts were routinely granted to and between public officials in the hope of some reciprocal benefit.[81] As the Hebrew God stated most clearly in Deuteronomy 10:17–18, '[I am] the God of gods and Lord of lords; the great, mighty, and terrible God who does not lift up faces and does not take [offerings], but secures justice to widows and orphans'.[82] The Hebrew God was not only the ultimate judge, but also could not be influenced by gifts or special favors – a verse seemingly contradicting the reality of routine sacrifices. Noonan notes that because this image of God was used as a model for the judges of Israel, and because sacrifices were often made to that God, the prohibition on 'offerings' or 'bribes' took form in the specific context of judgement.[83] The understanding was that justice existed outside of any favor a briber might be able to curry with a bribee. Nevertheless, as a matter of day-to-day business operations and intercultural interactions, special gifts (bribes) remained both common place and morally acceptable.[84]

It was not until the early Christians gained clout in the Roman Empire and mixed with Roman legal professionalism that morality and capitalism coalesced in the modern concept of the bribe. An authority to judge reciprocal benefits had to derive legitimacy from something above the highest state authority, and I want to suggest that 'the market' began to fill that void. According to Noonan, Rome's professional class of orators independently developed the immorality of gift-giving in the context of judgement because their 'profession would have been meaningless if the cases could have been decided by the highest bidder'.[85] Both ideas were accepted by the Christians, but escalated through judgment's connection to the soul.[86] For example, when Simon Magus attempted to purchase the Spirit of Simon Peter in Acts 8:9–24, Simon Peter rebuked him in the harshest of words: 'You and your money go to hell!'[87] In this and other Christian teachings,[88] it became clear that, for Christians, '[m]arket reciprocity is wrong in relation to the Spirit'.[89] Similar concepts can be seen in prohibitions on selling organs, fetuses, and perhaps even sex.[90] These concepts emerged concurrently in another Abrahamic religion: Islam. One crucial difference is that Islam distinguished between bribery paid for good or bad reasons. For example, if a bribe is paid in a situation where bribing is the only way to attain what is right, then it is forbidden only for the one who receives it. In Islamic teaching, the act of bribing is called رشا (*Risha*). The root word *Risha* refers to a rope that is tied to a pail which collects water from inside a well, and another form, *Rashwah*, refers broadly to a system of wage or gift giving in exchange for help or an advantage that would not have been given freely.[91] While there is little in the *Rashwah* word itself to distinguish it from employer–employee relationships, the *Rashwah* is usually used in contexts of the reverse power balance: gifts are given to those with the power to make decisions that could advantage the giver, not given by the powerful to the less powerful in exchange for labor. The act is not always in itself wrong: indeed, one school of Islam (Hanafi) provides an exception for the bribe as a *Wasaatah* – a justified intervention or mediation – which attaches immorality only to the individual receiving the payment, not to the one giving it.[92] Thus, unlike the Christian tradition which views grace or 'affirmative defenses' such as necessity or duress as justification for a wrong act, at least one Islamic tradition places the wrongness in the circumstances of a society – if certain social circumstances are present, the act itself is not wrong and therefore not occasion for justification. In Jewish and Christian traditions, it does not matter if the market (a social circumstance) demands bribes, the individual who accepts a bribe has breached a moral law. To summarize a long and nuanced point that could include many other traditions,[93] just as Simony broadened to describe inappropriate capital intervention in matters spiritual, bribery broadened to a general prohibition on selling justice, which always locates wrongness in individuals. It is therefore a moralization that is not universally held.

I want to suggest that one consequence of this thinking – that immorality resides categorically within the individuals engaging in the act without an overriding exception, not upon the consequences of the act – is the internationalization of a morality in IACIs that assumes individuals rather than systems should be the law's target.[94] By insisting that corruption has to do with moral virtue, the law tends disproportionately to ignore creatures which can have no morals. Specifically, it ignores amoral legal fictions, such as ICPs, Political Action Committees, tax havens, or transfer pricing rules in corporate accounting.

The status quo is that most IACIs require criminalization for individuals who engage in corruption but leave it to States to decide whether to criminalize corruption for legal persons.[95] For example, the OECD Convention Article 2 requires only that States 'establish the liability of legal persons for the bribery of a foreign public official'.[96] Meanwhile, the Convention's Art. 3 Sanctions specifically require that penalties for public officials 'shall, in the case of natural persons, include deprivation of liberty sufficient to enable effective mutual legal assistance and extradition'.[97] Yet for legal persons the Convention remains deferential: 'legal persons shall be subject to effective, proportionate and dissuasive non-criminal sanctions, including monetary sanctions, for bribery of foreign public officials'.[98] Although one might be tempted to explain this discrepancy through the Convention's emphasis on eliminating the official's motivation to accept bribes, the Convention clearly requires criminal sanctions for bribers – not just bribes – so long as they are natural persons. Similarly, while the UN Convention requires criminalization of bribery, embezzlement, misappropriation, or diversion of public funds, Article 26 (liability of legal persons) provides that '[s]ubject to the legal principles of the State Party, the liability of legal persons may be criminal, civil or administrative'.[99] The UN Convention also requires State Parties to consider criminalizing similar acts of natural persons in the private sector, but remains deferential when it comes to legal persons.[100]

ii. Transfer pricing

Transfer pricing is a term that usually refers to the pricing of cross-border transactions within an ICP – that is, internal to the organization at the same time as it transcends multiple States. It provides another example of a legal technology available to ICPs but not to natural persons or other legal personalities. Although there are legitimate uses of transfer pricing, the term is often associated with distasteful if not illegal attempts by ICPs to reduce tax liability, evade currency controls, or to conceal the origins of funds transferred abroad. Unlike bribery, which can be regulated and curtailed through the State, transfer pricing depends upon internationality, exists only through the precondition of differing State systems, and generates problems that cannot be resolved by any individual State. While efforts have been made to address these problems primarily at the OECD, a growing body of research suggests existing OECD remedies to transfer pricing abuse contribute to the ICP's use of tax havens.[101] Thus, it seems pertinent to analyze those instruments.

Somewhat ironically, while proponents of international deregulation for ICPs root justifications for their legal structure in a market logic which holds that inhibiting competition generates inefficiency, the lack of international regulation for ICPs promotes a situation in which ICPs create markets within themselves that ICPs then seek to shield from external competition. Indeed, by some estimates, intra-firm flows of goods account for 40–50% percent of world trade.[102] As the argument goes, internal ICP markets allow for the transfer goods, services, and knowhow between subsidiaries and affiliates without the uncertainties of 'free market' transactions, which reduces the overall costs of production and therefore enhances internal ICP efficiency and external competitive advantage. However, this enables an ICP not only to manage its international market, but to control that market across any number of States. (While relatively recent vintage, these legal technologies have ancient roots: recall from Chapter 1 Vattel's description of the State as owing separate 'internal' and 'external' duties rooted in separate theories of morality and Vitoria's description of international merchant morality as separate from the domestic citizen.)[103] Professor Muchlinski has offered one classic example to illustrate why the transfer pricing status quo is problematic:

> [W]here a subsidiary in country A is subject to a corporation tax rate of 40 per cent and a subsidiary in country B is subject to a rate of 20 per cent, the prices charged for transfers of inputs between them can be manipulated so as to ensure that the bulk of the profits earned by the two related undertakings appears in the books of the subsidiary in B. This can be done, first, by under-invoicing B for the cost of inputs bought by it from A, thereby reducing the profits made by A from sales to B, and increasing the profits of B by reason of cheaper inputs from A. Alternatively, should B supply inputs to A, A can be over-invoiced for the cost thereof, resulting in a reduction in A's profits, and in a corresponding transfer of the inflated purchase price to B's profit account.[104]

Not only does country A lose the revenue of every ICP with subsidiaries in country B; it potentially loses revenue from every ICP with subsidiaries anywhere with a corporate tax rate that is less than 40 per cent. And to this end, ICPs can move or manipulate balances through three basic techniques: (1) altering the timing of payments; (2) re-characterizing the nature of payments; and (3) changing the recipient. Option 3 provides the most salient international technique. ICPs consist of multiple intermediary entities (companies, trusts, partnerships, etc.) that can be created and dissolved as needed in jurisdictions with domestic taxation systems favorable to *inter alia* assets, transactions, or foreign income.

Broken down into basic components, most ICPs utilize these technologies through three categories of entities: (1) a Base entity; (2) a Conduit entity; and (3) operating entities. Base entities are created as citizens of States that do not tax the type of income the ICP wishes to avoid, for example, no income tax, no profit tax, or no tax on foreign income. The legal rationale for these entities is that they defer taxation from ICP profits so the ICP can reinvest them in other operations rather than distributing them to shareholders. Thus, the primary function of Base entities is usually to own things: shares in other affiliates in a corporate group, intellectual property rights, or tangible assets. More rarely, they provide services like insurance or shipping. However, the 'consulting' services for which prices are so often inflated are usually offered by entities located in financial capitals:[105] London, New York, Hong Kong, Frankfurt, Tokyo, Singapore, Shanghai, Sydney, and so on. These 'consulting services' are often the source of real decisions for the corporate group or network, but they avoid the appearance of 'control' for legal liability purposes.

Conduit entities are created in reaction to international taxation treaties between States that agree to reduce or eliminate source taxation to facilitate investment between the parties. While taxation treaties assume 'investors' are bona fide citizens of the partner State, ICPs headquartered anywhere in the world can create a citizen-Conduit in a State that has a taxation treaty that benefits the ICP. As such, the primacy function of Conduits is to channel flows of income. If the treaty allows it, income categorized as non-taxable can be directed through a Conduit and passed on directly.[106] If a treaty restricts benefits to active entities rather than passive (pass-through) ones, other strategies can be used. For example, a Conduit can rack up charges to another entity within the ICP for goods and/or services that fall within the treaty's protection and then use the proceeds to finance the same or another entity within the ICP (now tax-free). These strategies can even be used by domestic investors seeking to access the benefits usually reserved only to foreign ones, though such behaviors from local investors usually cross the (seemingly arbitrary) legal line into the category of 'tax evasion'.

Dodging for now the question of whether States (or cities) should compete to attract corporations seeking favorable tax rates, let us focus on the 'corruption' aspect of this – that is, how is this legally-blessed practice different from criminally sanctioned money laundering apart from a definition of money laundering that requires the money itself to have been illegally obtained? Usually when money is considered to be laundered, criminality attaches to any one of three phases: (1) the act of introducing illegal profits into the financial system, often by breaking up the profits into smaller deposits; (2) the process of disguising origins of revenue or control of assets, or using undisguised funds to facilitate the process of disguising such origins, usually facilitated by the transfer of funds from one account to another through various legitimate banks and business around the world; and/or (3) reintroducing the 'washed' funds back into the legitimate economy.[107] One can readily recognize parallel steps in transfer pricing practices, but transfer pricing entails a different circumstantial element: rather than seeking to wash the money of its illegal source, it seeks to 'wash' legitimately obtained profits of taxes levied on their source.

Efforts to regulate these practices have been awkward and ineffective, mimicking domestically applied principles from U.S. and UK corporate law. But effective regulation is tough given the status quo: the ICP operates subject to no single system and the OECD cannot claim the ICP as subject. Nevertheless, the OECD has attempted regulation via two primary means: (1) the 'Arm's Length' Principle (ALP) and (2) Comparable Profit Methods (CPM). The ALP essentially seeks to allocate the costs and benefits of an ICP's international subsidiaries as closely as possible to the allocation that would have occurred in an identical open free market transaction between unrelated corporate entities.[108] The most sweeping domestic example of this is likely the U.S. IRS Code, Section 482, which allows the State to reallocate corporate profits between entities, but this depends on the State's ability obtain complete access to an ICP's worldwide accounts.[109] At the international level, the method is even more problematic as it assumes the existence of 'free markets' which often do not exist. For example, markets that have been created by the ICP (e.g., the market for materials for which the ICP drastically increased demand), markets that could not exist but for the existence of the ICP (e.g., the market for consulting services regarding something exclusive to the ICP), markets with prices inflated by the actions of an ICP (e.g., if the ICP's monopolistic position disconnects price from true costs of production), or intangible determinations of price (e.g., if the ICP's marketing team created the gap between production costs and price due to a brilliant advertising campaign).[110]

To address problems of intangibility and inexistence that emerge from the ALP approach to transfer pricing,[111] some regulators have turned to CPMs. Some CPMs, such as the 'exact comparable' or 'inexact comparable' methods, are essentially variations of the ALP with slight methodological caveats.[112] Where such methods proved impractical or ineffective, especially when no exact or inexact comparable transactions exist, U.S. policy makers (and now the OECD)[113] have advocated for the use of 'basic arm's length rate of return' (BALRM), which involves an allocation of profits between related entities which seek to distinguish between profit that is attributable to the use of tangible assets and that which is derived from the use of intangibles. This is achieved by ascertaining the market rate of return on the tangible assets and factors of production used by each entity (which is done through a comparison with similar functions and assets employed by unrelated entities) and allocating that rate of return to the entity using the asset or factor of production in question. The remaining income would then be allocated to the owner of the intangible. In cases where the related transferee also owned intangibles that were used in exploiting the transferred intangible, the U.S. advocates for 'BALRM plus profit split': first, each party is allocated a return on the functions performed through the application of BALRM. And second, the remaining income (presumably derived from the use of intangibles) is split according to the relative value of the intangibles of each company.[114] The obvious subjectivity of ascertaining many of these values have rendered both CPMs rather unpopular, especially with the OECD,[115] which prefers the simplicity and predictability of the ALP. This is understandable. Even if intangible profit can float under the radar, at least subjective 'judgments' on their value do not acquire the appearance of principled legality.

iii. Tax havens

While it is possible for almost any State's laws to be used to avoid or evade another's taxes, Tax Havens are those State's whose laws are aimed to enable avoidance or evasion of another State's tax laws or regulations. The rise of the importance of tax havens to the world economy since WWI is somewhat understudied by international lawyers, perhaps because it is a problem generated by the 'sacred' notion of sovereignty. Another reason might be the relatively recent vintage of individual income taxation.[116] While haven jurisdictions sprouted with the interwar Havens in Luxemburg, Switzerland, and Liechtenstein, they exploded alongside the proliferating practice of State-levied taxes on individual income after WWII.[117] Corporate use of tax havens also trebled in the mid-1940s and throughout the 1950s as corporate tax rates in the United States and Europe often ranged from 40–50%.[118] In part because of the globalization of legal technologies accompanying first multinationals and now ICPs, the concealment of corporate wealth through these and newer tax havens is even more difficult to quantify than individual wealth.[119]

The widespread ICP use of tax havens has resulted in astronomical revenue loss to States. Using macroeconomic data to demonstrate that foreign firms are more profitable than local firms in tax havens but less profitable than domestic firms in their home countries, one recent study suggests that roughly 40% of multinational corporate profits are moved to tax havens on a yearly basis.[120] Other studies estimate that the total cost of tax revenue lost by States to tax havens hovers between $500 and $600 billion per year. To make matters worse, the OECD instruments that could address this have taken an approach that exacerbates the problem. This is because the OECD has directed most of its efforts in this realm toward transfer pricing – a practice which itself has a variety of methods through which firms can legally avoid taxation, as discussed previously. This is because the mere existence of transfer pricing instruments provides a sort of smoke-in-mirrors scapegoat (for the pessimist) or placebo (for optimists) when it comes to effectively addressing the more fundamental sovereignty issues raised by tax havens, in other words, does one State have a duty to help another State enforce its tax laws? Does a State harmed by the tax laws of another State have any remedy against that State? At what point is privacy a hinderance to transparency and vice versa in international financial transactions? Recent scholarship suggests the OECD's focus is misplaced because, first, transfer pricing involves easily ascertainable information, especially amongst OECD countries, so officials are more quickly drawn to this low hanging fruit when it comes to repatriating lost tax revenue.[121] Second, because of the availability of information in developed States (i.e., because of transparency), actions against other high-tax OECD countries are more likely to succeed than actions against, say, Bermuda.[122] And finally, successful actions between high-tax States are more likely to be enforced, either because they are members of a common regional governmental authority (e.g., the EU) or members of a common transgovernmental organization (e.g., the OECD).[123]

By the same token, if the goal of IACIs is to reduce the amount of State revenue channeled to private gain rather than public benefit, increasing the liability of the State itself by conceptualizing 'freedom from corruption' as a human right actionable against the State – as some commentators have suggested[124] – would harm some of the States most affected by 'corruption as bribery' while doing nothing to curtail the much more significant economic harms caused by 'corruption as tax evasion and avoidance'. Many of the States that receive the highest scores on Transparency International's 'corruption perception' index are those with administrative and legal structures that are already stressed and many already struggle to provide livable wages for citizens. This is not to say that public officials in those States do not steal from their citizens but creating a right to freedom from corruption actionable by a harmed individual against a State is unlikely to stop a *de facto* dictator from syphoning public funds offshore, for example. This is especially true because most States – and especially developing States – are not bound by the decisions of any international human rights court. At best, in this simple hypothetical, the State will pay out the complaining citizen at the expense of other citizens of the State rather than at the expense of the *de facto* dictator. At worst, the 'naming and shaming' of the State would stigmatize its citizens and its status in the global market to the detriment of public welfare.

iv. Deferred prosecution agreements

The idea that IACIs should focus on illicit transfers of State revenue rather than a moral interpretation of individual behavior is a double-edged sword. Where State revenue as a driving principle motivates States to spend fewer resources on the moralization of individual bribes and greater resources on devising methods to curb the export of corporate capital through tax havens and transfer pricing, the sword cuts against economically powerful States, which often benefit from base erosion in other States and enjoy favorable placement on indicators such as Transparency International's Corruption Perception Index. That edge of the sword fights for the peoples of weaker States whose resources are depleted by the practices of many ICPs. However, the revenue focus has also motivated economically powerful States to devise new legal technologies through which to appropriate damages incurred by weaker

States through the corrupt practices of the most powerful ICPs. One of the most effective of these technologies is the DPA. The first DPA emerged as an option for ICPs under UK law in 2015 but has spread quickly to other economically powerful States such as Japan, Canada, Germany, France, Singapore, Australia, and the United States.

A DPA is an option created through domestic law granted only to wealthy ICPs who wish to avoid the stigma of a criminal corruption conviction. While the specific legal parameters of DPAs vary across jurisdictions, the central features are that a DPA invariably involves an amount of money to be paid by an ICP against whom a strong criminal case can be made to the State prosecuting the case. DPAs always include a set of conditions in addition to payment that ICPs must meet to avoid prosecution, and the conditions are case specific. However, the conditions always involve third parties, as DPAs are usually justified on the grounds that corrupt ICPs can identify several 'smaller' corrupt actors that engaged in corrupt behavior with the ICP in the manifold jurisdictions in which it enjoys operations. Thus, for example, where Airbus, a German ICP, systematically granted gifts to the heads of small airlines throughout the world in exchange for orders, it was able to avoid prosecution in the United States for business it conducted in China by paying more than half a billion USD to the U.S. Treasury, and it was able to avoid prosecution in the UK by paying more than one billion USD to the UK Serious Fraud Office for bribes paid out to airline operators in Malaysia, Sri Lanka, Taiwan, Indonesia, and Ghana.

Proponents of DPAs would argue that, without the cooperation of Airbus, the reach of their corrupt acts and the implications of their consequences (which the United States alleged included risks to its national security) would not have been known. For this reason, DPAs are sometimes analogized to plea bargains in the United States,[125] though the analogy is a weak one. The analogy is weak because, rather than one prosecutor juggling multiple defendants seeking to trade small offenders for the 'big fish', DPAs allow economically powerful 'big fish' to purchase freedom on the condition that they provide evidence to pursue smaller offenders. The upshot is that economically powerful States are the actors from whom ICPs must purchase freedom, even though the crimes alleged often predominantly harm the publics of less economically powerful States (such as Malaysia, Sri Lanka, Taiwan, Indonesia, and Ghana). Considering this, critics of DPAs argue that such agreements remedy none of the problems with the current IACI status quo. Instead, they allow the largest offenders to purchase freedom and allow the richest States to appropriate and nationalize the financial harm caused to the publics of poorer States.

d. Environmental law

The primary international legal texts that concern the environment fail to address the ICP's potential to mitigate environmental damage largely because they are framed in terms that assume the primacy of international development. The two foundational texts are the 1972 Stockholm Declaration[126] – important because of discourse-shaping role as the UN's first international environmental agreement – and the 1992 Rio Declaration,[127] which served as a catalyst to implement ongoing State monitoring and goal setting meetings, such as the UN Climate Change Conference (COP), whose 25th meeting in Madrid recently ended in gridlock.

i. Stockholm

The Stockholm Declaration proclaims in Section 4 that '[i]n the developing countries most of the environmental problems are caused by underdevelopment . . . [t]herefore, the developing countries must direct their efforts to development'. Section 5 goes on to proclaim that '[o]f all things in the world, people are the most precious'. It also idealizes the achievement of a version of nature that is 'more in keeping with human needs and hopes.' It therefore appears to contradict Section 6, which speaks of the need to 'defend . . . the human environment' without any mention of what it might need defense from, except perhaps through the subtle caveat that the environment's defense must occur 'together with, and in harmony with, the established and fundamental goals of . . . worldwide economic and social development'.[128] The Declaration then goes on to set out a number of principles based on the initial proclamations, several of which deploy the language of rationality (e.g., 'rational management' or 'rational planning') in a matter that instrumentalizes nature as a tool for human aims, one of which is to ensure that future humans can also enjoy nature.[129]

ii. Rio and aftermath

Twenty years after Stockholm, the 1992 Rio Declaration more explicitly crystalized the UN Environmental Framework's obsession with 'development'. Whereas the Stockholm Declaration's full title is *The Declaration of the United Nations Conference on the Human Environment*, which notably frames the environment as the property of humanity, the Rio Declaration's full title is *The Rio Declaration on Environment and Development*, which explicitly couples the environmental with the economic on the UN's agenda. In 'seeking to build upon' the Stockholm Declaration, the Rio Declaration's Preamble asserts a need to 'protect the integrity of the global environmental and developmental system' – now coupling the environment with development but still failing to articulate what either system needs to be protected from. The Principles that follow make several assumptions, but two are notable here: (1) States have a right to the exploitation of nature and (2) the environment belongs separately to States, that is, each State has its own environment that other States are not to pollute (directly or through their policies toward corporate actors) without just compensation. Thus, the right to exploit appears juxtaposed against punishment for pollution, the latter keeping the former in check. Several of the other Principles suggest specters of an environmental tort remedy, with Principle 10 even calling for 'access to judicial and administrative proceedings, including redress and remedy'. However, by emphasizing that the 'national level' is the 'relevant level' for participation of 'all concerned citizens', and by stating that '[e]nvironmental issues are best handled with the participation of all concerned citizens', the language strongly cuts against the establishment of an international environmental court, much less an international environmental cause of action.[130]

The text also prioritizes economic health over State environmental legislation. For example, after demanding that States enact 'effective environmental legislation', Principle 11 declares:

> Environmental standards, management objectives and priorities should reflect the environmental and developmental context to which they apply. Standards applied by some countries may be inappropriate and of unwarranted economic and social cost to other countries, in particular developing countries.[131]

I do not criticize this formulation of the problem in order to suggest that developing countries should be economically and socially harmed in order to hasten international action on climate change. Rather, it is the complete absence of discussion on corporate actors to which I wish to draw attention. The language of the existing agreements assumes that States are the only actors that can curb environmental damage, and that they must do so to their own economic detriment. These are assumptions, not factual demonstrations. And here I would venture a causal claim: these assumptions excuse policy makers from thinking more creatively about how to address ICP regulation vis-à-vis environmental damage. Therefore, creative thinking on environmental policy is often stunted by assumptions about the economic viability of curbing environmental damage, or by parties interested in fortifying the notion that radical environmental policies would result in severe economic damage.

But setting aside my speculations and claims to causality for the moment, I want to highlight that these assumptions perpetuate at least three common notions of 'the natural' in the minds of international lawyers and economists. The first underlying notion is that economic advancement cannot occur without environmental damage. The second underlying notion is that, because States must implement standards, there will always be different levels of environmental damage occurring in different States. And the third underlying notion is that modes of production that cause greater environmental harm will produce greater profit margins and are therefore of greater benefit to developing States.

I want to offer at least two reasons why these notions should be challenged. First, all of these notions only make sense if we assume a future in which the economic inequalities that exist between States today persist indefinitely – that is, cheaper modes of production are beneficial to richer States because they export pollution from production to developing States and import the products at discount rates. Second, and more importantly for our purposes here, these notions assume that the ICP must be regulated through the intermediary of the State – that international law cannot apply directly to the ICP and in common to all ICP actions in every State. As the OECD notes with resignation in its report on environmental law in practice, 'political will and international cooperation will remain the crucial drivers for change'.[132]

The OECD is wrong about this. By now we have seen that domestic political will is often a small part of what drives and justifies binding public international law. At the very least, the statement overlooks crucial forces that shape political will and cooperation. As the various branches of international economic law have shown us, the market for capital, not diplomacy, serves as the most effective 'sword' to enforce the decisions of international courts.[133] It is commercial risk insurers and global suppliers of capital – *inter alia*, the IMF, the World Bank, the AIIB, institutional investors, and private foreign ICPs contemplating entry – that levy the most serious economic penalties over time on States that undermine commitments to comply with international agreements. If we are to take seriously the notion that the environment should be a subject of international law, that it should have rights enforceable against States, either all suppliers of capital must be on board with enforcement (which is unlikely so long as capital can be maximized through noncompliance) or a framework that is independent of enforcement by means of economic coercion is necessary.

e. *International economic law*

Although these topics fall under the umbrella of 'economic law', the ICP's privileged role in international investment arbitration and its role in shaping some aspects of the WTO Agreements is thoroughly discussed in other subsections. Thus, this subsection will focus on two slightly more obscure facets of the ICP's role in international economic law: (1) NIEO and (2) 'development'.

i. Legacies of the new international legal order

Two years after the Stockholm Declaration, the UN Secretary General released a special 1974 Report – the *Report of the Group of Eminent Persons to Study the Impact of Multinational Corporations on Development and International Relations* – that understood the corporation as intrinsically linked to international development. The Report observed that growing MNE international power, especially vis-à-vis developing States, required transnational organizations to create a new policy framework: 'a policy framework which may be adequate for dealing with national corporations needs to be modified when dealing with multinational ones'. The Report also noted that 'multinational corporations can use their power in a manner which may run counter to the needs of the societies in which they operate' and that 'Corporate power cannot, of course, be compared with the political power of Governments which possess both legitimacy and means of enforcement. Yet many developing countries may hesitate to exercise their governmental power because of the real or perceived costs entailed'. The language implies both vastness and illegitimacy on the part of corporate power, and these observations underpin 'the need for public involvement and for discussion of the goals and policies that multinational corporations should pursue and the means whereby corporate power may be oriented in the interest of world development'. The phrase 'world development' here is striking in its reference to the idea of a global public, to a call for law and policy rooted not in the interests of the State but in the interests of the world. The phrase is also striking in its possible breadth: 'the interest world development' could reasonably be understood as those interests which are mutually beneficial to the Earth and all of its inhabitants – that is, to Humanity, to the environment, and to non-human animals. Nevertheless, although the Report notes that its 'concentration on the relative capacity of nation States to regulate the activities of multinational corporations should not imply that corporations themselves have no responsibility for regulating their own conduct', the Report never suggests that international law could regulate corporations directly.

Given much of the language of the Report, it seems unlikely that the possibility of direct regulation did not occur to its twenty eminent authors. More likely, in 1974, no concept yet existed in international legal thought to describe the place MNEs came to occupy. This is one gap that a more coherent theory of the ICP could address. As the previous chapter has shown and as the next chapter shows, judge-made law since the early 1900s and international agreements since the 1970s have carved an ever-clearer picture of the ICP. Yet the questions of whether and how to assign duties are ever shifting and often opaque. The Secretary General's 1974 Report was the first international effort to clarify the space, but while its ambitions were focused on 'world interests' and 'hard law' – for example, policies and 'regulatory mechanisms defining more closely the interests to which corporate management should respond, the promotion of more competitive international markets, and promoting the countervailing power of trade unions' – it was eventually subsumed by later 'soft law' efforts that placed emphasis on corporate self-regulation, that is, Ruggie's Guiding Principles. Articulating a clearer theory of the ICP offers a chance to understand the corporation as a primary subject of international law, not an entity whose only two access points to international law are hard law initiatives from states and soft law initiatives calling for self-regulation.

If the ICP is to be a direct subject – as more international tribunals suggest is the case – what duties should it bare and to whom? I use the word 'subject' here to connotate a direct attachment. Just as the international law of armed conflict claims authority to hold liable individuals who violate the laws of war regardless of their status as agents of a State,[134] corporations too can be conceptualized as actors that – when exhibiting certain behaviors in certain contexts – can be liable for breaching duties that transcend any State; duties owed to humanity, to the Earth, to the Environment, or to some combination of these. An additional note: I am here using the word 'duties' rather than 'responsibilities' as the former to refers to hard legal requirements and the latter refers to both legal requirements and other forms of obligation, for example, social and moral ones.

Some commentators advocate for greater corporate liability at the domestic level but oppose direct subjectivity and the assignment of duties under international law.[135] These commentators believe direct duties would lead to an inflation of rights for corporations under international law, much like the one that has occurred in the United States. I believe this analysis is misguided because, as we have seen in Chapter 1, the rights associated with corporate personhood in the United States – where corporate personhood first took form – did not emerge from duties assigned by law. Rather, they emerged from a constitutional amendment that included the word 'person' rather than 'human' or 'citizen' in an environment in which people who had not previously been considered 'persons' under the law attained 'personhood' status. An analogous phenomenon is in the process of occurring on the international stage because the term 'investor' collapses both natural and legal persons into a single category that privileges capital over citizenry and foreign capital over domestic capital, thus creating what might be conceptualized as a shadow constituency. This concept will be discussed at greater length in the next chapter.

Sticking broadly into the U.S. history of the concept of corporate personhood, the Courts were tasked with the decision on whether other the persons mentioned in the 14th Amendment included legal persons. The concept of corporate personality was well-established and the process of grafting human rights onto legal persons proved faster and more effective than the process of guaranteeing legal equal protection for freed slaves.[136] Discussions on duties followed the rights that corporations obtained. These took form largely in tort law doctrines which transferred the duties owed by individuals to the corporate person, so long as the individuals concerned acted within the scope of their corporate roles and, in some cases, so long as the corporate veil could be pierced.[137]

On the international stage, the desire for corporations to hold duties to States predated the judge-made phenomenon of the ICP. In the 1974 Report, the Twenty Eminent Persons called on developing countries to 'monitor the distribution of benefits between themselves and the multinational corporations which operate in their economies'.[138] The Report also noted that the capacity to do so was not yet present. 'Not only should host countries be prepared to use, with knowledge and skill, the powers which belong to them as political entities, but they should develop sufficient knowledge to control the impact of multinational corporations on their economies as a whole'. Indeed, the Eminent Persons considered this knowledge a necessary precondition to 'formulating agreements with [multinationals] prior to their entry'.[139]

At the behest of that Report, the United Nations Economic and Social Council (ECOSOC) adopted Resolution 1913 in 1974, which created both the Intergovernmental Commission on Transnational Corporations and the Information and Research Center on Transnational Corporations, both of which are now defunct.[140] The ill-fated Commission failed in its principal task: it should have negotiated a code of conduct pertaining to multinational corporations. To its credit, the Code of Conduct (the Code) was actually drafted – indeed it was near completion in 1977 – but negotiations on its adoption derailed on the prospect of reciprocal duties in 1978. Subsequently, the Code suffered a slow decline throughout the 1980s and ultimately failed to gain the approval of the world's most powerful economies when the completed draft was circulated in 1990.[141] This lack of enthusiasm may be attributable to the fact that the world's most powerful economies and corporate representatives had latched to the idea that the Code should include State duties to corporations, first proposed by Henry Kissinger.[142] Developing countries felt this idea undermined the entire purpose of the Code.[143] Perhaps because of this, by 1992 the State-centered style of economic development favored in the 1970s and by the G-77 was no longer considered a 'viable option'.[144] The President of the 46th General Assembly opted for a 'fresh approach' to foreign investment: it folded the UN Center on Transnational Corporations into the UN Conference on Trade and Development (UNCTAD) and refocused the Center on producing documents such as its flagship *World Investment Report*. Needless to say, the vision of direct corporate subjectivity was stymied.

The vision suffered a slow death. Throughout the 1990s, even as corporate lobbying succeeded in making intellectual property a trade issue at the same time as agricultural subsidies in developed States undercut the neoliberal vision of development,[145] a sub-commission of the UN Human Rights Commission began to reposition itself vis-à-vis development. This sub-commission eventually created the Working Group on the Working Methods and Activities of Transnational Corporations. Developed over the course of five years beginning in 1999, the Draft Norms were submitted to the sub-commission of the UN Human Rights Commission in late 2004.[146] The Draft Norms were the final gasp of what began in 1974 as the Code of Conduct. Because the Draft Norms sought to attach human rights obligations directly to corporations, they drew strong criticism from the business community. The International Chamber of Commerce claimed that the Norms were a dangerous and irresponsible attempt to 'privatize' human rights: 'If put into effect, the Draft Norms will undermine human rights, the business sector of society, and the right to development'.[147] The Office of the High Commissioner for Human Rights subsequently consulted relevant stakeholders to produce a comprehensive review of all existing instruments and initiatives pertaining to the human rights and responsibilities of corporate actors. A few months after the Report's publication in 2005, the Commission requested that a special representative be appointed on the issue of human rights and transnational corporations. Then–Secretary General Kofi Annan appointed Harvard international affairs professor John Ruggie.

Ruggie – a non-lawyer whose massively influential Framework we have already discussed – quickly concluded that the Norms had too shaky a legal basis to extend direct obligations to corporations. His Report obfuscates a central question: whether his assessment was based primarily on legal issues or whether it was rather based on the business community's extreme dislike of the Norms. 'Indeed, in the [Special Representative's] view', wrote Ruggie in his initial Report, 'the divisive debate over the Norms obscures rather than illuminates promising areas of consensus and cooperation among business, civil society, governments, and international institutions with respect to human rights'.[148] Thus, Ruggie set out to draft a new approach – what eventually became the Guiding Principles on Business and Human Rights – which was endorsed by the HRC and enshrined as the UNGPs in 2011.

Where earlier efforts sought to push beyond CSR to create external standards to which corporations were bound, Ruggie argued that these efforts should rather 'buil[d] upon' the phenomenon of CSR. The UNGPs, for Ruggie, are a way to deepen and officialize trends in CSR – trends that ICPs initiated – that may eventually serve as a basis upon which future international legal regimes can build. Always the pragmatist, he viewed the Code and the Norms as failing because they lacked a clear legal basis to directly obligate corporations and he believed the UNGPs might provide to future instruments the legal clarity previous attempts lacked. As we have seen in our discussion on the OEIGWG's draft binding instrument, Ruggie's ideals remain a great distance from realization.

ii. 'Development' and the ICP

Many sections of this book, and most recently the sections detailing ISDS case law, environmental law, and business and human rights, reference the fact that 'development' is deeply intertwined with the activities of the ICP. Yet the State bears sole legal responsibility for manifesting 'development'. 'Development' serves as a justification for much of the international legal treatment of ICPs, in particular treaties that favor capital inflows from ICPs and other investors, but also international regulations on trade and taxation. And as we have seen, it also serves as a restraint on environmental regulation. But what is 'development'? Based on my own previous work, I will here provide three brief definitions of the term as a legal rather than economic concept.

DEVELOPMENT AS A HIERARCHY

This conceptualization usually makes tangential reference to the term 'development' in its economic sense. That is, not simply referring to economic growth, but referring to a series of specific metrics that define 'development' within the discipline of economics (e.g., per capita GDP, literacy rates, or corruption).[149,150] Nevertheless, I refer to this conceptualization as a hierarchy because it is always viewed in the legal texts in terms of 'levels'. While the economist's typical definition of development describes a stage in a process, referring to 'levels of development' employs the term in a static (rather than dynamic) time-locked sense. At the top of the hierarchy are the developed states. It is presupposed that those termed 'developing' are at a premature stage, the end goal of which is to 'graduate'[151] to the state of the developed States. A World Bank staffer described this "graduation" as the point at which a state becomes a donor to the World Bank rather than only a recipient of funds.[152] When the now-defunct TPP speaks of development as sets of policies to promote or as something that can and should be maximized by the TPP itself, as it does in Chapter 23, it is referring to a state of being 'developed' as an end goal for all States.[153]

DEVELOPMENT AS CREATION/IMPROVEMENT

The most common use of development is simply as a synonym for some perceived improvement or for the creation of something that does not exist but supposedly should. For example, economic development describes a perceived improvement toward higher incomes in a State, technological development describes improvements to the existing state of technology, and infrastructural development describes an improvement to the existing infrastructure in a given State.[154] NAFTA's reference to strengthening and developing laws which do not yet exist, as it does in its Preamble,[155] is an example of development as creation. This conceptualization of development is also used to describe a tool or set of tools made available by powerful actors to less powerful ones on the journey toward 'graduation'. This includes but is not limited to state actors. In the TPP Preamble for example, references are made to supporting businesses through developing supply chains, which in turn supports smaller businesses through 'enhancing their ability to participate' in international networks.[156] In TPP Chapter 23, the Committee on Development and its accompanying procedural mechanisms can be thought of as *instruments* to facilitate some form of improvement.[157]

DEVELOPMENT AS A CONTEXT

Development is often used to imply a certain conception of 'correct' context. For example, the assumption behind the phrase sustainable development is that development will occur whether sustainable or not, and thus, promoting sustainable development refers to promoting a type of context in which development can occur (i.e., a sustainable context).[158] The EU–Vietnam BIT Chapter 15, EU–Singapore Chapter 13, and CETA Chapter 22 (Trade and Sustainable Development), specify three 'pillars' of sustainable development in their respective Article 1.1 goal setting sections (Context and Objectives): 'economic development, social development, and environmental protection'.[159] In fact, sustainable development is a well-known legal concept today and has been recognized by various international decision making bodies.[160] The normative responsibility inherent in the concept of sustainable development is addressed to States and businesses alike.[161] One of the salient features of the concept of sustainable development is that economic interests are to be reconciled with needs in the social and developmental domains.[162] These 'domains' (economic, social, and environmental) are normatively expressed in international standards and principles that have been carved out over time and so solidify presuppositions with respect to the concept of development.[163] Likewise, supporting harmonious development implies that development could occur in another way, harmonious and unharmonious, and the law's role is to support a harmonious scenario. The assumption is that the context of development is inevitable, and while it may be true that the world is never frozen in place, the term is still a heuristic for values associated with the Washington Consensus (liberalization of trade, facilitation of foreign investment, etc.): development as a context describes different ways in which the law can shape an inevitable process.

There are, of course, other uses of the term development in international treaty texts. For example, *Development as an Occurrence*: 'Any Party that considers that this Chapter requires modification to take into account developments in the production process'. However, this and other uses of the term carry no evaluative judgments or implied legal significance, and therefore, are not of particular interest for our purposes here. The three definitions I set out previously all carry implicit normative judgments evaluating one condition as being superior to another. *Development as a Hierarchy* carries the implication that the condition of being developed is superior to the condition of being developing. *Development as Creation/Improvement* carries the implication that development is an instrument through which to achieve a superior condition or superior tool: better enforcement mechanisms, better legal regimes, better socioeconomic conditions, and so on. And finally, *Development as a Context* carries the implication that, while the process of development occurs almost synonymously with the inevitability of evolution, there are superior contexts in which that process can occur: sustainable is superior to unsustainable, harmonious is superior to unharmonious. For a detailed description of how I arrived at each of these definitions, please see my 2017 article *The Concept of Development in International Economic Law*, referenced in the endnotes.

f. OECD guidelines for multinational enterprises

Following the Code of Conduct efforts put forward at the UN General Assembly by the Group of 77 (G-77) in 1970s, the thirty member States of the OECD responded to the need to improve the supervision of the international activities of MNEs by drafting the non-binding Guidelines for Multinational Enterprises. In 1976, the OECD States along with a handful of other States adopted the Guidelines. In 2000, revisions to these made corrections to a flimsy supervisory mechanism and introduced a general obligation on MNEs to 'respect the human rights of those affected by their activities consistent with the host government's international obligations and commitments'.[164] These were again updated in 2011 to harmonize with Ruggie's Guiding Principles.[165] To be sure, the Guidelines push MNEs toward greater accountability in the States that adhere to them, but they can be viewed more cynically as undermining G-77 efforts to implement permanent sovereignty over natural resources. They can also be viewed as making States with minimal international obligations more attractive to MNEs thereby placing a chilling effect on collective action toward more radical efforts to manifest an international framework that understands natural persons or the environment rather than ICPs, investors, or capital flows as the immediate priority. This is illustrated by the fact that, from the outset, the Guidelines were adopted as a portion of the larger Declaration on International Investment and Multinational Enterprises, which seeks primarily to facilitate trade among OECD countries by requiring States to adopt the MFN and FET policies and by reducing conflict of laws amongst States with respect to MNE regulation.[166] Thus, the broader Declaration within which the Guidelines are set out primarily serves to encourage the opening of economies to foreign direct investment.

Criticisms aside, the Guidelines remain the most visible instrument articulating the international obligations of MNEs and serve important transparency goals. On the one hand, some provisions could serve to curtail the legal ambiguities with respect to ownership and control through which many MNEs have avoided international accountability. For example, Section III of the Guidelines refers to 'the obligation of all companies to disclose information on matters such as ownership and voting rights, intra-group relations, governance policies and enterprise objectives'.[167] On the other hand, the Guidelines serve the interests of States who wish to welcome foreign investment but are uneasy about the blurred line between public and private capital, particularly from firms investing the spoils of sovereign wealth funds (such as SoftBank Vision Fund, headquartered in London and Tokyo but animated by Saudi Arabia's Public Investment Fund), firms with virtually unlimited access to cheap loans and State capital (such as Huawei), or other sources of capital associated with State Capitalism.[168] Firms that wish to do business in States that adhere to the Guidelines are required to disclose this information to the States in which they operate, but not necessarily to the public. Always focused on economic concerns, these provisions are geared toward greasing the gears of investment: a State with misgivings about a foreign government's entanglement in its critical infrastructure may have national security concerns, but natural persons ultimately affected by ownership and control structures might not have access to that information.

III. The modern ICP's role in 'authoring' international law

By now we have seen that, through myriad avenues historically and presently, the private sector is no stranger to international law. Indeed, since the colonial era, the law of nations has been linked to the interests of chartered companies. Debatably, the interwar period is an exception, and without question the relationship between public international law and the private sector has undergone dramatic reformations since the colonial era. Nevertheless, the received understanding of international law in the present is still divided into two camps: private international law (private agreements, say, between businesses) and public international law (agreements between States). The distinction will often rigidly categorize the doctrines related to 'public' and 'private' concerns and will ignore the effects each set of agreements have upon the other. Many fields of international law resist this distinction, with international investment law blurring the lines most obviously (agreements between states that enforce private agreements between business or businesses and States). But the blurred lines are not always obvious; the category of public international law can itself be misleading insofar as the ontology suggests that 'public law' is law created primarily by the public – that is, State representatives and diplomats – for the public – that is, for the benefit of the citizens of all States involved. But neither of these things has ever been consistently true of public international law.

While it is true that only public representatives can enter into public international agreements, the private sector often influences how those international agreements are constructed and therefore how international law applies to ICPs vis-à-vis other actors. In an effort to better understand the ICP's place within international law, therefore, this section will explore three avenues through which the ICP plays a role in 'authoring' it. The ICP shapes international law (1) through 'consultant' or 'observer' status in negotiations at institutions across the UN through the ECOSOC access rules, (2) through lobbying and 'revolving door' access to government as illustrated by the WTO TRIPS Agreement's understanding of intellectual property as a trade issue, and (3) through political donations, as illustrated by recent empirical research on political spending and CEO policy preferences.

a. 'Consultant' or 'observer' status

The ECOSOC regulatory structure was developed early in the life of the UN. As such, it has provided a 'blueprint' for many later UN institutions and it continues to function as a gatekeeper for other UN institutions. To gain access to many international organizations, an association must first gain access to the ECOSOC. Article 71 of the UN Charter authorizes ECOSOC to 'make suitable arrangements for consultation with non-governmental organizations which are concerned with matters within its competence'.[169] Over the years, ECOSOC has adopted a variety of resolutions enabling NGOs to apply for accreditation 'for consultation'.[170] These resolutions require non-state actors to have 'aims and purposes' that align with the 'spirit' of the UN's work, and grant access to those organizations that can overcome a series of accountability and representative indicia, such as 'an established headquarters', a 'constitution' that provides for representation in policy-setting within the organization; an 'executive' that is 'responsive'; and 'authority to speak for its members through its authorized representatives.' At the ECOSOC, only non-profits are allowed, and they must obtain funding from 'national affiliate[s]' or 'individual members.'[171] When these financing criteria are not met, an organization can still gain access through the ECOSOC's Committee on NGOs.

Scholars have noted that the structure of the ECOSOC rules (which grant access to other UN institutions) presuppose that a feature of NGOs is their representativeness of a group with people or peoples with a certain stake or interest in international decision-making. Where Kenneth Anderson points out the lack of process to determine representativeness indicates a lack of legitimacy, Melissa Durkee suggests that the current rules err strongly on the side of optimism regarding the motives of actors that gain access. The bulk of the academic literature on this process, as Anderson has pointed out, assumes that 'global civil society . . . is about the leftwing Human Rights Watch and Greenpeace . . . and that it is committed to . . . the idea of global governance'.[172] However, recall that in accordance with ECOSOC's rules, business organizations can also gain access, so long as they are organized as a non-profit and report 'aims and purposes' that are 'consistent' with the UN's 'purpose' and 'spirit'. If one considers the fact that the UN – and particularly ECOSOC – holds 'economic development' as one of its primary purposes, it is not difficult to imagine how many business organizations are able to meet the ECOSOC criteria for accreditation.

In fact, as Durkee has noted, the ECOSOC's rules are not so much concerned with which interests are represented at UN Agencies, or whether they represent any particular 'public'. The rules are rather focused on whether the organization applying for accreditation has some means of maintaining accountability to the members the organization represents:

> Thus, business advocacy groups – trade and industry associations – may become accredited as consultants to the ECOSOC. In fact, they can become accredited alongside and on the same terms as NGOs who advance various social causes. However, *individual* businesses cannot become accredited to consult unless they are non-profits.[173]

As of January 2020, more than 700 of the 5,500 accredited organizations represented businesses or 'private sector' groups – almost 13%.[174] This number likely underrepresents the actual business presence at the ECOSOC because it only accounts for business groups and trade associations that are openly registered as 'consultants'. Businesses often create non-profit NGOs with 'front causes' to support business goals while obscuring the identity of the parent for-profit enterprise. For example, the National Wetlands Coalition serves U.S. oil companies and real estate developers, Consumers for World Trade was formed by industry to support the WTO's GATT, and World Vision – one of the largest recipients of USAID funding – supports an evangelical Christian version of 'development' in many non-Christian majority states.[175] Conditional aspects of U.S. funding have also imposed morally paternalistic restrictions on international aid recipients that would be illegal to impose if those recipients were headquartered in United States, for example, a requirement that a humanitarian organization publicly denounce prostitution.[176] Furthermore, businesses can gain influence over the distribution of funds and conditions imposed through sponsorship, board membership, or by effectively taking over struggling groups that have already received accreditation, sometimes many years prior.[177] A range of special industry and private ideological interests are therefore represented in UN international law and policy making, but these interests are in no way required to represent the interests of any particular 'public'.

b. The WTO's TRIPS agreement

In the United States, as in much of the world, IP law is characterized by a tension between the desire to avoid monopolies on markets (Anti-Trust Law) and the desire to spur innovation. Intellectual property rights produce both monopolies and incentives; they produce incentives because they produce monopolies. More than a decade ago, Susan Sell has showed us that, even in the United States, the exclusive right to own intellectual property was not initially conceived of as a 'right' at all. Rather, it was considered a 'monopoly privilege' – the privilege to exclusive ownership of an idea or creative work for a period of time.

The basis of intellectual property rights in the U.S. springs from Art. I Section 8 of the 1789 Constitution, which protects 'useful arts'. Article I itself was based on a Lockean vision of intellectual property – a natural law conception that views individual property as an outgrowth of individual labor.

But this 'individual' in the original conception was a national, not a global individual. The original U.S. IP Act protected the IP rights of citizens only, which spurred innovation through sub-economies of foreign IP appropriation, especially printed works first published in the UK. As the field of IP evolved from one dominated by printed works to one encompassing inventions, the directionality of appropriation began to shift. Changes in legislation over the past century have been driven largely by a need to adapt to technological change; as innovation becomes more costly, more incentives are necessary for research and development. Historically, the U.S. judiciary pushed back against increasing legislative protection of IP holders in favor of innovation: a series of Supreme Court cases beginning in 1917 (*Universal Pictures*) favored infringers (misuse doctrine), but this changed in 1980 with *Dawson Chem. Co.*, which placed innovation on equal footing with free competition.

As the judiciary swung back toward IP holders, and as the fame and influence of neoliberal economists such as Milton Freidman grew, Reagan-era policies adopted the Chicago School focus on price theory. Reaganomics saw anti-competitive business practices as those that reduced output and increased prices; business practices that expand output were pro-competitive. In contrast to classical approaches, a Freidman-infused Reaganomics believed that '[h]igh levels of market concentration and the exercise of market power may be indicative of efficiencies'.[178] On this view, a firm with an artificial IP monopoly could only decrease supply of its IP to the degree that its superiority generated demand over potential rivals; were this not the case, the expense of the IP would quash demand and an inferior but cheaper product would seize the market.

At the same time as these ideas were garnering influence, the U.S. legislature was quietly internationalizing its 'developed world' conception of IP rights. By 1984, the 1974 Trade Act Section 301 which set out power to deny benefits or impose duties on any country 'unjustifiably restricting US commerce' had transferred the power originally vested in the Executive to the US Trade Representative (USTR) in consultation with private industry. During Reagan's first term, the U.S. trade deficit had increased by 309%, and the overvalue of U.S. dollar put pressure on the administration to keep the United States competitive. This fueled a shift in the focus of U.S. trade policy. By 1988, just before Reagan left office, the Congress abandoned its previous categorical approach to international IP infringement in favor of the so-called rule of reason: practices are not prohibited outright, but only after an analysis of whether the practice had an anti-competitive effect weighed against pro-competitive attributes; a sort of balancing test that may be a distant relative of the TRIPS's approach to IP.

The internationalization of these developments in U.S. domestic policy took place because of a particular coalescence of Reagan-era protectionism and Clinton-era globalism. Over the course of about a decade, IP went from a domestic concern with World Intellectual Property Organization policies akin to 'best practices' to a homogenous internationally enforceable concept. In 1984, the efforts of Pfizer CEO, Edmund Pratt, who chaired the Republican Party's Advisory Committee for Trade Negotiations, persuaded the Reagan Administration to link IP to Trade along with other amendments to the 1974 Trade Act. In addition to creating the USTR, the 1984 Act granted the USTR the authority to initiate the Section 301 sanctions of the original

Trade Act on its own motion. With the USTR rather than the Executive initiating sanctions, international IP enforcement took on the appearance of administrative function rather than political decision. Thus, in 1985, the USTR initiated its first Section 301 IP case against South Korea; and in 1987, it initiated the first IP case that resulted in retaliation, or sanctions, against Brazil. In 1986, encouraged by the USTR's success, Edmund Pratt and a collection of private-sector lobbyists and CEOs from the United States, EU, and Japan formed the Intellectual Property Committee (IPC). The IPC included major cross-sectoral corporations such as Bristol-Myers, DuPont, FMC Corporation, GE, GM, HP, IBM, J&J, Merck, Monsanto, Pfizer, Rockwell Int., and Warner – companies that championed a U.S. Section 301-based IP enforcement model to be linked to the burgeoning international trade system under negotiation at Marrakesh (this, of course, would eventually establish the GATT 1994 and the WTO in 1995).

The IPC worked alongside Pharmaceutical Manufacturers Association to shape the NAFTA IP Chapter and the WTO's TRIPS Agreement. In doing so, it argued that firms lost 2.7% of sales (23.8 billion) to international patent infringement. (This figure was provided by the IPC firms.) Drawing from the work of private sector lobbyist veteran Jaque Gorlin, the IPC urged a GATT-based solution specifically because trade penalties were the best feasible way to enforce U.S. IP standards internationally. The sanctions authorized by the 1984 Trade Act's Section 301 also served as inspiration. The success of Section 301 generated a motive for less economically powerful States to accept IP as a trade issue: at least with TRIPS, the United States could not unilaterally impose sanctions based on infringement allegations – a neutral third party would decide whether a violation had occurred.

The key legal triumphs of the IPC in TRIPS can be summarized as follows: (1) a balancing approach to infringement cases, reaffirmed at Doha, which allows a WTO Panel or Appellate Body to balance the IP rights housed in one country against the public health of another (affirmed with the Doha Declaration); (2) the allowance of trade sanctions as retaliation for IP infringement; (3) a minimum 20-year patent protection for all WTO Member States; (4) a criminalization requirement for what was once legitimate entrepreneurial activity; (5) a compulsory licensing exception where public health is at issue (affirmed with the Doha Declaration); and (6) in order to attain the free trade benefits of GATT, TRIPS implementation was necessary.[179] Thus, intellectual property was solidified as an international trade issue. A collection of private ICPs, through the IPC, authored public international law.

c. CEO preferences and political spending

If ICPs can influence the establishment of an entire branch of international law through the IPC, and if they can participate in negotiations and consultations before a wide range of U.N. institutions, we should endeavor to understand the political preferences of those natural persons who hold the most influence over the political spending decisions of corporate ones. There is not a great deal of literature that documents CEO political preferences in general and the existing literature is admittedly U.S.- and Euro-centric.[180] Nevertheless, given the relative power of firms headquartered in these jurisdictions, given the power these jurisdictions display in the making of international law, and given the relative ease with which especially U.S. corporate persons can express their preferences through donations, a few points from this literature are worth mentioning.

First, U.S. CEOs tend to disproportionately favor the Republican party. With a few slight variances, this holds true across time, industry, region, and CEO gender. According to a recent 18-year study by Alma Cohen and her collaborators, about 57% of CEOs donate to Republican candidates, whereas only 19% donate to Democrats. Moreover, although Fremeth et al have shown that all CEOs tend to increase political contributions when they become CEOs, Cohen et al have shown that Republicans donate substantially more than Democrats – almost twice as much. They find that the median CEO directs 75% of his or her political contributions to Republicans. Their study includes 89% of all S&P 500 CEOs, 82% of the 'mid-cap' CEOs, and 72% of the remaining smaller company CEOs.

Second, again according to Cohen, Republican CEOs are less likely to be transparent to investors about political spending. It is true that, even in the infamous *Citizens United* decision, the Supreme Court has encouraged companies to be transparent when it comes to political spending, but disclosure in fact remains a largely private business decision. That is, although federal laws allow shareholders of public companies to submit proposals for a vote for disclosure, requirements are stringent. Thus, rather than manifesting the Court's intuition that 'with the advent of the Internet, prompt disclosure of expenditures can provide shareholders and citizens with the information needed to hold corporations and elected officials accountable for their positions and supporters', corporate actors are in fact unlikely to expose themselves to accountability, and significantly more so if run by an individual on the right wing of the political spectrum. The optimistic vision of shareholders that 'can determine whether their corporation's political speech advances the corporation's interests in making profits' and citizens that 'can see whether elected officials are 'in the pocket' of so-called moneyed interests' is not only unrealized – it is wholly unrealistic in light of the practical function of holding shares in a publicly traded company. That is, even if full disclosure were the norm, most shareholders own fractional interests in numerous companies and do not bother to vote their shares or track the political spending of each company in which they own shares. Moreover, a minority shareholder's ability to change the course of political spending is often negligible, so in practical terms, they would be left only with a choice between holding or selling the shares, which could pit financial interests against political ones. In reality, only majority shareholders – often institutional investors or other corporations themselves – could place systematic checks on whether the speech serves the corporation's profit interests. And all of these points can only proceed after accepting two false assumptions: (1) that full disclosure of political spending would be immediate and accurate; and (2) that a corporation's only purpose – or a shareholder's only legitimate interest in a corporation – is to maximize profits. Let alone the audacity of Justice Kennedy's suggestion that waiting two to six years to remove an official whose loyalties clearly lie with corporate rather than human constituents is an appropriate way to react to a blatant betrayal of democratic process.

Finally, and moving away from the United States, it is worth noting that campaign contributions are only one small ingredient in a potential legal calculus that seeks fairer political campaigning. For example, some States limit campaign spending but not contributions, which creates a threshold after which fundraising is irrelevant.[181] The downside of that approach is that, if one party gets one mega-donor, they can bow out of the race early and spend more time bashing their opponents. Other states place no limits on either, which seems to work well in many States that use it (e.g., Germany, Denmark, Norway, Sweden, Switzerland, Luxembourg, inter alia). But this is because voting is party-based, not candidate-based. The interchangeability of individual candidates thus decreases the appeal to wealthy donors and ICPs who may seek to purchase political favor. One must be cognizant of these and other potential legal constellations in considering what law and democracy can contribute to a fairer global distribution of wealth and power.

IV. No analogies: the ICP's unique status under international law

The ICP's ability to transcend legality is not as simple as the law not applying to some corporate activity. It is also that ICPs play a role in creating the laws that apply or the extent to which laws apply. But all law is created, and all law can ultimately be remade. In this and the previous chapter, I have identified twenty-two areas in which judges and texts have created rights and legal 'permissions' available only to ICPs or exercisable in a particular form only by ICPs. These special privileges can be characterized as follows. An ICP has:

(1) The ability to decide for itself whether or not it is subject to international law – for example, through the (re)structuring of 'control' – in accordance with the ICJ standard;
(2) The ability to assert substantive rights under international law independent of those rights authorized by the State;
(3) The capacity to violate international law independent from the State;
(4) The ability to assert both the State's sovereignty and its own corporate veil as shields against liability, and the ability to define the reach of both sovereignty and the veil under certain circumstances;

(5) A negative duty to uphold human rights but often a positive right to claim them;
(6) The ability to avoid fiscal liability through (re)structuring and undercapitalization;
(7) The ability to access courts of 'fourth instance', that is, to 'appeal' decisions from supreme domestic courts or petition for *de novo* review;
(8) The ability to extend jurisdiction beyond the State in which the controversy in question arose;
(9) The right to enforce a law in a jurisdiction not bound by that law but bound by a contract to honor that law;
(10) The ability to decide upon procedural remedies for violations of its international responsibilities with respect to human rights;
(11) The ability to select the level of law and enforcement for a violation of an international obligation, that is, domestic, regional, international, or some combination;
(12) The ability to claim a legally prescribed *mens rea* with respect to its actions rather than to expose itself to inquires into actual *mens rea*;
(13) An exemption from State requirements to criminalize the corrupt acts of 'individuals';
(14) The ability to create 'internal' markets and to limit the access of or exclude non-ICP actors;
(15) The ability to choose and simultaneously hold multiple citizenships and to thereby play the advantages of multiple domestic systems of its choosing against one another to the benefit of the ICP;
(16) The ability to purchase exemptions from international prosecution for corruption;
(17) The benefit of assigning responsibility for deliberate, cumulative environmental behavior to States and their ability to regulate and enforce restrictions;
(18) The ability to move capital and commodities freely across jurisdictions even as labor is immobile;
(19) Access to the benefits of legal reasoning and inertias of belief that favor corporate expansion through various concepts of development;
(20) Ownership that is separate from actions;
(21) An inflated ability to write and sustain the rules to which it is subject in relation to State governments, publics, capital, equity, humanity, and so much more; and
(22) The ability to be both a State-Owned Enterprise (SOE) and an ICP – to simultaneously be both a public and a private entity.

This list illustrates the contours of the ICP. It is non-exhaustive and, if current trends continue, it will grow longer in the years ahead. While it shows that the ICP veers closer to the State than individual, what should be clear from these findings is that the ICP is not analogous to anything – that, in

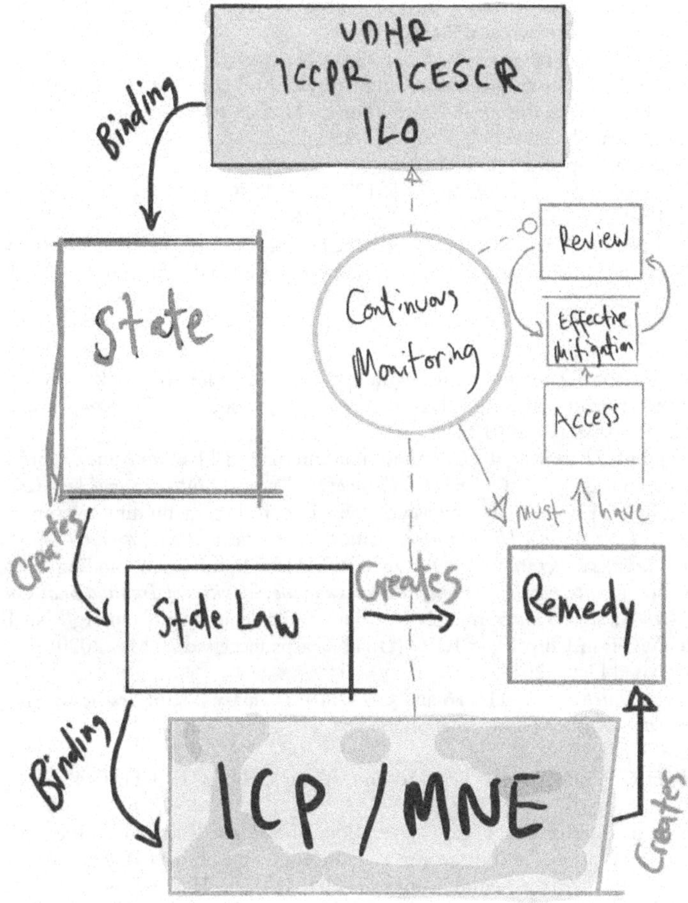

Figure 2.1 UNGP Corporate Liability Map

fact, overreliance on analogical reasoning is likely to obfuscate the reality of the ICP's legal status.

Notes

1 For example, sovereignty is used to justify tax havens and to prevent environmental regulation. A longer discussion of the flipped coin of sovereignty and veil piercing is included in Chapter 4 of this book.

2 E.g., Peter Muchlinski's seminal *Multinational Enterprises and the Law* (1995); Bart Wenaart, *International Law and Business: A Global Introduction* (2017).

3 The complete list of ILO Declarations is available at www.ilo.org/global/about-the-ilo/how-the-ilo-works/departments-and-offices/jur/legal-instruments/WCMS_428589/lang-en/index.htm (accessed 20 May 2020).
4 E.g., the ILO's databases provide an invaluable research resource, available at www.ilo.org/global/statistics-and-databases/lang-en/index.htm (accessed 20 May 2020).
5 Council of Europe, European Convention on Human Rights, available at www.echr.coe.int/Documents/Convention_ENG.pdf (accessed 20 May 2020).
6 *A v. Austria*, App. No. 9905/82 (1985).
7 *Autronic AG v. Switzerland*, App. No. 12726/87 (1990).
8 E.g., *Agrotexim v. Greece*, App. No. 15/1994/462/543 (1995).
9 United Nations, OHCHR, Guiding Principles on Business and Human Rights, Implementing the United Nations "Protect, Respect and Remedy" Framework (2011).
10 *Id.*
11 *Id.*
12 *Id.*
13 J.M. Amerson, "The End of the Beginning?": A Comprehensive Look at the U.N.'s Business and Human Rights Agenda from a Bystander Perspective, *Fordham Journal of Corporate & Financial Law* (2012).
14 Fleur Johns, Theorizing the Corporation in International Law, in Anne Orford & Florian Hoffmann (Eds.), The *Oxford Handbook of the Theory of International Law* (2013).
15 UN HRC, OEIGWG Chairmanship Revised Draft, Legally Binding Instrument to Regulate, in *International Human Rights Law, the Activities of Transnational Corporations and Other Business Enterprises* (2019); OEIGWG Zero Draft, Legally Binding Instrument to Regulate, in *International Human Rights Law, the Activities of Transnational Corporations and Other Business Enterprises* (2018). Both available at www.ohchr.org/EN/HRBodies/HRC/WGTransCorp/Pages/IGWGOnTNC.aspx (accessed 20 May 2020).
16 *Id.*, Revised Draft (2019).
17 See e.g., *Dutch BV* (C-116/16 and C-117/16) (January 2020); *Textile Workers Union v. Darlington Mfg. Co.*, 380 US 263 (1965).
18 Fed. R. Civ. P., Rule 12.
19 OHCHR, Report on the Fifth Session of the OEIGWG, A/HRC/43/55, 9 January 2020.
20 Center for International Legal Cooperation, The Hague Rules on Business and Human Rights Arbitration, Arbitration Rules on Business and Human Rights (2019), available at www.cilc.nl/cms/wp-content/uploads/2019/12/The-Hague-Rules-on-Business-and-Human-Rights-Arbitration_CILC-digital-version.pdf (accessed 20 May 2020).
21 Hague Rules, Art. 38; UNCITRAL Transparency Rules, Art. 1.
22 International Bar Association (IBA), Guidelines on Conflicts of Interest in International Arbitration (2014), available at www.google.com/url?sa=t&rct=j&q=&esrc=s&source=web&cd=&ved=2ahUKEwje7dfZreHpAhUb73MBHaXNAIIQFjAAegQIBhAB&url=https%3A%2F%2Fwww.ibanet.org%2FDocument%2FDefault.aspx%3FDocumentUid%3De2fe5e72-eb14-4bba-b10d-d33dafee8918&usg=AOvVaw2J_QfVS8ohoW1YobOau6SA (accessed 30 May 2020).
23 On this point, see e.g., Kai Möller, Justifying the Culture of Justification, *International Journal of Constitutional Law* (2019).
24 See e.g., Andrew Clapham, Workshop: Corporate Criminal Liability: New Developments in International Criminal Law, 6 *J. Int'l Crim. Just.* 899 (2008); see generally Special Issue – Transnational Business and International Criminal Law, 8 *J. Int'l Crim. Just.* (2010).
25 Indirect perpetration through an organization was originally conceived by German legal theorist Claus Roxin with the particular experience of Nazi state-orchestrated crime in mind. See Thomas Weigend, Perpetration through an Organisation: The Unexpected Career of a German Legal Concept, 9 *J. Int'l Crim. Just.* 91, 94–97 (2011).

26 For detailed analysis of this form of liability and its origins and application at the ICC, see generally Symposium: Indirect Perpetration: A perfect Fit for International Prosecution of Armchair Killers?, 9 *J. Int'l Crim. Just.* 85; Neha Jain, The Control Theory of Perpetration in International Criminal Law, in 12 *Chi. J. Int'l L.* 159 (2011); Florian Jessberger & Julia Geneuss, On the Application of a Theory of Indirect Perpetration in Al Bashir, 6 *J. Int'l Crim. Just.* 853 (2008); Hector Olasolo, The Criminal Responsibility of Political and Military Leaders as Principles to International Crimes, in 4 *Studies in International and Comparative Law*, 116–134 and 302–330 (Ed. Mochael Bohlander, 2009); and Harmen G. van der Wilt, The continuous quest for proper modes of criminal responsibility, 7 *J. Int'l Crim. Just.* 307 (2009).

27 Here, JCE is described as 'doctrines' rather than 'doctrine' because the evolution of JCE has produced three similar but separate doctrines, each with slightly different *mens rea* requirements. Jose Alvarez has cautioned generally about transposing such concepts of public law to the international investment arena, even as a way to generally inform arbitral interpretation, because the circumstances and stakeholders in the various branches of international law tend to differ so vastly. See the Alvarez article previously cited, 'Beware – Boundary Crossings'. See also ILC Guidelines, rule 20; Vienna Convention on the Law of Treaties art. 31–32, opened for signature May 23, 1969, 1155 U.N.T.S. 331 [hereinafter VCLT].

28 For a brief history of JCE's evolution, see Giulia Bigi, Joint Criminal Enterprise in the Jurisprudence of the International Criminal Tribunal for the Former Yugoslavia and the Prosecution of Senior Political and Military Leaders: The Krajišnic Case, in 14 *Max Planck Yearbook of United Nations Law* 51–83 (von Bogdandy & Wolfrum, Eds., 2010).

29 I recognize that the equation of an 'enterprise' in JCE to a 'corporation' under general international law is problematic, at least because of the different avenues through which corporations and JCEs are formed. Nevertheless, JCE is the only such tool in international law available to determine *mens rea*, and as such, could be considered by an ICSID Tribunal's interpretation of 'aimed'. This is because the ICSID Convention requires that the terms of treaties litigated under its rules be interpreted according to the VCLT art. 31. The VCLT Article 31(3)(c) stipulates that, in interpreting treaty language 'any relevant rules of international law applicable in the relations between the parties' be taken into account. And as an element of public international law to which virtually all the world's states are party, the ICJ Statute can inform the sources arbitrator use; specifically, Art. 38(1) of that statute stipulates that 'international custom' and 'general principles of law' can be considered, among other sources.

30 The Rome Statute requires that the "'aim' of each individual to further the criminal purpose of the enterprise, but the standard remains results-based for demonstrating 'common plan'. See Rome Statute, art. 28. The intent behind individual participation in the enterprise – the most controversial element of JCE III – is not at issue here.

31 See, e.g., Michael M. Kelley, The Top 25 Weapons Companies in the World (Excluding China), *Business Insider* (Dec. 15, 2014), www.businessinsider.com/the-top-25-weapons-companies-in-the-world-excluding-china-2014-12/?IR=T.

32 *Id.*

33 *Id.*

34 *Id.*

35 See Paul Bartrop & Michael Dickerman (Eds.), *The Holocaust: An Encyclopedia and Document Collection* 155 (2017), explaining the pre-WWII operations of Degussa and Degesch.

36 See Joanna Kyriakakis, Developments in International Criminal Law and the Case of Business Involvement in International Crimes, 94 *Int'l Rev. Red Cross* 981 (2012).

37 K Crow, International Law and Corporate Participation in Times of Armed Conflict, *Berkeley J. Int'l L.* (2019).

38 Rome Statute, art. 25 (emphasis added).

39 For a description of the test for aiding and abetting under customary international law, see the International Commission of Jurists Expert Legal Panel on Corporate Complicity in International Crimes (ICJ Expert Panel), Corporate Complicity and Legal Accountability, Vol. 2, International Commission of Jurists, Geneva, 2008, pp. 17–24. However, also note the decisions of the International Criminal Tribunal for the Former Yugoslavia that import a 'specific direction' requirement as a material element of aiding and abetting. This new requirement demands that to constitute an accomplice under international criminal law, a person must not only provide assistance that has a substantial effect on the commission of an international crime, but such assistance must additionally be specifically directed toward assisting such crime. See Prosecutor v. Perišíc, Case No. IT-04–81-A, Appeal Judgement, (Int'l Crim. Trib. for the former Yugoslavia Jan. 28, 2013); Prosecutor v. Stanišíc, Case No. IT-03–69-T, Trial Judgement, (Int'l Crim. Trib. for the former Yugoslavia May 30, 2013). While the introduction of a 'specific direction' requirement will have significant implications for satisfying aiding and abetting in the context of commercial relationships and international crimes, this section's primary aim is to apply doctrines that emerged from ICL in the context of IIL. Moreover, the Rome Statute, on which this section's argument rests, was not at issue in the 2013 ICTY decisions on aiding and abetting.

40 See *id.*

41 Prosecutor v. Tadic, Case No. IT-94–1-T, Trial Judgement (Int'l Crim. Trib. for the former Yugoslavia May 7, 1997).

42 See Prosecutor v. Brima, SCSL-06–16-A, Appeal Judgment (Feb. 22, 2008): '[t]he mens rea required for aiding and abetting is that the accused knew that his acts would assist the commission of the crime by the perpetrator or that he was aware of the substantial likelihood that his acts would assist the commission of a crime by the perpetrator' (quoting Prosecutor v. Brima, SCSL-06–16-T, Trial Judgment II (June 20, 2007); see also Prosecutor v. Sesay et al., Case No. SCSL-04–15-A, Appeal Judgment, Special Court for Sierra Leone (Oct. 26, 2009). The SCSL Appeals Chamber subsequently endorsed this Court's jurisprudence that awareness of a substantial likelihood is a culpable *mens rea* for aiding and abetting liability in customary international law. Interlocutory Decision on the Applicable Law: Terrorism, Conspiracy, Homicide, Perpetration, Cumulative Charging, Special Tribunal for Lebanon, Case No. STL-11–01/I (Feb. 16, 2011). In domestic legal systems this mental state ranges from being 'indifferent' to the result, to being 'reconciled' with the result as a possible cost of attaining one's goal. Elies van Sliedregt, *Individual Criminal Responsibility in International Law* (2012).

43 International Commission of Jurists Expert Legal Panel on Corporate Complicity in International Crimes, Corporate Complicity and Legal Accountability, Vol. 2, *International Commission of Jurists*, Geneva, 2008, 22–24.

44 *Id.*

45 See, e.g., S.C. Res. 808/1993, 827/1993, May 25, 1993 (Statute of the International Criminal Tribunal for the Former Yugoslavia); S.C. Res. 1315, Jan. 16, 2002 (Statute of the Special Court for Sierra Leone).

46 This is an old debate in U.S. jurisprudence, and different states still take different approaches. For an old but classic example of the scholarship on the issue, see generally, John S. Strahorn, Jr., Preparation for Crime as a Criminal Attempt, 1 *Wash. & Lee L. Rev.* 1 (1939).

47 See *Prosecutor v. Taylor*, Case No. SCSL-03–01-T, Judgment Summary, Special Court for Sierra Leone (Apr. 26, 2012), www.rscsl.org/Documents/Decisions/Taylor/1283/Charles%20Taylor%20Summary%20Judgement.pdf.

48 *Id.*

49 See *id.* See also *Prosecutor v. Charles Taylor*, Case No. SCSL-03–01-T, Trial Chamber II, Judgement, Special Court for Sierra Leone (May 18, 2012).

50 *Prosecutor v. Charles Taylor*, Case No. SCSL-03–01-T, Trial Chamber II, Judgement, Special Court for Sierra Leone (May 18, 2012).

51 See e.g., Kevin M. Clermont & Emily Sherwin, A Comparative View of Standard of Proof, 50 *Am. J. Int'l L.* 243 (2002).
52 See e.g., Jessica Durney, *Crafting a Standard: Environmental Crimes as Crimes Against Humanity Under the International Criminal Court* (2008).
53 Mohammed Saif-Ailden Wattad, The Rome Statute & Captain Planet: What Lies Between 'Crimes Against Humanity' and the 'Natural Environment'? 19 *Fordham Envtl. L. Rev.* 265.
54 Rome Statute.
55 *Id.*
56 For an overview on market share liability's emergence in the late 1970s and early 1980s, see e.g., Mary Jane Sheffet, Market Share Liability: A New Doctrine of Causation in Product Liability, *Journal of Marketing* (1983).
57 See e.g., Brent Fisse & John Braithwaite, *Corporations, Crime and Accountability* (1993).
58 See UN Office on Drugs and Crime, United Nations Convention Against Corruption, Preparatory and Negotiating Sessions of the Ad Hoc Committee for the Negotiation of a Convention Against Corruption, complete documents available at www.unodc.org/unodc/en/treaties/CAC/background/index.html (accessed 20 May 2020).
59 Tina Søreide, *Corruption and Criminal Justice: Bridging Economic and Legal Perspectives* (2016).
60 Alejandro Posadas, Combating Corruption Under International Law, 10 *Duke J. Comp. & Int'l L.* 345 (2000).
61 OAS, Inter-American Convention Against Corruption, art. VII.
62 OECD Convention Preamble.
63 OECD Convention, art. 3(1).
64 GRECO Criminal Law Convention on Bribery, ch. 2.
65 Forward to the UNCAC.
66 See generally African Union Convention; see also *id.* at art. 6.
67 FCPA, Section 78dd-2(g)(1), compare with FCPA, Section 78dd-2(g)(2)(A).
68 This has indeed been demonstrated empirically. See e.g., Sarah C. Kaczmarek & Abraham L. Newman, The Long Arm of the Law: Extraterritoriality and the National Implementation of Foreign Bribery Legislation, 65 *International Organization* 765 (2011).
69 E.g., Susan Sell, *Private Power, Public Law* (2003).
70 *Id.*
71 E.g., Alejandro Posadas, Combating Corruption Under International Law, 10 *Duke J. Comp. & Int'l L.* 345 (2000).
72 UNCAC, OECD, etc.
73 For an overview, see e.g., The Distinction Between "Mala Prohibita" and "Mala in se" in Criminal Law, 30 *Columbia L. Rev.* 74 (1930). For criticisms of this distinction, see e.g., Richard L. Gray, Eliminating the (Absurd) Distinction Between *Malum Prohibita* and *Malum In Se* Crimes, 73 *Wash. U. L. Q.* 1369 (1995).
74 The FCPA's influence on present-day international anti-corruption law is well-documented and well-discussed by many legal and political scholars. See e.g., Alejandro Posadas, Combating Corruption Under International Law, 10 *Duke J. Comp. & Int'l L.* 345 (2000); Cecily Rose, *International Anti-Corruption Norms: Their Creation and Influence on Domestic Legal Systems* (2015); Philip Urofsky & Hee Won Moon, A Resource Guide to the US Foreign Corrupt Practices Act: The US Government's Perspective on Enforcing the FCPA, in Mark Pieth, Lucinda Low & Nicola Bonucci (Eds.), *The OECD Convention on Bribery* (2015). One of the editors for this final volume, Mark Pieth, was one of the lawyers responsible for shaping the direction of the early OECD approach on bribery, which adopted wholesale the FCPA approach, without much thought as to why the FCPA moralized certain types of corruption as opposed to others through the practice and language of criminalization, and attempted to internationalize it. The results have been shoddy, but this branch of the OECD has not been quick to exercise critical self-reflection. The latest publications from the OECD Working Group on Bribery can

be found at http://www.oecd.org/daf/anti-bribery/latestdocuments/ (accessed 20 January 2021).

75 See, e.g., Deputy Attorney General, Department of Justice Memorandum, *Bringing Criminal Charges Against Corporations* (June 1999, updated March 2010), available at www.justice.gov/sites/default/files/criminal-fraud/legacy/2010/04/11/charging-corps.PDF (accessed 7 June 2019).

76 See e.g., Anthony Gray, Mandatory Sentencing Around the World and the Need for Reform, 20 *New Crim. L. Rev.* 391 (2017).

77 See Kofi Annan's Foreword to the 2004 publication of the UN Convention Against Corruption.

78 The most relied-upon source is Transparency International's 'Corruption Perception Index'; the 2019 report from that organization is available at www.transparency.org/files/content/pages/2019_CPI_Report_EN.pdf (accessed 20 May 2020).

79 Thomas R. Tørsløv, Ludvig S. Wier & Gabriel Zucman, The Missing Profits of Nations, National Bureau of Economic Research (NBER), Working Paper No. 24701 (2019).

80 See generally, John T. Noonan, *Bribes* (1984).

81 John T. Noonan, *Bribes* (1984).

82 New International Version.

83 John T. Noonan, *Bribes* (1984).

84 John T. Noonan, *Bribes* (1984).

85 *Id.*

86 Michel Foucault has also observed this phenomenon in the context of state-sanctioned punishment. See generally *Discipline and Punish* (1975)

87 New International Version.

88 See e.g., Daniel Graeber, *Debt: The First 5000 Years* (2011).

89 John T. Noonan, *Bribes* (1984).

90 See e.g., Daniel Graeber, *Debt: The First 5000 Years* (2011).

91 Kassim Salleh Ijtihad, Sejarah dan Perkembangannya (1989); Othman Haji Ishak, Fatwa Dalam Perundangan Islam (1981); Mahmood Zuhdi Abd. Majid, Pengantar undang-undang Islam di Malaysia (1997). See also Aris Munandar, *Beware of the Bribe* (4 December 2012), Syaria.com, available at http://syaria.com/361-beware-of-the-bribe.html (accessed 1 February 2019).

92 *Id.*

93 On file with the author; see also John T. Noonan, *Bribes* (1984).

94 This is because, at least in the Kantian understanding of 'categorical' and 'consequential' which has informed my thinking, categorical moral rules cannot have exceptions. If they do, they are more likely hypothetical imperatives rather than categorical imperatives.

95 This is apparent throughout the text of the OECD and UNCAC anti-corruption instruments.

96 OECD Convention, art. 2.

97 OECD Convention, art. 3.

98 *Id.*

99 UN Convention, art. 26.

100 See generally UNCAC.

101 See most recently Thomas R. Tørsløv, Ludvig S. Wier & Gabriel Zucman, The Missing Profits of Nations, National Bureau of Economic Research (NBER), Working Paper No. 24701 (2019).

102 See e.g., See World Bank, Arm's-Length Trade: A Source of Post-Crisis Trade Weakness, Global Economic Prospectus (June 2017); see also Sol Picciotto, *Regulating Global Corporate Capitalism* (2013).

103 Johannes Thumfart, On Grotius's *Mare Liberum* and Vitoria's *De Indis*, Following Agamben and Schmitt, 30 *Grotiana* 65 (2009).

104 Peter Muchlinski, *Multinational Enterprises and the Law* (2nd edition 2007).

105 See e.g., Capitals of Capital, *The Economist* (13 May 2014).
106 I am using 'non-taxable' for the sake of brevity; sometimes Conduits provide the benefit of low taxation rather than non-taxation.
107 This is derived from U.S., UK, and European definitions.
108 OECD Agreement on Transfer Pricing (2017).
109 Section 482, US IRS Code.
110 See Muchlinski, cited previously.
111 E.g., US Tax Reform Act 1986, Section 482; White Paper, U.S. Department of Treasury, 1988: 'Commensurate with Income' standard.
112 See Muchlinski, cited previously.
113 The OECD Transfer Pricing Guidelines for Multinational Enterprises and Tax Administrations (2010).
114 See Muchlinski, cited previously.
115 OECD Committee on Fiscal Affairs Report of January 1993.
116 See e.g., W. Elliot Brownlee, *Federal Taxation in America: A Short History*, Woodrow Wilson Center Press (2004).
117 See Gabriel Zucman, *The Hidden Wealth of Nations: The Scourge of Tax Havens* (2015).
118 *Id.*
119 *Id.*
120 Thomas R. Tørsløv, Ludvig S. Wier & Gabriel Zucman, The Missing Profits of Nations, National Bureau of Economic Research (NBER), Working Paper No. 24701 (2019).
121 Thomas R. Tørsløv, Ludvig S. Wier & Gabriel Zucman, The Missing Profits of Nations, National Bureau of Economic Research (NBER), Working Paper No. 24701 (2019).
122 *Id.*
123 *Id.*
124 E.g., Anne Peters, Corruption as a Violation of International Human Rights, *EJIL* (2018).
125 See e.g., Graham Brooks, *Criminal Justice and Corruption: State Power, Privatization, and Legitimacy* (2019).
126 Declaration of the United Nations Conference on the Human Environment (1972).
127 General Assembly, A/CONF.151/26 (Vol. I), Report of the United Nations Conference on Environment and Development, Annex I, Rio Declaration on Environment and Development (1992).
128 Declaration of the United Nations Conference on the Human Environment (1972).
129 See e.g., *id.* principles 13 and 14.
130 General Assembly, A/CONF.151/26 (Vol. I), Report of the United Nations Conference on Environment and Development, Annex I, Rio Declaration on Environment and Development (1992).
131 *Id.*
132 OECD, Translating Environmental Law into Practice: Progress in Modernizing Environmental Regulation and Compliance Assurance in Eastern Europe, Caucasus, and Central Asia (2007).
133 See e.g., Karen Alter, *The New Terrain of International Law: Courts, Politics, Rights* (2014). See also generally the work of Mikael Rask Radsen and Alter's other colleagues at iCourts in Copenhagen.
134 See Antonio Cassese, *International Law* (2002).
135 E.g., Barnali Choudhury & Martin Petrin, *Corporate Duties to the Public* (2019); Markos Karavias, *Corporate Obligations Under International Law* (2013).
136 For a more thorough discussion on the 14th Amendment jurisprudence, see Chapter 1 of this book. See also Adam Winkler, *We the Corporations: How American Businesses Won their Civil Rights* (2018).
137 G. Edward White, *Tort Law in America: An Intellectual History* (1980).
138 Report of the Group of Eminent Persons, The Impact of Multinational Corporations on Development and International Relations, U.N. Doc. E/5500/Rev.1, ST/ESA/6 (1974).

139 *Id.*
140 ECOSOC Res. 1913 (1974).
141 See e.g., Columbia Center on Sustainable Investment, United Nations Code of Conduct on Transnational Corporations: Experience and Lessons Learned, available at http://ccsi.columbia.edu/work/projects/united-nations-code-of-conduct-on-transnational-corporations-experience-and-lessons-learned/ (accessed 20 May 2020).
142 Jennifer Bair, Corporations at the United Nations: Echoes of the New International Economic Order?, *Humanity* (2015).
143 See Resolutions and Decisions adopted by the General Assembly during its 46th session: GAOR, 46th Session, Supplement No. 49 (1991–1992).
144 Jennifer Bair, Corporations at the United Nations: Echoes of the New International Economic Order?, *Humanity* (2015).
145 See Resolutions and Decisions adopted by the General Assembly during its 46th session: GAOR, 46th Session, Supplement No. 49 (1991–1992).
146 ECOSOC, Draft norms on the responsibilities of transnational corporations and other business enterprises with regard to human rights (1994); the most recent version, updated in 2003, is available at https://digitallibrary.un.org/record/498842?ln=en (accessed 20 May 2020).
147 Isabella D. Bunn, *The Right to Development and International Economic Law: Legal and Moral Dimensions* (2012).
148 E/CN.4/2006/97.
149 Each one of these metrics has its shortcomings. For example, the corruption index measures rates states as 'more' or 'less' corrupt using indicators such as transparency and frequency of bribes. However, one criticism at least of the bribery metric is that it depends to a large degree on the existence or non-existence of legal constructs that legitimize cash flow from and to various sources. The only difference between a bribe and a tax write off could be the construct that surrounds it, not the intrinsic 'corruptness' of it.
150 See e.g., David Jaffee, Levels of Socio-Economic Development Theory (1998). For an early critique of the economic and political construction of development, see Arturo Escobar, Power and Visibility: Development and the Invention and Management of the Third World, *Cultural Anthropology* (1988).
151 As former World Bank staffer Thomas Blinkhorn put it during a seminar on 'science, technology, and society' at Dartmouth's Thayer School of Engineering. He worked on infrastructural projects throughout the world, including the infamous Narmada dam project. According to Blinkhorn, that project taught him that he should 'listen to the people we are trying to help'. A video of the seminar is available at http://engineering.dartmouth.edu/events/the-mysterious-world-bank-history-evolution-and-future-under-jim-yong-kim/ (last accessed 4 December 2016).
152 *Id.*
153 TPP Chapter 23.
154 See e.g., TPP Article 18.3.
155 NAFTA, Preamble (stating that the parties agree 'to strengthen the development and enforcement' of certain regulations).
156 TPP Preamble.
157 TPP Chapter 23.
158 I recognize that the term 'sustainable development' has an economic context with specific criteria (although at times varying) for what constitutes sustainability. However, for the purposes of this book, I am looking only to what the phrase promotes or covers in the legal sense.
159 EU–Vietnam, Chapter 15, Art. 1(2); CETA, Chapter 22, Art. 22.1(1); EU–Singapore, Chapter 13, Art. 13.1(2).
160 International Law Association, Report of the Seventy-Second Conference, Committee on International Law on Sustainable Development, 467 (472 et seq).

161 UNGA, Resolution 42/187, 11 December 1987, Report of the World Commission on Environment and Development; United Nations, Report of the United Nations Conference on Environment and Development, A/Conf.151/26/Rev.1 (Agenda 21).

162 See *Iron Rhine ('Ijzeren Rijn') Railway (Belgium/Netherlands)*, Permanent Court of Arbitration, 24 May 2005, par. 59, available at http://legal.un.org/riaa/cases/vol_XXVII/35-125.pdf.

163 *Ibid*, 82 et seq.

164 OECD Guidelines for Multinational Enterprises (2000, 2011).

165 Jay Butler, The Corporate Keepers of International Law, *AJIL* (2020).

166 Declaration on International Investment and Multinational Enterprises (2000, 2011).

167 Lauge N. Skaavgard Poulsen, States as Foreign Investors, *ICSID Review* (2016).

168 See generally the collection of articles in ICSID Review, *30th Anniversary of the Review, Special Focus Issue: State Owned Enterprises*, Volume 31, Issue 1 (2016).

169 Charter of the United Nations, art. 71.

170 ECOSOC Res. 43 (21 June 1946); Res. 288 (27 Feb 1950); Res. 1296 (23 May 1968); Res. 1996/31 (25 July 1996).

171 Res. 1996/31 (25 July 1996).

172 Kenneth Anderson, Global Governance: The Problematic Legitimacy Relationship Between Global Civil Society and the United Nations, Am. Univ. Wash. Coll. Of Law Research Paper Series, Working Paper No. 2008–71 (2008).

173 Melissa Durkee, International Lobbying Law, *Yale L. J.* (2018).

174 I derived these numbers by searching the ECOSOC NGO Branch database; if current trends continue, industry representation will increase further. The database is available at https://esango.un.org/civilsociety/displayAdvancedSearch.do?ngoFlag=&method=getSearchByParameters (accessed 15 January 2020).

175 See Kevin Crow, The Use of 'Human Rights' and 'Development' by Evangelical Organizations, *OpenDemocracy* (June 2018), available at www.opendemocracy.net/en/how-us-evangelical-organizations-deploy-human-rights-and-development/ (accessed 20 May 2020).

176 E.g., USAID requires this, though the legality of this Bush II–era practice is working its way through the federal courts. For an *amicus curiae* that sums up the issues well, see Civil Action No. 05-cv-8209 (VM), ECF Case, Southern District of New York, available at www.aclu.org/sites/default/files/FilesPDFs/memorandum%20of%20law%20of%20aids%20action%20and.pdf (accessed 20 May 2020).

177 Melissa Durkee, International Lobbying Law, *Yale L. J.* (2018). (Noting that this process bought Philip Morris and British American Tobacco influence through the International Tobacco Growers' Association with the FAO, World Bank, and UNCTAD in the fight against WHO regulations.)

178 Marc Allen Eisner, *Antitrust and the Triumph of Economics: Institutions, Expertise, and Policy Change*, 105 (1991).

179 For a complete account of how the IPC drove IP law on the international stage, see Susan Sell, *Private Power, Public Law* (2003).

180 Adam R. Fremeth has done fantastic work in this area over the course of more than a decade; the fact that most of the results are focused on U.S. and European CEOs might also reflect cultures of greater transparency and the fact that many of the world's largest companies are headquartered in these regions. For the paper from which I derive the data used in this book, see Adam Fremeth, Guy Holburn & Richard Vanden Berg, Corporate Political Strategy in Contested Regulatory Environments, *Strategy Science* (2020).

181 Alma Cohen, Moshe Hazan, Roberto Tallarita & David Weiss, The Politics of CEOs, *Journal of Legal Analysis* (2019).

Chapter 4

Theorizing international corporate personhood

The previous chapters have shown that the ICP is a legal person that transcends States and sometimes State authority. It is composed of single or multiple businesses, owned by shareholders – some of whom are legal persons themselves composed of legal and natural persons – directed by directors and managers, and it executes tasks through the labor of employees. While these shareholders, directors, managers, and employees can span the globe, an ICP is nominally understood to be a 'citizen' of the State in which it is headquartered. Thus, the ICP's relationship with international law is one fraught with dissonance: it is neither understood as a direct subject of international law nor as a direct 'constituent' or active participant in the making of international law, yet it plays an active role in 'authoring' international law through consulting, lobbying, 'shadowing', and 'speaking' through cash donations and other forms of patronage.

The United States is important to conceptualizing the ICP not only because it is the jurisdiction in which corporate personhood emerged, but also because for the entire relevant period (post-WWII) it has boasted the greatest share of the world's largest ICPs. Since the 1960s, U.S. dominance in this arena has trekked a slow decline.[1] While this decline is overwhelmingly due to the rise of Europe, Japan, and China relative to the United States rather than due to corporate citizens leaving the United States, the loss of dominance has bolstered the narratives of private-sector lobbyists that claim that States should be competing through their legal systems to attract corporate citizens, often in the form of low corporate tax rates, large corporate tax breaks, and labor regulation that disempowers collective action. This results in what many regulators view as a Catch-22: although virtually every major economy struggles to pay for the social programs that justify individual income taxes, regulators cannot sufficiently tax ICPs – either because they will leave or because they will avoid taxes via the legal technologies discussed in the previous chapter – and they cannot raise taxes on citizens because they cannot raise taxes on ICPs. It also results in 'rights shopping' along with 'forum shopping': an ICP enjoys rights in a foreign jurisdiction that it would not enjoy at home and it can form groups and networks that render almost every jurisdiction both 'host' and 'home'. And as we have repeatedly seen, it can also access rights through international legal systems unavailable to citizens of any state. This is particularly true in the subfield of international investment law, which globalized to a large degree the U.S. law's treatment of corporations as persons by importing doctrines developed at the PCA, the ICJ, and the WTO, as well as several powerful domestic courts. This occurs through a phenomenon José Alvarez has called 'boundary crossing' in international law.[2]

Boundary crossing is the process through which legal doctrines developed in one international court used to adjudicate disputes between parties regarding the provisions of one international agreement wind up being applied to different parties in different legal systems with different legal personalities litigating provisions in a different agreement.[3] It occurs through a series of legal agreements that have been interpreted by many international courts as forming the corpus for legitimate sources of international law. The first of these agreements – the 1969 Vienna Convention on the Law of Treaties (VCLT, which actually entered into force in 1980) – sets out in its Articles 31 and 32 the two basic prongs for textual interpretation in international dispute settlement. Article 31 requires that treaties be 'interpreted in good faith in accordance with the ordinary meaning' of the text in light of a treaty's 'object and purpose', and in the context of the agreement as determined by the preamble, annexes, and other subsequent agreements connected to the conclusion of the treaty.[4] It also requires international adjudicators to 'take into account . . . any relevant rules of international law applicable in the relations between the parties'. Article 32 allows recourse to preparatory work and circumstantial evidence from the time a disputed treaty was concluded.[5] As one might suspect from the textualist and originalist leanings of the provisions, these Articles were drafted by a handful of English and American lawyers in 1969 – a period during which corporate common law doctrines were taking hold in much of the newly decolonized world.[6]

It is the 'relevant rules of international law' provision in Article 31(3)(c) that opens the door to claims that general international law should be taken into account when arbitrators interpret the provisions of international investment agreements and the 'relevant rules' for determining the sources of public international law can be found in Article 38(1) of the Statute of the International Court of Justice ('ICJ Statute'). The sources there listed include international conventions, 'custom' as determined by 'general practice accepted as law', 'general principles of law accepted by civilized nations', and at the bottom of the hierarchy (in theory), judicial decisions and the writings of highly qualified experts.[7] Many of the provisions of Article 38(1) are contentious.[8] For example, judicial and expert opinions play an outsized role in investment arbitration, and determining international law by examining the law of only 'civilized' nations is shot through with power dynamics entrenched through colonialism: who will determine which nations are civilized and how will that be determined? If international law excludes a significant number of states or people, can it really be said to be 'international'? Can its principles really be said to be 'general'? Questions such as these fuel a vibrant and growing body of Third World Approaches to International Law (TWAIL) and Critical Legal Studies (CLS).[9]

These questions also loom large in the background of our present concern: the mismatch between legal and economic realities concern the international corporate form. We may have a clear historical understanding of the purpose of corporate law within a given jurisdiction or the rights–obligations balance a given jurisdiction seeks to strike, but the legal–conceptual space the ICP occupies is a Rorschach of domestic legal systems and fragmented international legalities. The VCLT and ICJ Statute, both drafted in the immediate post-colonial period, provide the interpretive framework through which arbitrators and judges have transported and reinvented doctrines between courts and jurisdictions resulting in the formation of the ICP. And because corporate structures and the capital that flows within them can so easily span multiple jurisdictions and simultaneously shift with the tide, the international law that affects ICPs is largely reactive. It has evolved pragmatically to address specific problems but is not rooted in any unifying principle, purpose, or concept. Accordingly, this chapter seeks to address the yawning gap between theories that attach to existing international legal personalities and the ICP.

I. Conceptualizing the international corporate person

This section suggests that analogizing the ICP to Individuals, States, and other legal personalities detracts from a legal recognition of what I call 'corporate exceptionalism': the notion that MNEs and ICPs are not parallels to *anything* (a). It then stresses that the ICP has secured a class of rights under international law that have either been created exclusively for it or that are exercisable only by it – or both (b). Finally, it (re)introduces Jessup's emphasis on 'human problems' as an analytical framework for developing a non-analogous theory of the ICP (c).

a. Corporate exceptionalism

International lawyers who endeavor to conceptualize the ICP's relationship to international law have typically done so by analogy to the State, the individual, or to international institutions.[10] But as we have seen, the ICP is at best an uneasy parallel with other existing international legal personalities. Invariably, the ICP retains legal elements analogous to two or more of other legal personalities as well as elements that are foreign to all others. One crucial element of this is the fluidity of the corporate personality. Unlike any other personality, the ICP can rapidly expand and contract across jurisdictions in reaction to its needs, it can distance its ownership and its leadership from its actions, it can restructure both ownership and control relatively easily, and it can exercise political influence on the public institutions that create international and domestic law through a variety of forms that are either not accessible or not as varied as those available to other international legal personalities.[11] For example, the UN cannot fund domestic political campaigns,[12] an unaffiliated natural person cannot obtain consultant status at the UN through ECOSOC processes,[13] a State cannot lobby the domestic lawmakers of other States,[14] and so on.[15]

As a result of these and other features, the ICP can also channel assets and capital flows across jurisdictions, select its 'citizenship' for taxation purposes and create sub-economies within itself. The legal structures that facilitate these sub-economies often result in ICP 'efficiencies' that run counter to dominant economic conventions. For example, the law can create a situation in which it is efficient for a corporation to continually operate a subsidiary at a substantial loss in a jurisdiction with corporate income tax while channeling income through another jurisdiction that does not have corporate income tax, and it can then move capital between subsidiaries through a variety of legal technologies.[16] Certainly, a natural person can set up a legal person to obtain this class of rights and benefits; however, this is only if the natural person is not an 'employee' but rather an individual earning income based on contracts procured through the legal person.

This is what I refer to as 'corporate exceptionalism': the notion that MNEs and ICPs are not parallels to *anything* – that is, they are not analogous to States or Individuals or NGOs or IGOs or other international or transnational institutions. As such, they resist analogical reasoning vis-à-vis other international legal personalities. ICPs enjoy rights that are only available to this category of legal personality. They also have legally mandated motives that catalyze action and the ability to undertake actions not available to any other legal actor (e.g., intra-ICP international trade, cross-jurisdiction transfer pricing, legal control without legal ownership, opportunities created through State competition or fears of base erosion, creation of tax havens, multiple network legalities, choice of law within networks, etc.). On the private law end, international law creates a multitude of technologies through which ICPs can fulfill legally mandated profit motives in service to shareholders and to the exclusion of the 'public', both global and State-based (of course, many firms do not define 'purpose' in this way, but the point is to highlight to possibility). On the public law end, international law often washes its hands of corporate behavior: States regulate corporations; if liability is to attach to an ICP's headquarters in one jurisdiction for behavior in another, the corporate veil must be pierced, and the corporate veil – with all of its similarities to the shield of sovereignty – belongs to the realm of private law because it is concerned with relations amongst 'persons' rather than States.[17]

b. Beyond state, individual, and institution

One of the primary points that I have stressed in the previous chapters is that, beyond exceptionalism and analogy, the ICP has secured a class of rights under international law that have either been created exclusively for it or that are exercisable only by it – or both. Although this is certainly an incomplete list, the rights that I have identified as central to the ICP beyond the State, Individual, and Institution are: (1) the ICP's ability to decide for itself whether or not it is subject to international law – for example, through the (re)structuring of 'control' – in accordance with the ICJ standard; (2) the ICP's ability to assert substantive rights under international law independent of those rights authorized by the State; (3) the ICP's capacity to violate international law independent from the State; (4) the ICP's ability to assert both the State's sovereignty and its own corporate veil as shields against liability and the ability to define the reach of both sovereignty and the veil under certain circumstances; (5) the ICP's negative duty to uphold human rights but often a positive right to claim them; (6) the ICP's ability to avoid fiscal liability through (re)structuring and undercapitalization; (7) the ICP's ability to access courts of 'fourth instance', that is, to 'appeal' decisions from supreme domestic courts or petition for *de novo* review; (8) the ICP's ability to extend jurisdiction beyond the State in which the controversy in question arose; (9) an ICP right to enforce a law in a jurisdiction not bound by that law but bound by a contract to honor that law; (10) the ICP's ability to decide upon procedural remedies for violations of its international responsibilities with respect to human rights; (11) the ICP's ability to select the level of law and enforcement for a violation of an international obligation, that is, domestic, regional, international, or some combination thereof; (12) the ICP's ability to claim a legally prescribed *mens rea* with respect to its actions rather than to expose itself to inquiries into actual *mens rea*; (13) the ICP's access to an exemption from State requirements to criminalize the corrupt acts of 'individuals'; (14) the ICP's ability to create 'internal' markets and to limit the access of or exclude non-ICP actors; (15) the ICP's ability to choose and simultaneously hold multiple citizenships and to thereby play the advantages of multiple domestic systems of its choosing against one another to the benefit of the ICP; (16) the ICP's ability to purchase exemptions from international prosecution for corruption; (17) the ICP's right to the benefit of assigning responsibility for deliberate, cumulative environmental behavior to States and their ability to regulate and enforce restrictions; (18) the ICP's ability to move capital and commodities freely across jurisdictions even as labor is immobile; (19) the ICP's right to access to the benefits of legal reasoning and inertias of belief that favor corporate expansion through various concepts of development; (20) the ICP's right to ownership that is separate from actions; (21) the ICP's right to influence and sustain the rules to which it is subject in relation to State governments, publics, capital, equity, humanity, and so much more; and (22) the ICP's ability to be both SOE and ICP – to be both a public and a private entity simultaneously.

c. Human problems and corporate conceptions

At the outset of his 1955 Storr Lectures on *Transnational Law*,[18] the legendary international lawyer, diplomat, and professor Philip C. Jessup encouraged young lawyers to resist trends toward rigid compartmentalization of international law into 'domestic' and 'international' and, by implication, 'public' and 'private'. Jessup states:

> In the customary method of the study of international relations and international law, the stress is on the State or the nation factor. If the matter does not involve the government of one State in its relation with another government or governments, the matter is said to be 'domestic'. By and large, [this] orthodox approach precluded international consideration of a problem until at least it had a transnational dimension.[19]

For Jessup, writing during the post-WWII era of decolonization, such orthodoxies missed the point of international law – namely, the regulation and peaceful resolution of disputes between groups of humans. Problems between groups 'in general arise from conflicts of interest or desire, real or imagined'.[20] Thus, 'the State, in whatever form, is not the only group with which we are concerned'.[21] Indeed, 'States are not the only subjects of international law'.[22] International law's primary target should be the resolution of conflicts between groups; these conflicts are what Jessup saw as 'universal human problems'. For Jessup, an analysis should begin with identification of those problems and the groups involved – whether they be *inter alia* States, corporations, insurgents, cities, IGOs, NGOs, political parties, administrative bodies, or individuals – and then reach out from there to find the appropriate area of law to facilitate resolution. Jessup's approach has drawn some criticism: some take issue with his lack of distinctions between public and private legal principles; I am uncomfortable with the implication that international law should override States in the governance of humans and the accompanying broad power Jessup's interpretive authority vests in international judges, especially considering the not quite post-colonial era during which he wrote. Nevertheless, Jessup's approach is useful for the purposes of this chapter because it lends itself to pragmatic rather than analogical reasoning. That is, it reminds us that law is always a human creation in service to human interests (even if ecocentric rather than anthropocentric) and gives us permission to reconstruct international legal personhood with a focus on theory and utility.

Seeking a theory of the legal personality is nothing new. Neither are inquiries into the nature of the corporation. The literature covering the topic is vast and significant contributions dates back for over a century.[23] It is the international component of corporate legal personhood that is incompletely theorized; and a theory needs to consider both the human interests that gave rise to the international legal status quo as well as the amorphous nature of the ICP. Focusing only on a theory of the firm, one salient review from which I drew in Chapter 1 categorizes existing legal theories into three main groups: (1) Concession theories (also known as fiction theories), according to which corporations exist as creations of the state or the sovereign; (2) Participant theories, which identify corporations as primarily created by individuals; and (3) Institutional theories (also known as real entity theories), which understand corporations as 'institutions both formed according to legal rules and organized and run by individual people'.[24]

All these approaches entail assumptions that cannot be universally held, although proponents of one or another often draw rather far-reaching normative conclusions from their basic understandings of the corporation.[25] Nevertheless, it is worth noting the implications of various starting points. Take the two poles, for example: Concession and Participant theories. These can be understood as 'top-down' and 'bottom-up' views, respectively. That is, for a Concession theorist, a corporation's only legal entitlements are those granted by the State; the State can create and revoke entitlements at will and the corporation cannot exist but for the pleasure of the State. But this theory falls short in the ICP era, where corporations can un-incorporate and reincorporate freely in multiple States. It also sidesteps theoretical questions regarding whether corporations are reduceable to law or whether they can exist outside the law. Indeed, Concession theorist may argue that without law, limited liability does not exist. However, a Participant theorist would argue that corporate existence flows from the will of its members, not States. The State's monopoly on law and the political community's resulting ability to confer or revoke recognition and entitlements does not mean the State creates the corporation; it merely recognizes the corporation. Although fraught with false equivalencies, analogies might be drawn to the law's relationship to human slaves in the past – the fact that the law did not recognize the humanity of slaves did not mean that the lack of recognition made slaves inhuman. At any rate, both the strengths and the cracks in the analogy are clear: the law cannot banish to inexistence that which objectively exists but whether the corporation objectively exists is a question of ideology and belief. The notion that corporations have independent personality flowing from the will of the participants depends on a particular political ideology; it cannot flow directly from an analytic theory of the corporation.[26]

The difficulty in theorizing the corporation and especially the ICP is compounded by the ambiguity of the term 'corporation'. For example, while Concession theories generally understand corporations as legal platforms, Participant theories understand them as organizations. If a corporation is simply a form of contract, a legal arrangement, it makes sense to conclude that corporations exist only in 'contemplation of law', as the U.S. Supreme Court put it in *Trustees of Dartmouth College v. Woodward*. But if a corporation is a human organization, it obviously cannot be a 'mere creature of law'.[27]

The Institutional theory, favored and advanced by Professor Eric Orts, is an intermediate position. Orts summarized the theory as follows:

> The Institutional theory sees firms as socially established entities that are both authorized and recognized by governments and organized and managed by individual participants. The institutional recognition of the business enterprise as a legal 'entity' or 'person' interposes a conceptual separation between the political state and the firm's individual participants. Once a regular legal process for the governmental recognition and individual creation of firms has become established, business firms become social institutions. In legal terms, they become 'entities' and 'persons' with specified legal rights and obligations.[28]

The Institutional theory seems most suited to a 'high level' effort to theorize the ICP as terms such as 'authorized' and 'recognized' grant enough interpretive leeway to include ICP international institutions in the place of States, and terms such as 'organized' and 'managed' can (but do not necessarily) include States in the place of 'individual participants'. But one inapplicable factor in Ort's description is also immediately apparent: although ICPs certainly have specified rights under international law, their obligations are far less 'specified'. This is because, as we have seen,[29] ICP obligations under international law tend to be 'negative' in nature. ICPs are often understood only as having an obligation *not to* interfere with a State's international obligations.

As for specified 'rights' of ICPs, we might begin to understand them as fluid, constantly shifting as the ICP shifts, but falling broadly into two categories: passive and active rights.[30] Passive rights refer primarily to 'claim-rights'; that is, a right that someone else can exercise on behalf of the holder of the right. For example, an infant has a right not to be assaulted but it is up to a guardian to exercise that right on behalf of the infant. The guardian can only exercise that right to the benefit of the infant, not to benefit the guardian.[31] Similarly, an ICP might have a passive right to contract remedies in domestic courts or even human rights remedies in certain international courts, exercisable by a representative on behalf of the corporation. Passive rights are claims to which an entity has access. Without these, an entity cannot possess legal personhood; any object may have the same rights, but personhood describes only those entities that hold the quality of exercisability, through the self or through a representative. Thus, an ICP's personhood persists in part upon the passive rights its representatives can exercise on its behalf under international law.

Active rights are those that involve the ability to willfully act along with a contextual element – that act is considered an act-in-law. Active rights thus consist not only of a willful legal act but of the ability to incur legal responsibility for the act, usually either criminal or civil. These rights belong to actors that are free to take action, to make choices, and to accept responsibility for those choices. For example, if an infant willfully takes a piece of candy from a store without paying for it, under most circumstances neither the infant nor the guardian incurs legal responsibility for the act.[32] If a minor enters into a contract, the contract may well be legally void because it was not an 'act-in-law'; minors often lack legal ability to enter into contracts. Thus, the ICP's personhood persists in part upon the active rights it can exercise under international law: acts-in-law for which it can incur responsibility. The ICP's active rights are often those that involve contracts and various economic transactions.

In sum, an ICP is discernable in international law where its representatives can access international remedies on its behalf or where it commits acts-in-international-law for which it can incur responsibility. The former of these persists in the ICP's access to the ICJ, ICSID and other arbitration tribunals, and to human rights courts such as the ECtHR. The latter of these persists in the ICP's responsibility to shareholders under statutes such as the ATS, certain contract claims at arbitral tribunals, active interference with State obligations under international law, possibilities such as aiding and abetting under the Rome Statute, and potentialities such as the Draft Instrument on Business and Human Rights. Clearly then, the active and passive conceptions leave out important legal and normative orders within ICPs and within corporate groups. Transfer pricing and tax avoidance are international volitional acts, but they are rarely 'acts-in-international-law' as taxation and contract are relegated to the domestic realm.

This blind spot is the status quo. International law does not recognize the ICP's role in (and therefore responsibility for) market manipulations that tilt the focus of domestic systems to accommodate capital rather than to accommodate the public. To make matters foggier, States often do not merely accept the status quo; they actively promote collections of concepts that justify this focus on the grounds that State publics benefit from the status quo. States adopt the falsehood that natural market forces create the status quo, that negative consequences of market forces are 'externalities', that they should analyze policy decisions based on (monetary) cost-benefit analysis without inquiring as to whether and how those 'costs' are a product of choice, as if they exist as a natural fact, as if the market could not have been otherwise, as if intra-MNE economies do not exist, and so on. For example, if a State slices corporate taxation for fear of capital flight and base erosion, it can rightfully lay claim to the argument that attracting large companies attracts jobs for its citizen-constituents (and therefore a greater number of taxable citizen-constituents with no 'flight' option). This circle of reasoning reflects the self-validating logic of 'justice' Hans Kelsen first penned almost a century ago:

'[I]f [we assume that] only a just order is called law, a social order which is presented as law is [always simultaneously] presented as just'.[33]

In this way, both Kelsen and Jessup saw some form of salvation from the status quo in an empowered international judiciary. While Kelsen hoped for a judge empowered to strike down domestic law when it conflicted with international law, Jessup hoped for a judge empowered to select the law most suited to the 'human problem' – the interest giving rise to conflict. Kelsen's thought is representative of thinkers who envisage utopian global orders based on 'universal norms'. Jessup's thought, though perhaps emblematic of elite lawyerly fantasies, has pragmatism at its core. For this reason, and for the liberating qualities discussed earlier, I find it useful as a foundation for solution-oriented critique.

II. Constituency and sovereignty as human problems

Jessup's emphasis on 'the human problems' – an understanding of law and adjudication as societal functions fundamentally in service to the resolution of human problems – is a helpful analytical tool for international lawyers who seek to free their minds (and therefore their analysis) from disciplinary shackles that might insist on particular treaty understandings or interpretive conventions. A Jessupian approach attempts to first identify the dissonance between law and social or political goals that give rise to conflict, to distill the conflict (no matter what form its parties take) to human interests, and then to reach out from there to find appropriate tools within the international legal arsenal. Such an analysis is not always possible in a court of law, but it serves well to highlight underpinning contradictions that can remain like tectonic plates beneath the surface of the law until a social or political clash causes them to quake. Thus, it is through a Jessupian lens that I seek to highlight tectonic tensions between the ICP and constituency (a) and the ICP and sovereignty (b).

a. Constituency: IEL as a case study

Within a democratic State, the authority of a government to make and enforce laws depends in part on whether its political institutions and practices are justifiable to those who are governed by them. Hence, in democratic theory, the concept of constituency is linked to institutions that increase a government's (or governing system's) legitimacy. While there is no settled definition of constituency,[34] the uncontroversial elements appear to be that (1) constituencies are the stakeholders of political representation, and (2) they are made up of 'persons' with shared interests.

Two assumptions are often made about the concept of constituency that are worth bringing to the fore.[35] First, the concept of constituency is often linked to the institution of voting in the traditional sense, for example, one demonstrates citizenship, one human casts one ballot, the vote is cast for representation of interests, and the whole process often is linked to accountability through a future opportunity to reelect or replace. However, constituency need not be linked to voting or an office of representation. Voting is simply the institution that accomplishes political representation of a constituency and political representation can take place at varying levels of abstraction. In some States, political representation is focused on individuals, while the process of becoming a representative excludes virtually all constituents.[36] In other States, votes are cast for parties rather than individuals, and the process of representing the party requires an in-party political process wholly separate from constituent representation.[37] In any case, the fact that most human constituents are excluded from the possibility of direct representation has not particularly bothered democratic theorists. Instead, exclusion is often characterized as 'necessary' because, on the one hand, it increases the social distance between the humans governed by law and humans creating law (promoting legitimacy by removing inter-personal relationships),[38] and on the other hand, it tempers excesses in government through its quality- and deliberation-enhancing aspects (i.e., more qualified humans are voted into office and fewer humans makes for more compromise and progress).[39]

Second, the concept of constituency is often linked to territory,[40] for example, political representation is based upon physical residency in a town, city, district, county, parish, state, etc., as well as citizenship. However, there is nothing inherent to political representation or communities of interest that require constituencies to be territory-based. Constituencies have historically been based upon a variety of group features – for example, voluntariness, stability, or homogeneity – and with reference to a variety of purposes – for example group rights, fostering political collaboration, or representation of local interests.[41]

On the international stage, one strain of conventional wisdom is that the legitimacy of institutions derives from the fact that international law comprises a system of voluntary associations among States. While many states do not represent the publics within them – either because they are not democratic or because the actions of state negotiators do not represent the interests of the individuals within the states they represent[42] – the conventional wisdom holds that international or even transnational governance among States is legitimate so long as the sovereign controls the mechanism through which the State acceded. That is, the legitimacy of international law is rooted in State sovereignty, and the legitimacy of international courts therefore flows from State accession, not democratic political representation (much less decision-making). Other areas of international law – such as 'general principles' of non-intervention and the responsibility to protect[43] – tell us that State action loses its legitimacy where a sovereign either attacks or is incapable of protecting its own citizens. Apart from such rare instances, the wisdom of the sovereign in engaging with international law is trusted; the intention of the sovereign here is not a subject of general inquiry.

These wisdoms are also conventional in the historical sense. Similar lines of thought can be traced from James Harrington and James Madison through Francois Guizot and John Stuart Mill. Where Harrington's 1656 *Oceana* found the root of State authority in ownership over land and set out schemes to legitimate that authority through rotating redistributive authority via ballot,[44] James Madison saw territorial representation as a means to distill communities of interest into a 'vanilla' unified interest that could be contained in individual politicians.[45] And where Francois Guizot long insisted that universal suffrage sacrificed informed choice to the will of the masses,[46] John Stuart Mill's utilitarian democratism solved the suffrage problem with a sort of universal egalitarian engagement, nevertheless carefully insisting that pre-selected representatives should be the channels through which the masses would participate in this universal engagement.[47] All of these thinkers sought to remove the 'specialist' field of economic decision-making from democratic processes, particularly when it had to do with ideas regarding redistribution. And all of these thinkers adhered broadly to contours of 'legitimacy' as sketched by continental political philosophy.

It was not Harrington, Madison, Mill or other early democratic theorists that sought to specifically insulate the channels through which wealth and goods are moved and controlled across national borders. Rather, it was economist Friedrich Hayek and his lawyerly followers in Geneva, Chicago, and Germany who bore the greatest influence on the structure of international economic law since the 1971 collapse of the Bretton Woods system, especially in trade and investment law.[48] Hayek believed that international economic matters should be insulated from the whims of State political climate; all States would benefit from globally efficient markets, and as such, the international architecture should – in a sense – protect humans from themselves.[49] The role of international economic law (IEL), in Hayek's estimation, was to prize efficiency above all – efficiency understood in terms of minimized transaction costs and the absence of *active* market distortions.[50] (I will elaborate further on these themes in Section III.) Although Hayek's dream to eliminate economic discrimination and secure global economic prosperity was 'noble' in many ways,[51] it seemed to assume that law's constituency could simply be eliminated if its institutions focused narrowly on global market efficiency. This was a misguided belief, at least if the preponderance of legal and political theory as well as observations from the present status quo hold true.[52] Both the successful and the failed institutions of international law appear to substantiate a (hi)story that requires institutions of governance (especially those without access to military coercion as is the case with IEL) to dynamically demonstrate legitimacy and authority over the governed in a variety of changing contexts,[53] often by demonstrating their benefit (economic or otherwise) to some community of interest.[54] In this abstract sense, all legal institutions and regimes have a constituency; even authoritarian dictatorships have tiny clusters of constituents. International economic law also has constituents, many of which are not States.

Under the influence of Hayek and his followers, the present structure of international economic law reflects the perception that global markets are 'natural' and that legal instruments should insulate international markets from the 'political' processes that distort them, for example, nationalism, protectionism, or domestic economic interests. While citizen-constituencies were excluded from the revamping of the GATT and all three generations of investment treaties,[55] ICP-constituencies were able to rally political representation that served ICP interests. This resulted in one configuration of legitimate redistribution over another; one understanding of how 'right' should be constructed over another; one conception of where economic as opposed to criminal sanctions should be introduced over another; and so on. As the ICSID Convention overtook the Calvo Doctrine, or as the Uruguay Round's participants crafted the Post–Cold War globalist economy, ICPs did not need the power to vote, nor did they need to be confined to a geographic territory to attain political representation in WTO lawmaking, as can be seen through the Intellectual Property Committee and the structure of international investment law, discussed later. (Indeed, for voting purposes ICPs had always been superficially disenfranchised despite their ability to attain multiple citizenships.) Rather, ICPs rallied around shared collections of interests with respect to IEL, often promoted by trade groups represented a 'sector' rather than an 'actor'. These ICPs also share the legal purpose of increasing shareholder profit which results in pragmatic action to promote the globalization of economic dogma that serve this ICP legal purpose.[56] These phenomena, often floating on the tailwinds of economic theories discussed in the next few paragraphs, have situated industry sectors (each composed of ICPs and other types of private interests) as the primary constituencies shaping and legitimating international economic law.

To many economists, regulatory measures such as price ceilings, minimum wages, subsidies, or tax breaks are known as 'market distortions' in persistent reference to a mythical 'undistorted' market in which prices climb as high as the dictates of demand or as low as ordained by saturations of supply. The use of the term 'distortion' implies the 'naturalness' or 'purity' of a system of exchange in which both supply and demand can be converted into intermediary value in the form of currency. Indeed, government issued currency itself (a regulatory invention and legal fiction) is almost never considered a government distortion unless a government fails to guarantee its stability. The fact that a failure to guarantee is considered a distortion contradicts the notion that in the converse case the fact of stability is not considered a distortion but a feature of a 'pure' market. Similarly, when a government fails to uphold 'the rule of law', to protect intellectual and other property rights (at least a particular conception of them), or to permit anti-competitive or non-competitive behaviors, these are considered 'distortions', but when a government guarantees any of these things through interventions such as police powers or due process rights (i.e., through non-monetary intervention), the market retains 'undistorted' status. The core assumption upon which this language depends is that the 'undistorted' form of free monetary exchange is 'natural', a variation on a 'state of nature' – an uncorrupted natural condition. To Hayek and his followers, the international economic system's primary role is to restore and preserve this 'state of nature' to the greatest extent possible even as political and social interests at the State level seek to corrupt it through regulation. Thus, on this view, governments can be considered responsible both for *active* distortion – that is, wage and labor rights, taxes, and subsidies – and for *negative* distortion – that is, failure to ensure stable currency, competition, and the right of one actor to exclude others from various forms property over which the one has ownership or control.

The irony of this ordoliberal position is that so-called 'pure' market conditions cannot exist without regulatory and coercive protection. Ordoliberal globalism requires that its adherents place economic efficiency at the apex of State governmental purpose. It differs from raw *laissez faire* and libertarian views in that it welcomes interventions that serve 'efficiency' understood in transactional terms, that is, the prevention of *negative* distortions. In this vein, as Hayek and his followers sought to rethink the international economic system – especially as the Bretton Woods System began to crumble in the late 1960s – they sought also to legitimate rules that ensured particular types of political insulation for global markets. More specifically, they sought to ensure that governments would abstain from *active* distortions (e.g., through the 1980 ILO shift from structural inequality to employment equity,[57] and the Marrakeshian SCM Agreement, TBT Agreement, and GATT 1994)[58] at the same time as it required governments to prevent *negative* distortions (e.g., through the IMF's amendments releasing Special Drawing Rights in the late 1970s followed by a shift to global financial governance in the 1980s,[59] and the 1994 TRIPS Agreement).[60]

Of course, Hayek was not directly responsible for all of these structural assumptions. His ideas fused with the Chicago School Coase- and Posner-enthused 1970s 'law and economics' lawyers who bore great influence in the United States and on the international investment regime promoted by the World Bank (ICSID). Also instrumental were the Geneva School-influenced lawyers, such as Ernst-Ulrich Petersmann, whose imprint upon the form and function of international trade law (WTO) still looms large.[61] These schools of thought fused legal pragmatism with economic ordoliberalism to form a hybrid set of *Grundnormen* in international economic law. Where the Chicago–Coase approach contributed the *Grundnorm* that allocations of legal entitlements (e.g., property rights) were meaningless in the absence of *negative* market distortions because but for transaction costs markets 'naturally' produce 'efficient' and therefore 'just' outcomes,[62] the Geneva-Petersmann approach fused Hayek with Kant wherever it asserted a *Grundnorm* in the Marrakesh Agreement itself: free trade was constitutional in nature, it was essential to human dignity, a 'higher law',[63] even a human right though only private actors could use it.[64] These views breathe life into the 'personhood' of the ICP – a legal form possessing active and passive rights that neither States nor humans are capable of possessing. These views also complemented Geneva's fondness for Ricardian comparative advantage: the assertion that free trade provides the conditions for optimal allocation of resources and therefore that all States benefit regardless of strengths and weaknesses.[65] Together, these collections of concepts convinced swaths of lawyers and economists alike that an undistorted global market on which buyers and sellers can trade with each other under equal competitive conditions hence leads to overall welfare gains from which all countries participating in this exchange, rich and poor, can benefit.[66]

The human problems become obvious at the pressure points where this vision failed to manifest. Where global markets have enjoyed unprecedented growth in the post-WWII era (at least until COVID-19 abruptly halted it), international law is concerned with humans mostly insofar as their rights attach to States;[67] and where during the same period ballooning global capital has become more densely concentrated in the hands of the rich as production is consolidated in poorer States,[68] international law is concerned with capital mostly insofar as it can ensure that its movement is freed from State or government interference.[69] As Ingo Venzke put it in 2019, '[i]nternational law and its institutions assume the responsibility for increasing the size of the pie, but abdicate the responsibility for the distribution of the pieces to the national level of governance'.[70] And as Roberto Unger noted back in 1996, 'capital has become hypermobile while labor remains imprisoned in the nation-state – or in blocs of homogenous nation-states'.[71] Indeed, the very terms 'global market' and 'world market' so pervasive in the Marrakeshian instruments reflect a Ricardian assumption underpinning international economic law's status quo, that is, the assumption that State borders are or should be largely irrelevant to the channels, objects, and proceeds of economic activity; that borders are only for humans.[72]

All of this suggests that human problems associated with constituency – particularly the forms of exclusion endorsed by Madison, Mills, and other democratic theorists – are mirrored in the structure of international economic law. Whereas the democratic theorists sought governmental legitimacy through engaged deliberation but insisted that decision-making be insulated from the masses, the Hayekians sought international economic legitimacy through the accession of State governments but insisted that global markets be insulated from peoples. Hayekian-minded lawyers and other defendants of the international economic system tend to emphasize accession to the WTO system as a form of consent. As I have demonstrated elsewhere,[73] in order to adopt this *prima facie* approach to accession, one must assume that 'acceptance' is the same as 'agreement', and this assumption contradicts the prevailing view in ASEAN and other States in the Global South that view 'consensus' as the hallmark of legitimacy when it comes to international 'agreement'.

The choice of words used the WTO's founding Agreement presupposes that IEL – and by extension the global economy – does not 'belong' to all States equally. In fact, as we have seen through lobbying efforts in trade and investment law detailed in the last chapter, IEL does not 'belong' to States at all but to ICPs. At the very least it is clear that international trade law's constituency is not 'peoples' – it does not draw its legitimacy from individual citizen consent nor does it directly govern peoples through its institutions. Moreover, it would seem that if part of IEL's constituency is comprised of States, then some constituents are 'more equal than others', to borrow a euphemism from George Orwell's famous government of pigs.[74] As the Agreement on Trade-Related Aspects of International Property Rights (TRIPS) and Deutsche Bank and other examples have shown, Orwell's euphemism is reflected in the rules that constitute the *status quo* governing international trade – rules pushed and crafted predominantly by representatives from a particular collection of economically powerful States, who ultimately took cues from private industry.

Here I want to offer two points to narrow the focus on ICP constituency as a 'human problem'. First, although Marrakesh is an agreement between States, and although only States can initiate consultations at the WTO, States are not the actors that engage in most of the trading. Except for instances of State capitalism to which special rules sometimes apply,[75] States are severed from active market participation, banished to the artificial 'public' realm where they are implored to passively protect but not participate in or interfere with 'private' activity. Thus, it is the private sectors within States (or non-market actors in some economies) that trade with counterparts in other States: almost half of international trade is intra-ICP trade, that is, trade within a single collection of subsidiaries controlled by a single corporate parent.[76] The transnational corporate groups and networks that engage in this trade operate in many States and benefit from the Marrakeshian free movement of goods and services the WTO secures. These benefits ripple for ICPs up and down their supply chains, but the poorest States along those supply chains – in contrast to the ICPs that manipulate their internal markets – tend to benefit minimally or not at all as 'hosts' to providers of low value-added components.[77] A closer look at the legal structures that facilitate international trade reveal that the Ricardian understanding of 'benefit' espoused by the WTO naïvely assumes that increased production within a State results in increased wealth for its citizens. But within an international framework that ignores distribution amongst States, even a charitable view of the WTO's Ricardo must acknowledge that 'advantage' is understood narrowly as productive advantage, and therefore 'benefit' belongs to those that own and/or control the means of production. The law therefore clearly serves ICPs, and, as we have seen, some of the same ICPs it serves created and continued to legitimate the law. Perhaps because of this, the scales soon fell from the eyes poorer States; Marrakeshian trade did not necessarily benefit all States or peoples, especially not those relying more heavily on foreign capital. India's experience with the TRIPS Agreement is one example,[78] the collapse of the Doha Round is another.[79] These and other (hi)stories corroborate a more fundamental criticism, that is, that the goal of insulating global markets from the decisions of political State actors – even if protectionist or nationalistic – undermines at the outset claims that States are the WTO's primary constituency.

Second, when a State mobilizes the WTO's Dispute Settlement Understanding (DSU), it hardly ever does so for the benefit of an individual ICP. Rather, it overwhelmingly brings claims that benefit entire sectors,[80] industries depending on a specific commodity,[81] or for the benefit of State interests.[82] When a State brings claims that benefit specific ICPs, it almost invariably does so inadvertently – either because those ICPs occupy a large market share in a market with few players, as with Airbus and Boeing in the disputes between the EC and the United States,[83] or because there are intrastate monopolies.[84] The Complainant State never bases a complaint on harm to any particular ICP. Rather, complaints target measures or interpretations adopted by the Respondent State that causes some economic injury, often in the form of discrimination, to the Complainant. At first glance, this may seem to cut against the idea of corporate constituency as a human problem, but consider the effect of Most Favored Nation (MFN) and Fair and Equitable Treatment (FET) clauses in GATT (and for that matter in most BITs). Such clauses serve certain ways of conceptualizing commercial sectors on a transnational stage. They require an offending State not only change its behavior with respect to the Complainant but with respect to all States within certain communities of commercial interest.

In this way, the State can be understood as an intermediary – a touchpoint through which to access international law – for commercial sectors that transcend States and for ICPs that operate in multiple States, not just those States involved in the dispute. From this perspective, ICPs can be understood both as comprising and transcending the sectoral constituency. All of this indicates that, if legal structures *should* serve humanity generally rather than legally mandated purposes or legal fictions, at least one 'human problem' arising from IEL's corporate constituency is that this constituency is legally insulated from human problems.

b. Sovereignty as a strategy

The notion of 'sovereignty' as the basis of international law's legitimacy has followed lines similar to those of constituency. One clear example can be found in the 1960s and 1970s, when economically powerful States used the concept to undermine NIEO efforts to leverage sovereignty as a justification for economic autonomy measures.[85] ('Sovereignty' as a shield against non-intervention was condemned as 'relativist' by those same States.)[86] For instance, where the 1963 UN Resolution 1803 (Permanent Sovereignty over Natural Resources or PSNR) sought to ensure that rights of 'peoples and nations' to benefit from domestic natural resource exploitation (for the 'well-being of the people of the State concerned'),[87] powerful States encouraged international institutions to focus on 'nations' to the exclusion of 'peoples'. By the same sovereign token, international law was and is inaccessible to peoples whose governments deny access to the spoils of lucrative licensing agreements, sovereign wealth funds, and investment profits derived therefrom.[88] It is governments, not peoples, that are empowered to license, grant access, exploit, and redistribute. Governments hold the economic rights of 'peoples' in a nearly impenetrable trust, safe from international adjudication. Thus, where resource abundance might intuit visions of national wealth, the reality is that redistributive decisions are often insulated from the people and abundant natural resources often paradoxically promote poverty rather than wealth.[89] This collection of conditions is what many commentators have termed the 'resource curse'.[90]

The classical theory of international legal personhood – not of the ICP specifically – is that only sovereign States can have international legal personality because the applicability of international law is contingent upon State consent. This is a view associated with Heirich Triepel, Dionisio Anzilotti, and Lassa Oppenheim, all of whom held monumental influence on the development of 20th century international law.[91] In 1927, the PCIJ seemed to agree with this position when it stated in the *Lotus* case: 'International Law govern relations between independent States. Rules of law binding upon States therefore emanate from their own free will'.[92] In this view, international law touches non-State persons only through the interposition of domestic law, and therefore, it does not and cannot touch an ICP – it can only touch individual States that in turn touch the ICP.

The classical perception gradually gave way to accommodate non-governmental organizations such as the UN and NATO, and to address dissonance between outcome and principle with respect to the application of international treaties. For example, both the widespread notion that armed opposition groups are not directly bound by common Article 3 of the Geneva Conventions and Additional Protocol II and arguments that root justification for international condemnation or prosecution in an alleged consensus flowing from 'the international community' share an assumption that States are the only legitimate subjects of international law.[93] Objections to these and other approaches have led to modified versions of the States-only view.

The dominant modification to the classical view is the notion that States can confer derivative international legal personhood upon non-State entities, but there is a presumption against it. As discussed in Chapter 1, this view draws from the ICJ 'nature of the entity' standard set out in *Reparations for Injuries* in 1949. In that case, the ICJ stresses that States are the 'typical' subjects of international law, but nevertheless 'it is a mistake to deduce from this state of affairs the sovereign States alone are subjects of international law'. What emerges is a foggy legal definition in which States have 'discretion' to confer legal personality on any other entity, but it remains unclear whether this means that all States in the 'international community' need to collectively confer personality, whether parties to given dispute need to do this, whether a group of States can create an international legal personality that should then be recognized by other States, or whether one State can do this unilaterally. While expert views diverge, the mainline understanding is that individual imposition of legal personality onto an entity is primarily a question of interpretation. As Georg Schwarzenberger put it in *A Manual of International Law*:

> The rules government recognition are so elastic that there is no limit to the objects, which, by recognition, may be transformed into subjects of international law. Thus, the international personality of individuals is not a question of principle, but simply one of fact: is there enough evidence to substantiate the claim that the individual, the basis of national and international life, is more than an object in existing international law?[94]

Schwarzenberger's observation quite clearly references natural persons rather than corporate ones, but it points to a key component in the dominant theory of international legal personality. Namely, international law does not create new international legal persons. Rather, it leaves open the possibility that new international legal persons can come into existence through States. But Schwarzenberger's conventional view that States create international law has been convincingly challenged.[95] As we have seen, it is not far-fetched to imagine that international law has not only played a dominant role in creating most of the world's post-colonial States, but it has also played a large hand in creating and sustaining the current conceptions of States and that international systems they occupy. I would submit that, if origins are unclear, we should accept a degree of truth from both notions. That is, we should not solely understand State sovereignty as breathing life into international law, nor should we understand international law as a source of State sovereignty. Rather, we should view them as continuously reproducing each other – at the same time as international law articulates and legitimates a collection of concepts that sustain States in the international legal order, States articulate and legitimate international law through participation and adherence.[96]

Schwarzenberger's observation also gives us a clear standard through which to articulate corporate subjectivity. Rather than attempting to provide definitive answers on the nature of subjectivity and objectivity generally, Schwarzenberger poses a flexible question that is consistent with the standard for subjectivity set out in *Reparations for Injuries*: is there enough evidence to substantiate a claim that an ICP is more than an object? Although philosophers certainly debate the nature of objectivity, international courts consistently assume that an object is something that can be thought about or talked about, not necessarily something with definite physical substance.[97] Thus, where a person or a vessel in international waters might be considered an object, so too can an abstract concept like a security or (by some theories) a corporate form, or even a State be considered an object. The notion that individuals, not States, are the 'primary' subject of international law had been brewing as early as the turn of the 20th century at the Danube Commission,[98] and as we have seen, today many regional agreements provide both natural and legal persons rights actionable against States. The cases in the previous two chapters indicate a broad collection of factors that can move an ICP from objecthood to subjecthood. These are again collected and categorized in relation to active and passive rights in Table 4.1.

However, the concept of State sovereignty can be used a shield to undermine notions of subjectivity – to insist that ICPs cannot be direct subjects or to insist that States incur no duties to other States. For example, where a State's tax code attracts ICPs seeking to avoid taxes in other States, those States have used sovereignty to insist that they have no obligation to assist other States in enforcing their tax codes. And where international efforts to curb the negative environmental impacts of ICP activity, States have used sovereignty as a shield against international regulation, linking sovereign territory to a fragmented view of the environment as if each State's environment was insulated from all others. And to a degree this is true. For example, if Brazil stands to gain economically from clearing sections of the Amazon for commercial use,[99] what right do other States have to tell Brazil it cannot clear those sections? The legal systems we have created chain environment and people to territories but set capital free to go wherever it believes it can reproduce. Environmental degradation and tax avoidance and evasion have become global problems, yet the solutions advanced by international law still link coordinated action to State buy-in and consent. But this approach will never be free of collective action problems.[100] Environmental instruments link policy change to economic interests and incentives – especially development – to such a degree that international environmental law is becoming all but irrelevant. Indeed, even international lawyers interested in climate change tend to view environmental degradation as an economic problem because it is primarily caused by economic actors (business activity and governments who accept environmental degradation to promote business activity).[101] Sovereign authority and territorial integrity are ironically succeeding in degrading much of the territory over which sovereigns have authority.

ICPs also use sovereignty as a strategic component in legal argument. For example, ICPs have argued that, because States have the sovereign right to tax as they see fit, ICPs not only have the right to exploit States with favorable tax rates to their advantage, they also simultaneously have no right to criticize those low tax rates and no duty to assist other States in acquiring the revenue they would have acquired but for the low tax rates in the favorable States. Similar 'no fault' notions have been used in arguments regarding environmental degradation and capital redistribution. While the ICP is the entity that engages in the volitional act – for example, setting up a trust or shell in a tax haven, emitting toxins in a lax jurisdiction, or 'aligning incentives' through outrageous CEO compensation packages whilst exploiting obscenely cheap labor on offer from countries locked in the throes of a 'middle income trap'[102] – it is State sovereignty that absolves these international actors of international responsibility.

All of this begs the question: if international law creates, sustains, and reshapes States, if States create ICPs, if international law recognizes ICPs as subjects as of international law based on a factual question ('is it more than an object?'), and if ICPs have the power to reshape and redefine their own parameters with relative rapidity, does this not place a large degree of discretion within the ICP itself as to whether to accede or exempt itself from law? If so, an argument can certainly be made that the ICP itself is to some degree sovereign, at least according to definitions that do not link sovereignty to territory but vest it in a 'person'.[103]

III. The public–private delusion

If corporations serve or fund the public, if they are owned by the public or by States, or if they can even be understood as 'sovereign' by some conception of the term, the widespread notion that most international corporate behavior occupies the realm of 'private' law appears suspect. The history of this public–private distinction suggests that it emerged from the effort of powerful actors to locate liability, in some sense to insulate it.[104] Corporations were thought to be answerable to other parties with which or with whom they interacted, not answerable to the public at large. There may have been good reasons for this innovation initially,[105] but theory and practice both indicate that the evolution of the ICP has outgrown the reasons driving the creation of and present justification for the public–private divide. A new theoretical foundation is needed.

With this chapter, I am not attempting to articulate a full-blown theory of the ICP but rather to sketch the contours of a theory and, drawing from a Jessupian approach, to provide what might be considered a foundation. As a first step, (re)theorizing the ICP calls for a return to one of the most fundamental questions in corporate law. What is the legal purpose of a corporation in relation to its shareholders and the public(s) it affects? As we have seen in Chapter 1, before the ICP era but after the colonial, two conceptions of the corporation co-existed in public life and law, both emerging from Anglo-American common law: the property conception and the social entity conception. Beginning in the late 1970s and gaining force in the 1980s, a great 'crisis in corporate theory' pushed the property conceptions to the fore, born on the wings of economic theory far more than legal theory. Most famously, Milton Friedman and his colleagues at the Chicago School publicized the notion that, if corporations pursued any means apart from maximizing profits for their shareholders, their managers were effectively imposing a unilateral, undemocratic tax on their shareholders.[106]

The two basic conceptions of corporate purpose warrant explanation. First, the 'property conception' views the corporation as the private property of its stockholder-owners. On this view, the corporation's purpose is to advance the purposes of its owners because, after all, they own it. Since shareholders may have multiple purposes, the idea of 'shareholder purpose' takes the form of a broad common denominator of assumed rational interest. This results in a legal assumption that all rational shareholders wish to increase their wealth. In fact, this sometimes means 'increase wealth ruthlessly', since the 'limited liability' through which the corporate person absorbs risk by acquiring liabilities on behalf of its shareholders translates to 'no liability' for the shareholders themselves. If this shareholder interest is assumed, the remainder of the legal structure requires adherence: the corporation's directors are agents of the shareholders, and as such, their primary legal obligation is to serve the financial interest of the shareholders.

Second, and by contrast, the 'social institution conception' views the corporation as an entity that comes into being and continues to exist only with governmental concurrence. This derives from the Concession theory described earlier; it follows the concession logic through to the question of ultimate ownership. The state creates and blesses the corporation, protects it through its legal institutions, grants it legal personality and perpetual life, and endows it with a limited liability that it does not vest in natural persons. Because the legal benefits derived from incorporation cannot exist but for the public's endorsement of the State, and because the corporation exists only insofar as it is facilitated by public institutions, its existence is justified through its service to the general welfare. The directors' duties therefore extend beyond the financial interests of the shareholders to include a duty of loyalty to all those interested in or affected by the corporation. Some have called this a 'stakeholder' theory of fiduciary duties.[107]

These two conceptions of purpose have at their core fundamentally different understandings of where 'public' ends and 'private' begins. The property conception views the corporation as a 'thing'; the shareholders who purchase a part of that 'thing' are the only ones with any interest in it and the only ones to whom it should answer. But can a corporation be a 'thing' if it is also a person? Ordinary 'things' like cars and rocks and apples cannot exercise rights, and in the case of most 'things', no other party can exercise rights on their behalf. (Of course, there are some rare domestic-law exceptions.)[108] The public institution conception views the corporation as a 'public body'; managers owe fiduciary duties to anyone who might be affected. But if this is so, where is the line between the corporation and the State? The following subsections explore briefly how the public–private divide emerged (a) and provide examples from international economic law indicating that a clear line has always been a 'delusion' – the division has always been a moving target and has rarely been rigid.

a. Background

Both domestically and internationally, corporate law has evolved largely as a judge-made construct. While the corporate law of post–Cold War 'social market economies' like China tend to focus on state on enterprises rather than on entrepreneurial capitalist business, and while China, Japan, and several other Asian countries provide for personal liability for 'legal representatives' of corporations, at a broad level these countries use forms and conventions drawn from American and other Western judicial decisions. Indeed, the early statutory law in the West regarding the formation and governance of corporations was brief and simple, so judges tended to fill in the gaps. Codifying these principles, corporate (or company) statutes have grown considerably more complex over the past century, and while different states emphasize different features, today corporate law is relatively homogenous across the globe. The reasons for this should not be difficult to guess: Western European States (mostly England, France, and Germany) constructed the corporation, because it facilitated first the legal immortality of the Church, then the extension of sovereign authority in colonies, still later the collecting of taxes to execute public projects, and finally the modern profit-seeking enterprise. Most non-European countries either copied or received their corporate foundations from those States. Nevertheless, even where legislators rather than judges have played a larger role in shaping the modern law – in places like China, Malaysia, and Vietnam, where previously State-run companies become 'corporatized' rather than 'privatized' – similar public–private tensions in conceptions of the corporation persist.[109] Indeed, the oft-touted narrative that the purpose of the corporate person is simply to spur entrepreneurship and innovation has little or no basis in global corporate history.[110] Rather, from the late 1700s to the horizon of the 21st century, diverging conceptions of the corporation co-existed and diverged differently in different places, with the most thorough histories documented in the United States, England, Prussia/Germany, and Japan.[111]

While England and the United States shared the late 1700s default conception of the corporation as a public-purpose entity, it drifted in the early 1800s as the two States embraced different constructs of the 'private' and the 'public' in law, spurred in part by differing attitudes regarding desirable competition.[112] On the one hand, perhaps as a feudal hangover, the English common law viewed competition as hostile to property and capital well into the 1800s, and the law placed responsibility for injury due to competition not on the competitor, but on the customer. For example, according to Blackstone's famous illustration, a mill owner builds a mill with the understanding that the owner's community will use the mill to process grains and so undertakes to build the mill – a public benefit – in reliance on future private gains. Another person is free to build another mill in the vicinity, but any person who processes their grains in that mill may incur liability to the original mill owner.[113] On the other hand, the United States drew its corporate law initially from municipalities, granting joint-liability partnership rather than corporate status to private business enterprises, but extended corporate status initially to insurance companies on the grounds that they provided an invaluable public service. As new companies successfully drew analogous justifications for limited liability corporate status,[114] and as corporations used the public conception to suppress competition through arguments leaning on public property rights to exclusion,[115] a patchwork of judicial decisions created a schizophrenic version of the corporation – one that was a private law construct when it came to ownership but a public law construct when it came to financial liability. Only here did arguments emerge that the public should rightfully absorb the debts of, for example, a corporate bankruptcy – even a corporation that existed solely for private gain – because of the public benefits incurred through corporate innovation spurred by limited liability. Thus, Milton Friedman and his progeny saw no contradiction in declaring that, although the public absorbed the risk of corporate default, 'the social responsibility of a corporation is to make money' because the corporation is privately owned by its shareholders, and as such, bears no 'social responsibility' to any other stakeholder. Even today, as Corporate Social Responsibility initiatives and Ruggie's Guiding Principles gain traction, this remains the conventional wisdom, if not the 'legal truth', not just in the United States but in most of the world.

As U.S. corporations gained global prominence after WWII, so too did the prominence of the private property conception of the MNE. Although there are significant deviations from Anglo-American shareholder control and executive compensation structure (e.g., present-day Germany and Japan), corporate *purpose* as defined by the bylaws of corporate charters is almost ubiquitously some variation of 'any and all lawful business'. However, with the emergence of the ICP through international judge-made law, and with the freedom from single-jurisdiction liability the ICP enjoys, this understanding of corporate purpose may be losing some traction on the international stage. Even in the United States, a non-binding statement emphasizing a stakeholder- rather than shareholder-focused purpose was signed by 181 leaders of America's largest MNEs at the Business Roundtable in Washington, D.C., August 2019.[116] Businesses are responding not only to public outcry, but also a change in the international legal tides with respect to the ICP. Through counterclaims in international investment tribunals, ICSID arbitrators have teased the possibility of holding ICPs liable for human rights violations typically understood to be solely the responsibility of the State.[117] And more visibly, rising global awareness regarding the consequences of climate change and the ICP's role in causing and perpetuating it has spurred resilient interest in international corporate liability across jurisdictions and in the construction of international corporate duties.[118] International economic law has encouraged ICPs to structure GVCs to maximize profit without regard to environmental damage,[119] and at the same time, international human rights law has done nothing to address redistribution of those profits.[120] Indeed, 'development'-focused organizations such as the IMF and World Bank encourage the free global movement (and therefore exportation) of capital at the same time as they insist that redistribution is a problem from States, not for international organizations or international law.[121] Yet largely due to judicial interventions and private-sector innovations,[122] international law with respect to the ICP is encountering a moment in which lawyers can reimagine what international corporate law should become. While these new trajectories are cause for optimism, they entail a variety of complex problems. For example, are corporations liable to individual states or to some global body for human rights violations? Are these violations rooted in customary international law, and, if so, is the most pragmatic solution for domestic courts to incorporate them as torts? If an international body is necessary for torts, should that take the form of an international tort court? Should climate change can be considered a crime against humanity under the Rome Statute? Each question begets others, like a set of Matryoshka dolls nesting endlessly in both directions.

If we accept the notion that the ICP does not exist for any global or international public purpose but, rather, is the private property of its shareholders, who are members of many different publics and are often themselves ICPs, we are confronted with two significant problems. The first problem is that there is a mismatch between the idea of private ownership and the tools available for public regulation on the international stage. If it is true that the ICP is disconnected from any domestic public purpose, and if one adopts the traditional State-centric understanding of international law's legitimacy, the ICP is also disconnected from obligations to the global public. More specifically, when the corporation was a purely domestic legal person, it held clear duties to the public in which it was domiciled in the form of compliance with tax, labor, criminal, and other domestic laws, but the modern ICP's reach and its ownership transcend any individual 'public'; it can only uniformly be thought to belong to a global public, yet there are no global rules of corporate taxation, criminal liability, or labor and environmental standards. The second problem follows from the first: even if global systems of tax, labor, criminal, or environmental law did exist, it would be inconsistent with domestic treatment to speak of the ICP's relationship with these systems as 'duties'. They would rather take the form of 'obligations' – at least if the ICP is to international law what the domestic corporation is to domestic law. Wherever the

ICP's relationship to international law is analogized to domestic civil and criminal concepts, contradictions are quick to follow.

b. *Insurance and SOEs: examples from international economic law*

In a recent historical institutionalist account of the rise of ISDS, Taylor St. John thoroughly tracked the process through which institutional actors, primarily at the World Bank, hatched the ICSID Convention's approach to the international law of investment arbitration, then brokered it to private actors who took up the institution's cross over time. As St. John put it,

> The new politics of investor-state arbitration is that investors, law firms, and related interest groups have a strong preference for access to arbitration. This preference emerged after several decades of institutional development. This preference does not precede the institution; instead, in this explanation, the existence of investor-state arbitration created a constituency that, over many decades, realized it had a strong incentive in the maintenance of arbitration.[123]

Some of the sources through which St. John draws conclusions on investor preferences are questionable,[124] but his central observation rings true: 'A new policy or institution can cause the development of a constituency or client group with an incentive to push for the institution's maintenance and expansion'.[125]

While investment arbitration against a State had existed since the establishment of the Permanent Court of Arbitration in 1899, the World Bank's initiatives in the 1960s and 1970s quietly obtained buy-in from the newly decolonialized States that formed its primary client base and to whose service the Bank's mandate was devoted.[126] Yet the Bank, if it can be considered 'public', produced a draft that drew most significantly from the efforts of Hermann Abs, the (in)famous financier and former president of Deutsche Bank. Some have argued Abs' efforts in pushing for ISDS at the OECD were self-interested or born out of the trauma of national expropriation; others have suggested that the German government kept an interested but substantial distance from Abs' efforts.[127] Whatever his relationship to the State, the efforts of Abs and others gained the support of governments at the OECD. And while the OECD gave way to BITs as the Draft Convention's multilateral structure proved unworkable, the push of a private banker and a handful of other place international investment expropriation in the realm of public international law remains successful to this day.[128]

The dominant narratives of the ISDS system's genesis both acknowledge the non-constituency of human persons: one narrative infers causality from the actuality of private sector benefit and emphasizes the private sector's influence on the development of the current ICSID-driven ISDS system; and St. John's narrative claims that diplomatic records do not support those causal assumptions and rather places the catalyst for the present in technocratic lawyers of the past, particularly those at the intergovernmental World Bank. Both narratives paint a picture of non-State actors pushing for solutions that move the risk of fiscal liability from the private sector to the State. But the aims of the ISDS system – most saliently to provide a fiscal remedy for expropriation of international investment – could have been achieved in a manner which did not call on a State, and therefore its public, to bear the risk of fiscal liability. For example, investors who invest in a politically risky climate could insure themselves against the event of expropriation; the nominal cost without expropriation would fall on the investor and the fiscal burden in the event of expropriation would fall on the insurer. In both instances, the system could have been contained within 'private law' as traditionally perceived.

But traditional legal perceptions cannot long reflect legal actualities when it comes to the ICP. Even the idea of the ICP as a 'private' entity is increasingly misleading. Today, the ISDS system accommodates claims not only from ICPs and other private investors, but also from SOEs. As a 2013 UNCTAD World Investment Report noted, SOEs 'are increasingly internationalizing and becoming leading players in world investment'.[129] Under the terms of most investment treaties, SOEs can bring claims against a host State so long as the SOE is engaged in 'commercial activity' not attributable to the State. Again, the separation of ownership and control is vital. And both these issues – whether an SOE activity is purely 'commercial' and whether its management makes decisions independent from the State – are questions for arbitral tribunals.[130] Interestingly, the range of possibilities created by the international investment regime to not permit arbitral tribunals to inquire about the 'purpose' of investment, since in a globalized capitalist world, investment purpose is almost always legally assumed to be 'profit'. In the case of SOEs, this legal blind spot has potential to pose national security risks.

In international trade law, the WTO's Subsidies and Countervailing Measures Agreement (SCM Agreement) attempts to draw rigid textual lines between State and private enterprise for purposes of legal duties, but judge-made law radiating from the WTO's Appellate Body has so far routinely shifted the contours of 'the private' and 'the public'. A recent paper titled 'WTO – EU's proposals on WTO modernisation' aptly illustrates the problem. In it, the European Commission took issue with the AB's concept of "public body" over time.[131] The Commission claimed that the AB's jurisprudence allows a considerable number of SOEs to escape SCM Agreement obligations because the AB interpreted the phrase 'public body' to exclude several SOEs, whereas otherwise subsidies to SOEs would be included in a manner similar to all other State subsidies.

In *US – Anti-Dumping and Countervailing Duties (China)*, the AB considered whether certain Chinese SOEs and State-Owned Commercial Banks

(SOCBs) are 'public bodies' under SCM Article 1. Drawing from existing jurisprudence, it sets out three conceptual approaches.[132] The first approach (the *governmental control approach*) holds that governmental control over an entity is the criterion that determines whether such an entity is a 'public body'. The second approach (the *governmental function approach*) holds that an entity is a 'public body' if such entity performs a governmental function. The third approach (*the Governmental Authority to Perform Governmental Functions approach)* is the one ultimately adopted by the Appellate Body. It is a hybrid approach that considers (1) whether an entity is performing governmental functions and (2) whether it is doing so with governmental authority, considering all relevant factors. If this seems vague and unworkable to you, dear reader, you are not alone.[133] Nevertheless, according to the AB in *US – Anti-Dumping*:

> What matters is whether an entity is vested with authority to exercise governmental functions, rather than how that is achieved. There are many different ways in which government in the narrow sense could provide entities with authority. Accordingly, different types of evidence may be relevant to showing that such authority has been bestowed on a particular entity. Evidence that an entity is, in fact, exercising governmental functions may serve as evidence that it possesses or has been vested with governmental authority, particularly where such evidence points to a sustained and systematic practice.[134]

Moreover, in determining whether governmental authority backs a government function,

> [T]he standard applicable to the public body enquiry under Article 1.1(a)(1) of the SCM Agreement [is that] of 'meaningful control' . . . [It is only] where evidence shows that the formal indicia of government control are manifold, and there is also evidence that such control has been exercised in a meaningful way, [that] such evidence may permit an inference that the entity concerned is exercising governmental authority.[135]

The standard of 'meaningful control' at the WTO thus requires a showing of unspecified 'formal indicia'. One might assume this includes government funding, titles, uniforms, and public statements, but WTO jurisprudence shows that it may also include, for example, procurement contracts with the government for essential materials at rates considerably below market.[136]

In both examples – international investment law and international trade – the public–private divide is a moving target. Rather than bemoan this fact and cry out for 'definite' standards as many international lawyers have done,[137] perhaps we should admit that the corporate form resists such clear-cut distinctions and embrace its amorphous nature. Such an approach would therefore welcome both worlds of law – that is, both private and public – into the realm of potential applicability to corporate behavior. This would in affect bring the international judge closer to the capabilities described in Jessup's Storr lectures:[138] Begin the analysis with the human problem and reach out from there to solutions available in domestic and international law, private and public.

c. *Sovereignty and the veil*

State sovereignty and the corporate veil are two sides of the same conceptual coin. Sovereignty is a shield against external interference concerning a State's territory and citizens and the veil is a shield against external interference concerning corporation's assets and shareholders – where the sovereign buffers citizens and heads of state, the veil buffers shareholders and directors.

Veil piercing is rare. It belongs to the 'private' realm of tort law. However, while the characterization of 'tort' as 'private' in modern law is suspect in any sense, I want to suggest that veil piercing specifically cannot be classified as 'private' on the international stage, especially in the field of IIL. Tort law is fundamentally about fairness, not moral aspirations. Where criminal law (i.e., public law) evolved to address intentional and malicious harms, tort law evolved to address intentional but not necessarily 'wrong' harms, often isolated incidents.[139] The torts of battery, trespass, nuisance, conversion, and defamation, as well as torts arising generally from negligence are addressed to one-off events resulting from an intention, but not necessarily an 'immoral' intention on the part of a perpetrator to act.[140] By contrast, modern tort law evolved to address the existence of accidents and a systemic increase in exposure to risk. Thus, strict liability torts such as products liability seek to recognize the public harm caused by decreased consumer trust in manufactured goods when they are improperly manufactured. This type of tort compensates the individual, but its design seeks fairness to the public, not necessarily fairness to the individual.

It may seem paradoxical to speak of fairness to the public in the context of IIL, which has the power to public coffers into the pockets of private investors. But as we have seen, even 'investors' cannot be so neatly categorized as 'private'. When the IIL system was taking its present form during the 1950s and 1960s, 'investments' were predominantly the tangible, definable, brick-and-mortar assets one might associate with factories and refineries developed by 'investors'. But today, much of what counts as foreign investment consists of intangible assets that limit exposure to arbitration such as intellectual property and financial instruments. We have also seen that nature of the 'investor' has changed. On the one hand, various shell subsidiaries are used to route investments through multiple jurisdictions to decrease tax exposure, take advantage of favorable regulatory frameworks, limit legal liability, and fulfill other strategic motivations. On the other hand, both domestic investors and foreign SOEs can access arbitration against a given State, placing strain on bedrock IIL principles like non-discrimination. Add shareholders behind corporate investors, and you have an 'investor' with shareholder-citizens flung across the globe with a range of values and interests, none of which may have anything to do with the State in which the corporate investor's assets are situated. Traditional treaty terms are now interpreted to include ever-broadening and increasingly amorphous notions of investment and investor far beyond what the original negotiations had envisioned.

To be sure, States still wish to attract and protect foreign capital, but to fulfill obligations to human constituents, they should only seek to attract certain types of foreign capital. The policy debates on these issues rarely focus on the 'purpose' of the investment but rather focus on the proposed investment's contribution to the domestic economy. As Sonia Rolland and David Trubek ask,

> If the investment is short-term, precarious, or purely a pass-through entity, should it really be considered as an investment, and benefit from the full range of treaty protections? At a more fundamental level, if the investment does involve some real and long-term local assets, but the benefits to the local economy are minimal or negative, should the operation be treated differently than investments having positive local impact, or at least deliver what it was contractually bound to produce? Is it appropriate to extend BIT benefits to investments and investors that may be of a considerably different nature than those the treaties were originally drafted to protect?[141]

Through the categories of 'investment' and 'investor', the State cracked its sovereign shield, and through the evolution of veil piercing in law pertaining to the ICP, the shield is beginning to shatter. At the domestic level, a typical veil piercing case occurs as follows: a controlling shareholder sets up a corporation to incur obligations to a third party, undercapitalizes a subsidiary with existing capital commitments to a third party, or maintains a subsidiary in a state of undercapitalization in the face of fiscal liabilities to third parties. When the debt is due, the subsidiary does not have enough assets to repay it and the controlling shareholder is shielded by the subsidiary's limited liability from incurring personal liability.[142] The subsidiary can declare bankruptcy and the third party bears the burden of the unpaid debt. In such situations, a court or tribunal may intervene to prevent such injustice and pierce the corporate veil by holding the controlling shareholder liable (although this is typically rare).[143]

In the context of IIL, veil piercing involves reaching outward from the parties to the dispute and bringing in the parties that have not signed an arbitration agreement. These could be parent companies, subsidiaries, private individuals, governmental and quasi-governmental entities, or States, or some combination of these. Moreover, veil piercing in IIL can occur on the basis of a variety of legal contexts, including as human rights, environment, and tax, and the principles on which the adjudicators rely are diverse, not so much in their numerosity but in their unpredictability.[144]

Under the domestic law of most jurisdictions, shareholders are not allowed to bring claims on behalf of the company in which they own shares. However, in the international system, the inclusion of 'shares' into the definition of 'investment' in a BITs and other international investment agreements – as many do – generates a status quo in which the veil can be pierced, but only for the benefit of the shareholder. Disputes settled in accordance with the ICSID Convention are somewhat different, not least because their Awards do not need to be enforced in accordance with the New York Convention.[145] ICSID Tribunals permit corporate parties of ICSID proceedings to submit claims on behalf of non-parties. These non-parties are typically either the investor's shareholders or subsidiaries. Because Tribunals usually do not 'implead' such third parties, such claims amount to piercing the corporate veil. Nevertheless, if one of the parties does not agree to join a third party, controversy can still arise, and the corporate veil will need to be pierced in the more traditional sense to overcome the non-joining party's objections.[146]

The crucial difference here is that issues associated with ICSID Tribunal jurisdiction, including veil piercing, are resolved on the basis of international – not domestic – law. This is due to several provisions in the ICSID Convention, but Article 25(2)(b) specifically addresses veil piercing:

> [A]ny juridical person which had the nationality of a Contracting State other than the State party to the dispute on the date on which the parties consented to submit such dispute to conciliation or arbitration and any juridical person which had the nationality of the Contracting State party to the dispute on that date and which, because of foreign control, the parties have agreed should be treated as a national of another Contracting State for the purposes of this Convention.[147]

The language of Article 25 suggests two criteria must be present in order to determine jurisdiction and therefore allow for veil piercing: (1) nationality and (2) 'foreign control'. While the former is relatively clear-cut, the latter was a heavily debated concept during the formation of the ICSID Convention. After gridlocked negotiations, the drafters decided to leave 'control' undefined and defer it to each arbitral tribunal to decide the definition individually. These Tribunals in turn reference each other, and through the network of treaties briefed at the beginning of this chapter, public international law more generally. Thus, what has emerged is a set of criteria similar to those discussed in the context of the WTO's SCM Agreement presented here. Just as a corporation or SOE is considered a 'public body' at the WTO when it is 'controlled' by a government, a foreign corporation is one that is 'controlled' by a foreign parent as defined a fluctuating set of factors. These factors most often include controlling share ownership or overlap in business operations as demonstrated through shared management personnel, directors, internal policies, assets or liabilities with the parent, or other ambiguous criteria such as 'common purpose' or lack of adherence to the 'arms-length' principle.[148]

Thus, the IIL regime has the potential to melt both sides of the sovereign coin. It can hold a State liable for policies legitimately passed by the domestic legislature that harm a foreign investment and it can loop in parties not subject to an adjudicated agreement through third-party representation or on behalf of shareholders. In each of these modes of liability, the State public's interest is not recognized, but the ICP's 'public' – or, more precisely, its shareholders – have both standing and potential liability even where no relevant treaty touches the State in which those shareholders hold citizenship.

IV. The ICP and a bundle of sticks

The ICP is undoubtedly a bearer of rights under international law. Its duties are less clear. This section aims to parse through the approaches to ICP duties and responsibilities in order to move toward a more cohesive theory of the ICP. In particular, this section emphasizes the differences rather than similarities in how the ICPs duties can be simultaneously approached, and the unique features of the ICP that make it fit uneasily with existing legal tools.

By now it should be clear that, even though corporations are not typically considered direct subjects of international law, international law's subjects are not limited to States. Post-WWII scholarly acknowledgement of this began, at the latest, in 2007, with Nijmann's insight that international law's primary subjects are natural persons and that legal persons (such as States) are secondary subjects charged with ensuring rights to the primary subjects. More recent and provocative scholarship has suggested that international law created States rather than the other way around.[149] In international investment and trade law;[150] in international human rights law; in international criminal law and corporate law;[151] and, most prominently (though not always most coherently),[152] in discussions related to business and human rights, international lawyers have recognized the need to address asymmetries between rights and duties that ICPs enjoy as both beneficiaries of the rights ordinarily accorded to natural person and potential subjects of international law without any clear duties to natural persons under international law. As we have already seen, many international investment arbitral awards have muddied the distinctions between States, investors (ICPs and natural), and non-investor natural persons. And as recently as 2014, a UNCITRAL Award found in *Al-Warraq v Indonesia* that an IIA both imposed obligations on investors under international law and granted states a right to enforce them.[153]

One common means of addressing the possibility of corporate responsibilities under international law roots the ICP's duties to humanity in States – in other words, an ICP has a duty not to interfere with the State's obligations to natural persons. However, this approach fails to account for the interstate nature of ICP behavior; it may fulfill its obligations in one State in ways that indirectly harm the public of another (a). Another common means of addressing corporate responsibilities is through liability mechanisms between and amongst corporate groups and networks. However, an effective international liability scheme on this front would require an international system that allowed direct civil liability for corporate actors; that is, traditional liability structures that require passage through the State, such veil piercing and domestic tort law, might need to be bypassed for effective enforcement of ICP responsibilities under international law (b). Finally, a means through which corporate responsibilities might be addressed through international law is through the concept of personhood itself. Personhood should be granted equally to all entities with a stake in law. Because international law is unabashedly anthropocentric, it does not typically accord standing to nature, to animals, or to the environment. Standing belongs to humans or legal persons who can show legal harm and a court's ability to redress. Indeed, the international legal texts that address the environment tend to assume that nature is the property of humanity, but not the property of any individual or distinct group, and that each State has a separate environment. These texts chronically link environmental issues to economic interests. The final remarks in this subsection will explore how the ICP might fit into and possibly tilt this state of affairs in favor of stakeholders rather than shareholders (c).

a. Duties: civil and criminal

There are many justifications that scholars have offered to advance the attribution of corporate legal duties to the public, global and domestic.[154] I want to suggest that five of these apply to virtually all ICPs. These are (1) the relative power of ICPs vis-à-vis other domestic and international actors, (2) the role of ICPs as both domestic and international rule-makers, (3) the ability of ICPs to exploit differences in domestic legal regimes as international actors, (4) so-called 'externalities' of ICP activity that negatively affect various publics, and (5) the ability of ICPs to sue various publics as represented through States.[155]

These justifications suggest several different possible duties that ICPs could incur internationally. Some of the justifications indicate that criminal law should attach to ICPs in order to ensure power is not abused and international norms are geared toward mutual advantage.[156] Other justifications indicate tort law duties should attach internationally, but as we have seen, the traditional veil piercing approach is ineffective especially on the international stage and therefore more creative forms of liability should be explored.[157] Choudrey, Petrin, Miles, Jarrett, and many others have written elegant books on these themes; full references are available in the endnotes.[158] In the criminal law space, three highlights are worth mentioning: first, both criminal and tort liability can be justified in international courts for ICPs on numerous grounds. Second, criminal law has special procedural and substantive features that are particularly well-suited to the goals of transparency, norm-setting, and signaling functions, and, as such, it seems particularly well suited to serve as a vehicle for more radical international change. Finally, although corporations cannot be imprisoned, criminal sanctions are not limited to jail time; they can take the form of fines, garnishes, or other economic sanctions. Criminal sanctions are about restrictions on the freedoms enjoyed by other 'persons' similarly situated. Thus, for these reasons amongst others, criminal liability for corporations is not simply a replication of civil liability; it is a theoretically sound mode of liability for ICPs.

In tort law, direct liability for ICPs can only be attributed to a legal entity if a higher-ranking corporate agent – an 'organ', 'managing agent', or 'directing mind' – has a committed a tort. However, as Choudrey and Petrin have noted in a recent book,[159] tort law provides an inroad through 'vicarious liability' that is not available in criminal law and not properly utilized on the international stage. Vicarious liability is the doctrine through which torts committed by an entity's lower-ranking employees can be attributed to the organization as a whole. Nevertheless, for a variety of reasons already covered, systemic torts or environmental torts are difficult to attribute to single individuals and difficult to claim vicariously against an ICP. One way in which international lawyers could reimagine vicarious liability is, therefore, a sort of aggregate effect vicarious liability. That is, vicarious liability incurred through the aggregate effect of the actions of many lower-level employees that the corporation knew or should have known would, in the aggregate, result in harm to the public.

Both forms of liability – criminal and tort – suffer from the anthropocentric approach to corporate liability and international law more generally: liability attaches to and duties are held against persons, natural and legal. *Mens rea* requirements or requirements of reasonable foreseeability attach to individual minds, often precluding an inference of liability from a result of corporate action. These are problems that may well require new trajectories in law that reimagine individual and corporate activity as small parts of a much larger ecosystem – perhaps one that moves beyond the limitations imposed by State-based conceptions of property. Suggestions along these lines will be put forward in the next chapter.

A form of international legal liability that does not fit neatly into tort or criminal law is that which unfolds under international investment law. As we have seen, IIL creates the possibility for States to be sued by ICPs for engaging in behavior that causes harm to an ICP's investment, but States cannot initiate a claim against an ICP on an international stage if the ICP engages in behavior that harms a State's international economic interests through the ICP's investment. If the State wants to sue the ICP, it is predominantly limited to domestic venues. The one exception to this is the rare situation in which an ICP sues a State and the Agreement on which the suit is based allows the State to bring a counterclaim against the ICP.[160] Some of these cases are detailed in previous chapters; none of them have been successful on the international stage. Nevertheless, the point is worth raising here because the IIL status quo has led many international lawyers with a variety of ideological bents to call for duties to be imposed directly on ICPs to correspond with the rights they receive through most international investment agreements: access to international arbitration, the ability to choose at least one arbitrator, a legal inroad to apply international rather than domestic legal standards, and so on. When a State loses in international arbitration, it is often a vast sum that is lost, and, unlike a losing ICP which will often lose only the costs of the arbitration itself, a losing State's costs are borne solely by the public. Meanwhile, losing ICPs have the option of undercapitalizing the liable subsidiary and shielding the parent from liability behind the corporate veil. So far, the only corresponding duties on investors recognized in IIL have been those attaching to the State via *jus cogens* norms. As noted in Chapter 2 and as a colleague and I have noted elsewhere,[161] this trend may shift if more tribunals rely on the concept of *erga omnes* rather than *jus cogens* as a source of duties owed to all individuals. Only time will tell if this form of what some might call 'humanity law' will manifest,[162] but the legal possibility has already converted into a potentiality.

b. The amorphous liability of corporate groups and networks

Another avenue through which ICP responsibilities might take form is through clearer liability structures for corporate groups and networks (see definitions and distinctions in Chapter 1). Group and Network liability is a tricky and largely undertheorized topic, but Christian A. Witting has written a particularly illuminating book on this.[163] Professor Witting identifies the important elements of a Group as follows: (1) a Group is comprised of two or more persons (2) collectively undertaking tasks in a coordinated manner, that is, not two or more persons simply acting in parallel, (3) with a common purpose and (4) a commitment to the group. The final two elements here – 'common purpose' and 'commitment' – are cause for some debate. Some scholars believe it is not necessary that any individual member act toward or even have knowledge of the purpose of a Group so long as each individual is engaged in a coordinated effort toward a given task. Others believe that commitment to the Group should supplant the 'common purpose' element. Doctrinally speaking, common purpose is more closely aligned to theories of enterprise liability found in international criminal law, whereas theories that focus on individual commitment to the Group or intent to coordinate are more closely aligned with common law tort theories of liability.[164] To make room for both of these views in a theory of the Group, individual persons within a Group should have sufficient overlap in commitment or purpose with respect to the activities of the Group as a whole.

Membership in a Group brings with it a pressure to conform to the purposes of the Group. Professor Witting observes that expectations of conformity within Groups combined with individual choices to join Groups give standing to each member of a Group to reproach others. In effect, the Group extinguishes individual autonomy. Indeed, as List and Pettit wrote in their influential work on Group Agency:

> In domains where relevant obligations rule, the parties can address claims to others; expect others to comply; and inn case of non-compliance, have a complaint others must endorse, on pain of having to reject the conventions. And in such domains, parties must acknowledge that others occupy a reciprocal status: they too may address claims, expect compliance, and make compelling complaints about failures.[165]

These observations supplant the notion that a Group can be jointly liable for the individual actions of its members so long as the individual members are acting in their role within the Group. It cuts against the notion that liability for a breach of duty by some member should not extend to other parts of the Group. In articulating a theory of the Corporate Group, Witting first notes that Organizations feature all the attributes of a Group, but add to them hierarchy, structure, and a formalized decision-making process. Witting then offers five elements for a theory which I will summarized as follows: (1) the Corporate Group is characterized by structure, and this structure can be manipulated to serve the ends of the ultimate parent company. For example, subsidiaries can be established and dissolved in various jurisdictions, and assets and liabilities can be reorganized amongst them. (2) The Corporate Group is characterized by downward decision-making; subsidiaries are expected to conform to the interests of the Group as defined by its 'head'. (3) The Corporate Group is characterized by coordination, whether organized in a top-down manner, or whether managerial functions are 'outsourced' to the parent company acting as an 'agent' on behalf of the subsidiary. (4) The Corporate Group is characterized by economic unity. Economic unity is distinct from economic interdependence in that it is not necessary for each member of a Corporate Group to succeed economically so long as it serves the economic interests of the Group as a whole. As Witting puts it, 'While the strategic decision-making direction is downward, profits move upwards'.[166] (5) The Corporate Group is characterized by a common group identity. This could take the form of common color schemes and logos, but common identity need not manifest in aesthetics. I want to suggest that a subjective criteria is most useful to determine common identity. Rather asking about internal branding or policies, one should ask whether it is difficult for outside observers to appreciate the legal distinction between a subsidiary and its parent.

Members of Corporate Networks do not feature the same degree of collapsed individual autonomy. While it is true that members may form interdependent relationships, they do not act with the economic unity that is characteristic of Groups. Networks have weaker ties between companies, and each participant in a Network is loyal to its own 'home' company. Indeed, disputes frequently arise between members of Networks over contracts and pricing. The underlying tensions resulting from divergent economic interests prevent Networks from developing the sort of Group Individual – a concept that would be essential for direct parent liability.

From the previous discussion, it should be clear that some aspects of Corporate Groups invite direct enterprise liability, but the problem is most Corporate Groups avoid the outward appearances of Witting's five factors listed earlier. Indeed, a glance through the promotional webpages of many a corporate law firm's international advisory practice group will reveal articles and commentaries cautioning actors against exhibiting Witting's features and providing tips on how to structure group control in a way that would remain legally ambiguous in court.

c. Hume and Hohfeld

Drawing from the classic 'Bundle Theory' made famous by David Hume and a more recent Hohfeldian theory of personhood set out by Visa AJ Kurki,[167] I want to suggest that ICP obligations under international law flow primarily from 'passive' subjectivity to international law. The Hohfeldian analysis of law is rather mathematical: legal concepts can be defined by opposites and correlatives. Opposites follow the formulation, 'Where there is X there is no Y', whereas correlatives follow the formulation, 'Where there is an X, there is also a Y'. For Hohfeld, rights could not exist without duties, only privileges could exist without duties; rights and duties were correlatives whereas privileges and duties were opposites. Kurki divides rights into 'active' and 'passive' categories, each corresponding to different types of duties. Active rights are those that require some degree of volition, some sort of *mens rea*; passive rights are those to which one merely has access. This corresponds to passive and active concepts of subjectivity to law. For example, where passive subjectivity describes an entity's capacity to be a tortfeasor, active subjectivity describes an entity's capacity to choose to commit a tort or sue another for committing a tort.

Hume's relevant assertion was that a thing consists of its properties, nothing more. For example, where Plato's famous cave shadows were mere representations of a 'thing in itself', figures that both resembled and obscured the object casting its shadow, Hume would argue that the shadow was the thing, one could recognize it as a shadow because it had the properties of being dark, extending from a blockage to light, physical detachment from the surfaces upon which it is cast, and so on. Bundle Theory has long been considered a useful way to think about property law because it explains how all the properties of a thing can have different sets of rights attached to them. Thus, I can 'own' a tract of land without owning the minerals below it or the sky above it. The section that follows suggests that this is also a useful way to think about ICPs.

V. Toward a theory of the ICP

The central goal of theorizing the ICP is to determine whether and how the passive/active nature of the 'rights' that define the ICP's 'bundle' square them off with correlative duties under international law. We should again distinguish between 'duties' and 'responsibilities'. The former denotes hard legal obligations, and the latter describes legal as well as moral and social obligations. Most commentators seem to think ICPs should have some direct duties under international law, and those that do not (apart from the corporations themselves) have based their assessment on a traditional conception of the corporation in international law that is para-institutionalist and proxy-based (see Chapter 1). For example, the Guiding Principles also understand ICPs in this way: the Principles assume that direct subjectivity to international law cannot attach to corporations but must rather travel through States or be based on a conception that States can create liability in the future. However, as we have now seen, the past decade has brought judge-made law and international agreements that resist a clean, rigid understanding of the corporation's place in international law. Moreover, the emergence of the ICP marks an uneasy fit with the clear-cut doctrines that govern the corporate form in domestic law. It is not cleanly private or public; it is not cleanly domestic or transnational; it can dodge obligations imposed by States and can continue to exist internationally even where domestic law ceases to animate it; it can penetrate a sovereign State and can do so on behalf of shareholders who have never set foot in that State; it is a constituent to international law composed of constituents to capital; it is an agent composed of agents, a person composed of persons. In sum, the ICP is not cleanly analogous to anything.

I want to suggest that the lack of a coherent ICP theory flows partly from a misplaced reliance on analogical reasoning. The ICP cannot be understood with reference to sets of legal doctrines substantiating the State or the individual's role in international law. Framing ICPs analogically unnecessarily forecloses possibilities for what the international corporate form could become, indeed should become. A better starting point might be to first distinguish between those rights and privileges that animate the ICP: Limited liability, the right to commit to cross border contracts, the right to sue sovereigns for expropriation or lobby them for tariff reductions, the right to speak and to participate in politics, and so on. From there, one can see that the ICP is not animated by any single family of rights but by a 'bundle' of rights, and one can classify these into the two broad categories Visa Kurki described: passive rights and active rights.[168] The former category highlights the ICP's capacity as a 'legal platform' to which legal possibilities can be assigned; the latter category highlights the ICP's capacity as an agent, actively exercising rights to pursue interests. Finally, bearing in mind the different implications saddled with each category, one can understand the ICP's relation to its rights and corresponding obligations as responses to human problems – clashes of legitimate interest calling for legal (non-violent) solutions – and one can reach for solutions in bodies of law that fit the problems. Let us now apply Jessup's human focus to the concepts to passive and active ICP rights.

What are the bodies of law that are best suited to ascribe correlative duties to the ICP's passive rights (e.g., ability to be a tortfeasor, access to arbitral tribunals, etc.)? I want to suggest that the corporate law surrounding fiduciary duties best fits passive rights because passive rights and fiduciary duties exist in a default, no-conflict state. They both facilitate a sort of 'best practices' approach to ICP behavior toward various international publics (not to be confused with the 'global public'). Here's why: first, passive rights are rights that arise as a property of the fact of being a corporation. For example, because an organization cannot be a corporation unless it has limited liability, a corporation has the right to shield itself from liability by the nature of its very existence. The concession theory of the corporation applies most readily to this part of the ICP's personhood: limited liability is a right ascribed by the State, created at the same time as it legislates corporations into existence. The State's public will bear the costs of that liability when a domestic corporation defaults, so the duty is owed to the State's public. The only way to consistently apply that ideal to the ICP is to acknowledge that, when an ICP holds itself out to an international public, it gains a correlative duty to that international public. This includes not only the publics in which it operates but all publics whose domestic laws allow for its operations to persist. The correlative duty is rooted in the enabling function of domestic law and owed to the domestic public of any enabling State.

Second, fiduciary duties are most appropriate for a generalized duty to the public because in corporate law they flow from a corporation's management to its directors and shareholders on the basis of a trust relationship similar to that owed by a State to its citizens in a functional democracy.[169] This is not to draw an analogy between the State and the corporation but rather to extend duties to the ICP from those accrued through a State's responsibility to its citizens. For example, a State has a generalized duty to the public to provide access to drinking water, and when it contracts an ICP to provide that service, the ICP's fiduciary duties to stakeholders should absorb the State's duty to provide drinking water insofar as the State acts on the basis of public trust in good faith.

Finally, a general fiduciary duty to the public is correlative with the ICP's passive rights because passive rights do not require any agency on the part of the ICP. 'Private' fiduciary duties to the public also impose negative obligations on the ICP; for example, just as managers have a duty not to use material non-public information for personal enrichment at the expense of shareholders, ICPs as collective persons should have a duty not to use proprietary knowledge in ways that harm the publics of States the information affects. On a more general level, the ICP has continuous passive access to rights in international law granted to it by the State, and this continuous access should require continuous transparency, taxation based on access to public benefits rather than artificial territorial boundaries, and registration of all economic activity including capital gleaned from and transported throughout the territories in which it has interests.

What are the bodies of law that are best suited to ascribe correlative duties to the ICP's active rights (e.g., agency to pursue sustainable production, ability to select clients and sue specific individuals or States, etc.)? I want to suggest that international criminal law is best suited to assign duties and liabilities for breaches involving corporate agency because it has established legal doctrines that deduce para–*mens rea* elements to accompany the volitional acts of enterprises. For example, where the ICP has a right to choose the clients with whom it does business, it has a duty to refrain from engaging with certain clients if it has knowledge that those clients will, in the ordinary course of events, pursue a purpose that may amount to widespread and systematic attacks against civilian populations.

This passive-active categorization is not intended to set out an all-encompassing theory of the ICP. But it my hope that this, along with an emphasis on human problems as a starting point for the ascription of rights and duties, will provide a useful analytical framework for lawyers and policy makers concerned with reimagining the platform elements and agency elements within an international legal framework. The ultimate aim is to promote those elements of the ICP that promote human happiness on international and global levels while curtailing those elements that harm human happiness. Passive-platform rights can ground duties rooted in a fiduciary relationship: greater transparency, global taxation, and global wealth registry requirements, for example. Active-agency elements can ground duties arising from specific choices an ICP takes with respect to its operations in diverse locales: for example, human rights violations, political engagement environmental duties, and compulsory licensing for pharmaceutical patents to publics that cannot afford expensive but necessary drugs. Understanding the ICP's duties as correlative to different rights in the bundle that comprise its personhood could facilitate legal responses that complement the amorphous nature of the ICP. It would respond to the need for a dynamic approach that resists one-size-fits-all understandings of ICP obligations to international law at the same time as it retains the flexibility necessary to curtail ever-shifting opportunities for international legal exploitation. Keeping the focal point for ICP legal analysis on the resolution of human would also resist international law's tendencies to answer to non-human constituents, especially in the realm of international economic law.

VI. Changing gears: a summary thus far

Here I would like to offer a summary of the learnings from the first four chapters, since the next chapter switches gears from what *is* to what *could be* through a discussion of legal trends that are pushing the boundaries of the ICP in new directions. Framing the unique legal structures animating the ICP as 'features' rather than 'rights', the contours of the ICP summarized in the previous chapter can be categorized as follows:

Table 4.1

Passive Claim Features – The ICP as a Platform	*Active Substantive Features – The ICP as an Agent*
The ability to assert substantive rights under international law independent of those rights authorized by the State	The ability to decide for itself whether or not it is subject to international law – for example, through the (re)structuring of 'control' – in accordance with the ICJ standard
The capacity to violate international law independent from the State	A negative duty to uphold human rights but often a positive right to claim them
The ability to assert both the State's sovereignty and its own corporate veil as shields against liability, and the ability to define the reach of both sovereignty and the veil under certain circumstances	The right to enforce a law in a jurisdiction not bound by that law but bound by a contract to honor that law
The ability to access courts of 'fourth instance', that is, to 'appeal' decisions from supreme domestic courts or petition for *de novo* review	The ability to decide upon procedural remedies for violations of its international responsibilities with respect to human rights
The ability to claim a legally prescribed *mens rea* with respect to its actions rather than to expose itself to inquiries into actual *mens rea*	The ability to extend jurisdiction beyond the State in which the controversy in question arose
An exemption from State requirements to criminalize the corrupt acts of 'individuals'	The ability to select the level of law and enforcement for a violation of an international obligation, that is, domestic, regional, international, or some combination
The benefit of assigning responsibility for deliberate, cumulative environmental behavior to States and their ability to regulate and enforce restrictions	The ability to create 'internal' markets and to limit the access of or exclude non-ICP actors

Passive Claim Features – The ICP as a Platform	*Active Substantive Features – The ICP as an Agent*
Access to the benefits of legal reasoning and inertias of belief that favor corporate expansion through various concepts of development	The ability to choose and simultaneously hold multiple citizenships and to thereby play the advantages of multiple domestic systems of its choosing against one another to the benefit of the ICP
Separation of ownership from actions	The ability to purchase exemptions from international prosecution for corruption
The ability to be both SOE and ICP – to simultaneously be both a public and a private entity	The ability to move capital and commodities freely across jurisdictions even as labor is immobile
	An inflated ability to write and sustain the rules to which it is subject in relation to State governments, publics, capital, equity, humanity, and so much more
	The ability to avoid fiscal liability through (re)structuring and undercapitalization

The ICP's 'features', though non-exhaustive, show that it is not simply a platform but an active agent in the production of international law. This framework gives weight to the notion that top-down regulation is desirable in the sense that ICPs should be regulated by a community representative of its agency rather than by the patchwork bottom-up regulation that emerges from the cumulative actions of independent domestic systems. Whether top-down or bottom-up, whether a monistic or dualistic theory of law holds sway, whether the international system is stymied by the primacy of the State or the primacy of global governance institutions, or whether we are mired in the primacy of humanity over the primacy of ecosystem – the point remains that we have the power to change law, to remake it, to defy it and to redefine it. As Hans Kelsen put it in his *General Theory of Law and the State*:

> [I]f [we assume that] only a just order is called law, a social order which is presented as law is – at the same time – presented as just; and that means [we assume that] it is morally justified. The tendency to identify law and justice is the tendency to justify a given social order. It is a political, not a scientific tendency.[170]

Accepting that the international system cannot *inter alia* regulate tax havens, stymie the use of subsidiaries or trusts to avoid taxes and dodge liability, undertake a redistributive economic role amongst States, or impose a global corporate tax is to treat law as if it is 'given' – as if it is impossible for it to realize a role or function that primarily serves the interests of its creators rather than its creations. Treating law in this way forecloses possibilities that could become potentialities, likelihoods, and actualities and fails to conceptualize international law as fundamentally in service to human beings – a collection of doctrines and institutions geared toward the peaceful resolution of disputes and the facilitation of greater justice for all. What kind of order can facilitate justice? In a previous section, I alluded to Kelsen's famous answer to that question: '[A just] order regulates the behavior of [humans] in a way that is satisfactory to all [humans], that is to say, so that all [humans] find their happiness. It is happiness that [humans] cannot find as isolated individual[s] and hence see[k] in society. Justice is social happiness'.[171]

Taking Kelsen's cue, the next chapter departs from theory to focus on an analysis of *what is* and *what could be* in light of what is. It emphasizes that, unlike natural and other legal persons, the ICP is both bodyless and political. The ICP's bodylessness does not preclude it from utilizing rights ordinarily attached to bodies. In this way and many others, the legal reality of ICPs and MNEs more generally does not match their economic, social, or political reality. The question becomes, as Kelsen might put it, how can law facilitate greater social happiness utilizing the systems that are both animator of and habitat to the ICP?

Notes

1 See e.g., OECD Industry Newsletter: Multinational Enterprises in the Global Economy: Heavily Debated but Hardly Measured (May 2018).
2 Jose Alvarez, 'Beware: Boundary Crossings' – A Critical Appraisal of Public Law Approaches to International Investment Law, *Journal of World Investment & Trade* (2016).
3 *Id.*
4 United Nations, Vienna Convention on the Law of Treaties, 23 May 1969, United Nations, Treaty Series, vol. 1155.
5 *Id.*
6 Henry Hansmann & Reinier Kraakman, The End of History for Corporate Law, Olin Center for Law, Economics, and Business, Discussion Paper No. 280 (2000); Franklin A. Gevurtz, The Globalization of Corporate Law: The End of History or a Never-Ending Story?, *Washington L. Rev.* (2011).
7 Statute of the International Court of Justice, 33 UNTS 993, art. 38.
8 In 1920 Elihu Root, one of the presiding jurists at the Second Hague Conference, speaking on the authority of a handful of European countries to lay down 'universal' declarations, resolved the problem as such: '[W]e here come from but a few countries. We cannot come from more than ten if there are only ten of us. But let us see that the people of other countries from which no citizen sits here understand that we are going to consider in our work not only the feelings of the people of the countries from which we come, but the feelings and the opinions of the people of all countries. Let us lay down in some such declaration as this a broad foundation of unanimous international consideration of international subjects'. Elihu Root, The Constitution of the International Court of Justice, 15 *Am. J. Int'l L.* 1–12 (1921). That same year, concerned by the suggestion that the ICJ follow 'the principle of equality', he actively sought to keep 'all those backward nations [which] would have a vote' from having equal say in what 'justice' would look like at the ICJ. Advisory Committee of Jurists, *Procès-Verbaux of the Proceedings of the Committee, June 16th – July 24th, 1920 with Annexes at 6* (1920). Nevertheless, today, the former U.S. Secretary of State's portrait hangs in Harvard Law School and he is endowed with revered 'founding father' status by many international lawyers.

9 For an intro to this literature, see Antony Anghie, *Imperialism, Sovereignty and the Making of International Law* (2005); José-Manuel Barreto (Ed.), *Human Rights from a Third World Perspective: Critique, History and International Law* (2015); Sundhya Pahuja, *Decolonizing International Law: Development, Economic Growth and the Politics of Universality* (2013); Balakrishnan Rajagopal, *International Law from Below: Development, Social Movements and Third World Resistance* (2020).

10 There is a lengthier discussion on this in Chapter 1, and references in Chapters 2 and 3.

11 *Id.* There is also a list of specific legal actions available only to the ICP at the end of this chapter.

12 See e.g., UN Dep't of Political and Peacebuilding Affairs, Elections, available at https://dppa.un.org/en/elections (accessed 20 May 2020).

13 See UN Rules of Procedures for the Economic and Social Council, E/5715/Rev.2 (1992).

14 There are at least preventative measures against this type of lobbying activity in most States, though shadow companies and ICPs themselves often blur the lines between the public and the private when it comes to foreign influence on elections.

15 See e.g., Frank R. Baumgartner et al, *Lobbying and Policy Change: Who Wins, Who Loses, and Why* (2009).

16 E.g., trusts or shell companies opened in offshores under one name that wholly own subsidiaries in other jurisdictions to which they can transfer washed funds.

17 Gregory Keating, Is Tort Law Private?, in J Oberdiek & P Miller (Eds.), *Civil Wrongs and Justice in Private Law* (2019); see also generally Doreen Lustig, *Veiled Power: International Law and the Private Corporation, 1886–1981* (2020).

18 Philip Jessup, *Transnational Law* (1956).

19 *Id.*

20 *Id.*

21 *Id.*

22 *Id.*

23 For an overview of the historical corporate personality debate, see Alfred F. Conard, *Corporations in Perspective* (1976), 417–45. Some examples of English-language treatises of corporate personality are Ernst Freund, *The Legal Nature of Corporations* (2000), originally published in 1897; John Dewey, The Historic Background of Corporate Legal Personality, *Yale Law Journal* (1926); Arthur W. Machen, Corporate Personality, *Harvard Law Review* (1911); and Frederick Hallis, *Corporate Personality: A Study in Jurisprudence* (1930). Karl Olivecrona, *Studier över begreppet juridisk person i romersk och modern rätt* (1928).

24 Eric W. Orts, *Business Persons: A Legal Theory of the Firm* (2013).

25 Visa Kurki, *A Theory of Legal Personhood* (2019).

26 The connection between political philosophy and corporate theory is apparent in the title of Frederick Hallis's doctoral dissertation: Frederick Hallis, An examination of some modern theories of the relation of law and state with special reference to the juristic doctrine of corporate personality: a study in jurisprudence (D.Phil. thesis, University of Oxford, 1927).

27 *Trustees of Dartmouth College v. Woodward,* 17 US 518 (1819).

28 Eric W. Orts, *Business Persons: A Legal Theory of the Firm* (2013).

29 See Chapter 2.

30 Visa Kurki, *A Theory of Legal Personhood* (2019).

31 The term 'benefit' here refers strictly to the right. There can of course be psychological benefits and indirect monetary benefits for the guardian.

32 This assumes the guardian was unaware of the infant's willful act and there was no prior training of the infant to engage in this behavior on the part of the guardian.

33 Hans Kelsen, *General Theory of Law and State* (1949). The English translation first appeared in 1945, but the original unpublished German version was likely from the 1930s.

34 Societies in known history have based constituency on factors ranging from territory to race to profession; they can be more or less formal, assembled for general or specific purposes, voluntary or involuntary, and express interest through a variety of channels. But most definitions coalesce around the idea that there is some shared interest amongst members.

35 Andrew Rehfeld, in the context of the United States and its institutions, has undertaken this project far more brilliantly and thoroughly than I can hope to do here, but I do hope to draw on some of his observations in the context of ICPs in international law. For the U.S. context, see Andrew Rehfeld, *The Concept of Constituency: Political Representation, Democratic Legitimacy, and Institutional Design* (CUP 2005).

36 E.g., a U.S. citizen who is a black woman in rural Mississippi is more likely to be struck by lightning than to serve in Congress; this is not the case for a U.S. citizen who is a white man in urban Jackson, Mississippi. See *id.*

37 This is the case in most European and other parliamentary democracies.

38 For thinking along these lines, see e.g., Benjamin Barber, *Strong Democracy: Participatory Politics for a New Age* (Berkeley 1984); John Burnheim, *Is Democracy Possible?* (UCLA 1985); Jean-Jacques Rousseau, *On the Social Contract* (first published 1762); Iris Marion Young, *Justice and the Politics of Difference* (Princeton 1990).

39 For thinking along these lines, see Francois Guizot, *The History of the Origins of Representative Government in Europe* (2002); James Harrington, *The Commonwealth of Oceana* (first published 1656); David Hume, Idea of a Perfect Commonwealth; James Madison, *The Federalist* No. 10; John Stuart Mill, *Considerations on Representative Government* (first published in 1861); Iris Marion Young, *Inclusion and Democracy* (OUP 2000).

40 Andrew Rehfeld, *The Concept of Constituency: Political Representation, Democratic Legitimacy, and Institutional Design* (CUP 2005).

41 *Id.*

42 E.g., classically, Richard Steinberg, *In the Shadow of Law or Power, International Organization* (2002).

43 Jessup cleverly noted that the international judge's resort to 'the general principles of law' is not fundamentally different from the frequent U.S. domestic judge's appeal to 'wisdom of the founding fathers' or the 'spirit of the constitution' or the 'rule of reason'. *Transnational Law at 96* (1956).

44 Harrington had an agrarian view of land ownership: an owner ought to be limited by the amount of value land could produce, not the amount of land. Neoliberal economists would likely suggest that markets accomplish the same effect as the quantity of land is less important than its use-value. But such concepts are temporally restricted; we need not limit ourselves in the present to adopting only Agrarian valuation on land. We could place limits on individual ownership with respect to use-value, which shifts over time. See James Harrington, *The Commonwealth of Oceana* (originally published 1656).

45 James Madison, *Federalist* No. 10 (originally published 1787).

46 See e.g., Aurelian Craiutu, *Guizot's Elitist Theory of Representative Government, Critical Review* (2003).

47 See John Stuart Mill, *Considerations on Representative Government* (first published in 1861).

48 For a deterministic but nevertheless thorough and compelling intellectual history of this process, see Quinn Slobodian, *Globalists: The End of Empire and the Birth of Neoliberalism* (HUP 2018).

49 Friedrich Hayek, *The Constitution of Liberty* (Chicago 1960); see also generally Hayek's magnum opus in three volumes: *Law, Legislation, and Liberty, Vol. 1: Rules and Order* (Routledge 1973); *Law, Legislation, and Liberty, Vol. 2: The Mirage of Social Justice* (Routledge 1976); *Law, Legislation, and Liberty, Vol. 3: The Political Order of a Free People* (Routledge 1979).

50 See Section III.

51 For an inspiring take on Hayek's 'noble dream' and some reasons why it failed to come true ('it just did not happen that economic growth would lift all boats'), see Ingo Venzke, International Law and the Spectre of Inequality, Rede, in verkorte vorm uitgesproken bij de openbare aanvaarding van het ambt van hoogleraar International Law and Social Justice (16 May 2019).

52 I am certainly open to the possibility that all of these theories do not hold true, but in the absence of compelling argument otherwise, Hayek's assumption cuts against the bedrock principle that legal institutions must justify their authority at least periodically to those persons or entities governed by them. The observations I refer to here reference the current international economic system, which has not succeeded in attaining 'pure' markets even though it implemented the designs Hayek and his followers held dear. Instead, in many ways, it has entrenched many of the economic asymmetries established in the colonial era by legitimating such asymmetries as legally 'neutral'. For an argument along these lines, see e.g., John Linarelli, Margot Salomon, and M Sornorajah, *The Misery of International Law* (OUP 2018).

53 See Karen Alter, Laurence Helfer & Mikael Madsen, How Context Shapes the Authority of International Courts, iCourts Working Paper Series No. 18; 79 *Law & Contemporary Problems* 1 (2016); see also Cossette Creamer, Dilemmas of Delegation: The Politics of Authority in International Courts, Doctoral Dissertation, Harvard University, Graduate School of Arts & Sciences (2016), available at http://nrs.harvard.edu/urn-3:HUL.InstRepos:33493262 (accessed 6 March 2020).

54 Andrew Rehfeld, *The Concept of Constituency: Political Representation, Democratic Legitimacy, and Institutional Design* (CUP 2005).

55 For an overview of these 'generations', see e.g., Diane Desierto, *Public Policy in International Economic Law*, Ch. 4 (OUP 2015).

56 For an account of how this came to be so and why it need to be so in the future, see Kevin Crow, *International Corporate Personhood: New Trajectories in Law* (Routledge, forthcoming 2020–2021).

57 See e.g., Sandrine Kott, ILO: Social Justice in a Global World? A History in Tension, 11 *International Development Policy* 21–39 (2019).

58 These international agreements seek to reduce regulatory measures are analogous to what economists often consider 'distortions' in domestic markets: the SCM Agreement is concerned with subsidies and 'counter-veiling' measures, the TBT Agreement seeks to reduce technical barriers to international trade (such as differing testing or certification procedures), and the GATT seeks to eliminate tariffs (or taxes).

59 See IMF Factsheet, Special Drawing Right (SDR) (6 April 2016), available at www.imf.org/external/np/exr/facts/sdr.htm/ (accessed 6 March 2020).

60 The TRIPS Agreement requires WTO Members to adopt the IPC's conception of intellectual property and to criminalize intellectual property infringement, which means that States cannot 'negatively' distort the market by failing to enforce patent and copyright laws.

61 See Slobodian, *Globalists* (HUP 2018).

62 For a classic critique of Coase, see Mark Kelman, Consumption Theory, Production Theory, and Ideology in the Coase Theorem, 53 *S. Cal. L. Rev.* 1187 (1980).

63 Robert Howse, From Politics to Technocracy – and Back Again: The Fate of the Multilateral Trading Regime, 96 *AJIL* 105 (2002).

64 See e.g., Ernst-Ulrich Petersmann, The WTO Constitution and Human Rights, 3 *J. Int'l Econ. L.* 19 (2000).

65 See WTO, Understanding the WTO: Basics – The Case for Open Trade, available at www.wto.org/english/thewto_e/whatis_e/tif_e/fact3_e.htm (accessed 12 March 2020). In a section justifying the status quo to novices on the WTO's official website, a large section is devoted to comparative advantage: 'The theory dates back to classical economist David Ricardo. It is one of the most widely accepted among economists. It is also one

of the most misunderstood among non-economists because it is confused with absolute advantage. It is often claimed, for example, that some countries have no comparative advantage in anything'. Without thinking much more about it for him- or herself, the anonymous author simply ends the section like this: 'That is virtually impossible. Think about it'. *Id.*

66 See Christian Tietje, in Tietje (Ed.), Internationales Wirtschaftsrecht, § 3, 158–236, para. 11. Professor Tietje points out that, although the Ricardian approach has many critics, for mainstream economic law scholarship and teaching it remains the most convincing rationale for many, especially international trade practitioners.

67 Even binding instruments with special courts such as the ECtHR or the IACtHR have jurisdiction only to review state compliance with the instruments they adjudicate.

68 This point was popularized by Thomas Piketty, *Capital in the Twenty-First Century* (HUP 2013).

69 This is in some way the essentially the aim of both international trade and investment regimes, as well as the way organizations such as the OECD approach multinational corporations, transfer pricing, tax havens, corruption, and other issues through international instruments.

70 Ingo Venzke, International Law and the Spectre of Inequality, Rede, pg. 7, in verkorte vorm uitgesproken bij de openbare aanvaarding van het ambt van hoogleraar International Law and Social Justice (16 May 2019). Venzke illustrates point with reference to a joint report produced by the International Monetary Fund, the World Bank, and the World Trade Organization in which the international monetary behemoths claim credit for increasing per capita global production at the same time as they place responsibility for 'those left behind' on 'countries' that implement the 'right policies'. See IMF, WB, WTO Report, Making Trade an Engine of Growth for All: The Case for Trade and for Policies to Facilitate Adjustment (2017), available at www.wto.org/english/news_e/news17_e/wto_imf_report_07042017.pdf (accessed 10 March 2020).

71 Roberto Unger, *What Should Legal Analysis Become?*, 38 (Verso 1996).

72 The WTO's legal instruments are shot through with examples of this: The Preamble of the Agreement on Trade in Civil Aircraft desires 'to provide fair and equal competitive opportunities for their civil aircraft activities and for their producers to participate in the expansion of the world civil aircraft market'. See Agreement on Trade in Civil Aircraft, Preamble, para. 4. The Preamble of the Agreement on Agriculture aims at 'correcting and preventing restrictions and distortions in world agricultural markets'. Agreement on Agriculture, Preamble, para. 3. And according to Art. 6.3(d) of the SCM Agreement, 'serious prejudice' may arise, inter alia, if 'the effect of the subsidy is an increase in the world market share of the subsidizing Member in a particular subsidized primary product or commodity'.

73 See Kevin Crow, Bandung's Fate, in Ingo Venzke and Kevin Jon Heller (Eds.), *Contingency in the Course of International Law* (2020). See also Kevin Crow, Acceptance: *International Law in Post-Colonial Asia*, 1955–1995 (book forthcoming in late 2022).

74 See George Orwell, *Animal Farm* (1945). Orwell, always a master of double-speak, tells the tale of a government controlled by pigs who proclaim that 'all animals are equal, but some animals are more equal than others'.

75 See e.g., the chapter on SOEs in the now-defunct TPP and its reincarnation in the CPTPP.

76 For 2013 data, see UNCTAD, *World Investment Report: 2013*, ch. IV, "Global Value Chains: Investment and Trade for Development" (2014).

77 Id. See also e.g., Alessandro Nicita et al, Global Supply Chains: Trade and Economic Policies for Developing Countries, UNCTAD, *Policy Issues in International Trade and Commodities*, Study Series No. 55 (2013).

78 Charan Devereaux et al, TRIPS Part II: International Trade Meets Public Health: TRIPS and Access to Medicines, Harvard Kennedy School Case Study, HKS482-PDF-ENG (2008).

79 See Andrew Charlton, In Brief . . . The Collapse of the Doha Round, LSE Centre for Economic Performance, *CentrePiece* (Autumn 2006); see more recently WTO News, DG Azevêdo's address to the MC10 closing ceremony (19 Dec 2015), available at www.wto.org/english/news_e/spra_e/spra108_e.htm (accessed 6 March 2020).
80 E.g., WTO, US – Gambling, AB Report, DS285 (2005); WTO, EC – Energy Sector, Panel Report, DS476 (2014) (on appeal at AB); see also most SCM Agreement cases.
81 E.g., WTO, EC – Bananas III, AB Report, DS27 (1997); WTO, Korea – Beef, AB Report, DS161 (2000), WTO, US – Tuna II, AB Report, DS381 (2002).
82 See e.g., the WTO's 1994 Government Procurement Agreement (GPA).
83 See e.g., WTO, EC – Large Civil Aircraft, AB Report, DS316 (2011); WTO, US – Large Civil Aircraft (2nd Complaint), AB Report, DS353 (2012).
84 See e.g., Robert Anderson et al, Competition Policy, Trade, and the Global Economy: Existing WTO Elements, Commitments in Regional Trade Agreements, Current Challenges and Issues for Reflection, WTO Staff Working Paper ERSD-2018–12 (2018).
85 Although there were other NIEO efforts, see primarily UN Resolution 1803 (XVII); UN Resolution S6/3201 (SVI), 'Declaration on the New International Economic Order'; UN Resolution 29/3281 (XXIX), 'Charter of Economic Rights and Duties of States'; UN Resolution 41/128, 'Declaration on the Right to Development'.
86 See Kevin Crow, Bandung's Fate, in Ingo Venzke and Kevin Jon Heller (Eds.), *Contingency in the Course of International Law* (forthcoming, OUP 2020). I also wrote about this extensively in my PhD thesis, which I will publish as a book in the coming years. See recently the U.S. Dep't of State's Statement on ASEAN Human Rights Declaration.
87 GA Resolution 1803 (XVII), 1962.
88 To borrow a phrase from Genesis 45:18, KJV: 'I will give you the good of the land of Egypt, and ye shall eat the fat of the land'.
89 See seminally Jeffrey Sachs and Andrew Warner, Natural Resource Abundance and Economic Growth, NBER Working Paper No. 5398 (1995).
90 Richard Auty, Economic Development and the Resource Curse Thesis, in Morrissey & Stewart (Eds.), *Economic and Political Reform in Developing Countries* (Palgrave Macmillan 1995).
91 Astrid Kjedlgaard-Pederson, *The International Legal Personality of the Individual* (2018), p. 17.
92 S.S. Lotus (Fr. v. Turk.), 1927 P.C.I.J. (ser. A) No. 10 (Sept. 7).
93 Geneva Conventions, art. 3; Optional Protocol II.
94 6th Edition, p. 64 (1974).
95 L Eslava & S Pahuja, The State and International Law: A Reading from the Global South, *Humanity Journal* (2020).
96 This can explain at least one phenomenon in international lawmaking: at the same time as they have the loudest voice and heaviest influence on the articulation of international law, the most powerful States have the least incentive to adhere to it.
97 See George Manner, The Object Theory of the Individual in International Law, *AJIL* (1952); see also enlighteningly Jessie Hohmann & Daniel Joyce (Eds.), *International Law's Objects* (2018).
98 See Danube Convention Regarding the Regime of Navigation on the Danube, available at www.danubecommission.org/uploads/doc/convention_orig_1948.pdf (accessed 1 June 2020).
99 E.g., Anne Lappé, Follow the Money to the Amazon, *The Atlantic* (4 Sept 2019).
100 See e.g., Russell Hardin, *Collective Action* (1982, original 1940).
101 See e.g., Stockholm and Rio Declaration discussion in Chapters 2 and 3.
102 This is a phrase economists use to refer to the process by which a State attracts foreign investment through the promise cheap labor thereby facilitating 'development', but when in turn 'development' creates new wants in the improved lives of wage laborers, including the want of higher wages, the foreign investment moves on to another cheap labor location, thereby increasing the supply of labor in the first location and thereby driving wages lower again. Rinse and repeat.

103 'The freedom to choose to exempt oneself from law' or 'he who decides the exception'. The first quote paraphrases Barkan, the second paraphrases Schmitt, both referenced in Chapter 1.
104 Mortin Horowitz, *The Transformation of American Law, 1780–1860* (1977).
105 See e.g., David Millon, Theories of the Corporation, *Duke Law Journal* (1990).
106 Milton Friedman, The Social Responsibility of Business is to Increase its Profits, *New York Times Magazine* (13 Sept 1970).
107 See e.g., R. Edward Freeman, *Strategic Management: A Stakeholder Approach* (1984).
108 See, for example, the nature examples in Chapter 5.
109 See generally the collection of articles in *ICSID Review, 30th Anniversary of the Review, Special Focus Issue: State Owned Enterprises*, Volume 31, Issue 1 (2016).
110 I have found no source prior to the early 1900s that explicitly offers this as the primary justification for limited corporate liability.
111 See e.g., Kenneth Pomeranz, *The Great Divergence: China, Europe, and the Making of the Modern World Economy* (2000).
112 Seminally, see Mortin Horwitz, *The Transformation of American Law* (1977).
113 William Blackstone, *Commentaries on the Laws of England* (1765). See also Mortin Horwitz, *The Transformation of American Law* (1977).
114 This process in the United States is well-documented in Adam Winkler, *We the Corporations: How American Businesses Won their Civil Rights* (2018).
115 See e.g., OECD Policy Roundtables, Competition Policy and Intellectual Property Rights, DAFFE/CLP(98)18 (1997).
116 See e.g., Claudine Gartenberg & George Serafeim, 181 Top CEOs Have Realized Companies Need a Purpose Beyond Profit, *Harvard Business Review* (20 August 2019).
117 Kevin Crow & Lina Lorenzoni Escobar, International Corporate Obligations, Human Rights, and the Urbaser Standard: Breaking New Ground?, *Boston University Int'l L J.* (2018).
118 E.g., Barnali Choudhury & Martin Petrin, *Corporate Duties to the Public* (2019); Markos Karavias, *Corporate Obligations under International Law* (2013).
119 See e.g., Deborah Elms & Patrick Low (Eds.), *Global Value Chains in a Changing World*, WTO / Fung Global Institute / Temasek Foundation (2013).
120 A point nicely made by Ingo Venzke, 'International Law and the Spectre of Inequality' [2019] Inaugural Lecture No. 607, University of Amsterdam, available at http://cf.bc.uva.nl/download/oraties/oraties_2019/Venzke_Ingo.pdf (accessed 12 October 2019).
121 *Id.*
122 These are the subject of Chapter 5 of this book.
123 Taylor St. John, *The Rise of Investor-State Arbitration: Politics, Law, and Unintended Consequences,* (OUP 2020), 24.
124 He appears to base this assertion about investor preferences on a handful of ICCs from the 1960s and 1970s and fudges the line between aggregate firm interest and individual firm influence.
125 Taylor St. John, *The Rise of Investor-State Arbitration: Politics, Law, and Unintended Consequences* (2020).
126 *Id.*
127 *Id.* See also Werner Plumpe, Alexander Nützenadel & Catharine Schenk, *Deutsche Bank: The Global Hausbank, 1870–2020* (2020). This seminal account tracks the bank's 150-year history over the course of roughly 1,000 pages and leaves few previous secondary sources unexamined.
128 Werner Plumpe, Alexander Nützenadel & Catharine Schenk, *Deutsche Bank: The Global Hausbank, 1870–2020* (2020).
129 UNCTAD Investment Report (2013).
130 See generally the collection of articles in *ICSID Review, 30th Anniversary of the Review, Special Focus Issue: State Owned Enterprises*, Volume 31, Issue 1 (2016).

131 Council of the European Union, Document WK 8329/2018 INIT, Brussels (5 July 2018).
132 Ru Ding, Public Body or Not: Chinese State-Owned Enterprises, *Journal of World Trade* (2014).
133 For a good rant on the topic, see Marc Benitah, China's Industrial Subsidies, *International Economic Law and Policy Blog*, posted 18 May 2019, available at https://ielp.worldtradelaw.net/2019/05/chinas-industrial-subsidies-is-the-wtos-ab-jurisprudence-about-definition-of-a-public-body-an-instan.html (accessed 20 March 2020).
134 WTO, *US – Anti-Dumping and Countervailing Duties* (China), WT/DS379/12/Add.7 (2012); WT/DS449/15 (2014).
135 *Id.*
136 WTO, *US – Pipe and Tube Products* (Turkey), WT/DS523/7 (2019).
137 See e.g., Marc Benitah, China's Industrial Subsidies, International Economic Law and Policy Blog, posted 18 May 2019, available at https://ielp.worldtradelaw.net/2019/05/chinas-industrial-subsidies-is-the-wtos-ab-jurisprudence-about-definition-of-a-public-body-an-instan.html (accessed 20 March 2020).
138 See the discussion on 'Human Problems' earlier in this chapter. See also Philip Jessup, *Transnational Law* (1956).
139 Gregory Keating, Is Tort Law Private? In J Oberdiek & P Miller (Eds.), *Civil Wrongs and Justice in Private Law* (2019).
140 *Id.*
141 Sonia Rolland & David Trubek, *Emerging Powers in the International Economic Order: Cooperation, Competition and Transformation* (2019).
142 Lee Buchheit et al., The Dilemma of Odious Debts, 56 *Duke L. J.* 1201, 1248 (2007).
143 See Yaraslau Kryvoi, Piercing the Corporate Veil in International Arbitration, 1 *Global Business Law Review* 169 (2010).
144 The principles themselves are relatively homogenous, but when and how they are evoked is diverse. See e.g., Anthea Roberts, *Is International Law International?* (OUP 2017).
145 Convention on the Recognition and Enforcement of Foreign Arbitral Awards, June 10, 1958, 21 U.S.T. 2517, 330 U.N.T.S. 38 [New York Convention]; see also International Legal Framework, 1 *World Arb. Rep.* 1 (1994)
146 See e.g., David K. Millon, Piercing the Corporate Veil, Financial Responsibility, and the Limits of Limited Liability, 56 *Emory L. J.* 1305 (2007).
147 ICSID Convention, 575 U.N.T.S. 159 (1965), art. 25.
148 See OECD, *Transfer Pricing Guidelines for Multinational Enterprises and Tax Administrations 2010*, Chapter 1, The Arm's Length Principle (2010); OECD, *Risk Management and Corporate Governance* (2014); see also e.g., Deloitte, *A Roadmap to Accounting for Business Combinations* (2019).
149 Luis Eslava & Sundhya Pahuja, The State and International Law: A Reading From the Global South, *Humanity Journal* (Winter 2019).
150 E.g., Christian Tietje & Kevin Crow, The Reform of Investment Protection Rules in CETA, TTIP, and Other Recent EU-FTAs: Convincing?, in Stefan Griller, Walter Obwexer & Erich Vranes (Eds.), *Mega-Regional Agreements: TTIP, CETA, TiSA. New Orientations for EU External Economic Relations* (OUP 2017); Alessandra Arcuri, The Great Asymmetry and the Rule of Law in International Investment Arbitration, in Lisa Sachs et al (Eds.), *Yearbook on International Investment Law and Policy* (2019).
151 E.g., K Crow, International Law and Corporate Participation in Times of Armed Conflict, *Berkeley J. Int'l L.* (2019).
152 See e.g., Ludovica Chiussi, The Role of Internationnal Investment Law in the Business and Human Rights Process, *International Community L. Rev.* (2019).
153 *Al-Warraq v. Indonesia*, UNCITRAL Award (2014), available at www.italaw.com/sites/default/files/case-documents/italaw4164.pdf (accessed 2 June 2020).
154 E.g., Barnali Choudhury & Martin Petrin, *Corporate Duties to the Public* (2019); Markos Karavias, *Corporate Obligations Under International Law* (2013).

155 Christian Tietje & Kevin Crow, The Reform of Investment Protection Rules in CETA, TTIP, and Other Recent EU-FTAs: Convincing?, in Stefan Griller, Walter Obwexer & Erich Vranes (Eds.), *Mega-Regional Agreements: TTIP, CETA, TiSA. New Orientations for EU External Economic Relations* (OUP 2017).
156 See e.g., Harold Koh, Why Do Nations Obey International Law?, *Yale L. J.* (1996–1997).
157 See e.g., M Anderson, Human Rights Approaches to Environmental Protection, in Martin Dixon et al (Eds.), *Cases and Materials in International Law*, 4th ed. (2003).
158 Barnali Choudhury & Martin Petrin, *Corporate Duties to the Public* (2019); Kate Miles, *The Origins of International Investment Law: Empire, Environment and the Safeguarding of Capital* (2013); Martin Jarrett, *Contributory Fault and Investor Misconduct in Investment Arbitration* (2019).
159 Barnali Choudhury & Martin Petrin, *Corporate Duties to the Public* (2019).
160 See Christian Tietje & Kevin Crow, The Reform of Investment Protection Rules in CETA, TTIP, and Other Recent EU-FTAs: Convincing? in Stefan Griller, Walter Obwexer & Erich Vranes (Eds.), *Mega-Regional Agreements: TTIP, CETA, TiSA. New Orientations for EU External Economic Relations* (2017).
161 See Kevin Crow & Lina Lorenzoni-Escobar, From Traction to Treaty-Bound (working paper under revision, on file with author, forthcoming 2021).
162 Ruti G. Teitel, *Humanity's Law* (2011).
163 Christian A. Witting, *Liability of Corporate Groups and Networks* (2018).
164 *Id.*
165 Christian List & Philip Pettit, *Group Agency: The Possibility, Design, and Status of Corporate Agents* (2011).
166 Christian A. Witting, *Liability of Corporate Groups and Networks* (2018).
167 Visa A J Kurki, *A Theory of Corporate Personhood* (2020); see seminally Wesley Newcomb Hohfeld, *Fundamental Legal Conceptions as Applied in Judicial Reasoning and Other Legal Essays* (1919).
168 Visa A J Kurki, *A Theory of Corporate Personhood* (2020).
169 For a fuller discussion along these themes, see e.g., Evan J. Criddle, Fiduciary Principles in International Law, in Evan J. Criddle et al (Eds.), *The Oxford Handbook of Fiduciary Law* (2019); Evan J. Criddle & Evan Fox-Decent, *Fiduciaries of Humanity: How International Law Constitutes Authority* (2016).
170 Hans Kelsen, *General Theory of Law and the State* (1945).
171 *Id.*

Chapter 5

Political bodies and the bodyless

I. Political bodies and the bodyless

In many contexts, rights are understood as owed by the State to the body of a natural person or to the communicative and contract capacity between and amongst legal and natural persons. Just as some rights can only be attached to bodies – for example, the right to life – the ICP's bodylessness also creates a distinct class of legal rights. These rights are distinct from those accorded to ILPs more generally because they are not defined by any coherent political apparatus composed of natural persons. Thus, unlike natural and other legal persons, the ICP is both bodyless and political. The ICP's bodylessness also does not preclude it from utilizing those rights ordinarily attached to bodies – even those normatively rather than textually constructed – in accordance with the political interests of the ICP.[1] In this sense, a core element of the ICP's unique status within the broader category of MNEs is its capacity to act independently as a creator and shaper of law unattached to any particular polity, partially subject to many, but wholly subject to none. While a creature of inertia, it remains strikingly autonomous. This begs the question, what *should* ICPs become?

We have now seen that the ICP has at least three core features that distinguish it from other international legal personalities. The first is that its existence is not linked directly to any static political constituency; the second its ability not only develop internal private normative rules but also to enforce them across State boundaries; the third is its exclusive access to the passive and active rights identified in Chapters 3 and 4. Both persons and things can have passive rights, but only persons can have active ones. Not all MNEs are 'persons' in the sense that they can collectively choose to access international rights and remedies; the ICP describes the subcategory of MNEs that can do so. Through the fluidity of its legal form, it can retain alternatively or simultaneously elements of both personhood and thinghood.

The aim of this chapter is to focus to a greater degree on present forms and functions of the ICP and the possibilities they present – what *could* (or *should*) be? The chapter begins by exploring how GVCs render ICPs unlike any other subject of law in their capacity to make law applicable only to disjointed parts of the whole subject or 'person' (**II**). Justifications for ICP treatment are inconsistent with the treatment of 'things' that either have agency or have bodies but not both; trends in international courts show tensions in the concept of personhood as accorded to corporations and the dissolving lack thereof with respect to nature, animals, and AI (**III**). After Sections II and III challenge the linking of 'personhood' and 'thinghood' to the concept of agency, I explore how liability structures might more accurately reflect the legal reality of ICPs or MNEs more generally (**IV**). Finally, the chapter attempts to gather fresh ideas from a number of scholarly threads (old and new) that may be relevant for reform, while keeping in mind that the ICP can be (and sometimes is) reappropriated by natural humans as vehicles for positive change (**V**). Indeed, in many ways, ICPs are more flexible and more adaptive than traditional 'sovereigns' and other international legal personalities; some can mobilize a store of wealth and power that far outmatches many States. As such, ICPs may have the potential to address some of the world's greatest challenges most rapidly; definitions of purpose and attachment to narrow constituencies nevertheless tilt their interests toward capital accumulation and endless growth.

II. Persons as disjointed things

This section demonstrates that ICPs are unlike any other subject of law in their capacity to make law applicable only to disjointed parts of the whole subject or 'person'. This is the result of a pervasive cycle of disjointed State policy goals rather than a result of cohesive ICP regulation. Namely, foreign firms create internal 'law' that determines domestic firm behavior, State policy caters to export led growth thus increasing dependence upon foreign buyer firms, buyer firm multi-sourcing tactics increases competition amongst supplier firms thus decreasing their ability to redirect capital gains to the domestic market, and the power of the State to change this dynamic is undermined by the weakness of domestic policy when it comes to the needs of its exporting firms (**a**). While ICP use of CSR and investor use of ESG can put a 'human face' on the global economy, that face does not represents the multifaceted nature of a given ICP's actions (**b**).

a. The ICP and GVCs

Beyond 'external' legal systems both domestic and international, and beyond 'internal' systems of governance within firms are networks of value production that rely upon and link to law across jurisdictions and within firms. These systems, which I discussed briefly in Chapters 3 and 4, are often termed Global Value Chains. GVCs are not contained within single corporate groups or networks or within any unified system of governance,[2] yet they link to many of these.

Law is in some sense always operating within boundaries; GVCs can be thought of as channels linking many of law's discrete boundaries toward a business goal as internally defined by one of many ICPs or MNEs. Courts have jurisdiction over particular treaties or issues within particular geographic spaces, texts are subject to interpretation within the boundaries of 'legitimate' discursive space, justification must proceed from some premise or *Grundnorm*: for example, human dignity, economic efficiency, original textual intention, and so on. Whole fields of legal research are organized around other boundaries: for example, private and public, local and global, law and non-law, public regulation and private ordering, form and substance, rules and norms, firm and contract and firm and state, and so on.[3] As a locus of inquiry, GVCs traverse and transcend virtually all of these boundaries. In this way, they provide a particularly poignant avenue through which international lawyers may cast off overly stringent disciplinary boundaries in search of wholistic understandings of legal phenomena, particularly those related to inequality and climate change. As one group of GVC researchers put it:

> Focus on the role that legal frameworks play at different levels of a particular chain, and on the politico-economic power dynamics that operate behind competing legal norms, can help facilitate a critical assessment of the structural and distributional dimensions of GVCs – and the global economy more broadly – that are often taken for granted or normalized. Such an imaginative legal exercise can then help to elucidate alternative and potentially more progressive sites of intervention by scholars, policymakers and civil society groups.[4]

Just as the boundaries between multiple legalities, practices, conceptions, and disciplines of law are increasingly blurred, so too are the boundaries between what is hard law and what is soft law, or how and whether private ordering mechanisms should accrue legal 'legitimacy'. The GVC is an area of study particularly fruitful for forcing a re-examination the boundaries themselves, and whether they should be sustained.[5] For example, sometimes the 'soft law' outcomes within GVCs are more effective than 'hard' international law, not least because GVCs generate unique inter-firm and cross-border norms of business practice such as chain-wide corporate codes. Such efforts can drive behavior as powerfully as legal commands emanating from legislation.[6] In addition to this, novel public–private regulatory arrangements such as the Bangladesh Accord on Building and Fire Safety show how public and private GVC norms are entangled with and responsive to rapidly changing business practice and policies.[7]

Mapping GVCs from a legal perspective poses complex challenges for basic questions of positive legal analysis, including matters of territorial jurisdiction, governing law, private regulation through contract and sovereign authority.[8] As we have seen in previous chapters, this is partially because ICPs and their GVCs frequently traverse legal forms, geographic and jurisdictional boundaries, and multiple layers of potentially applicable law. Nevertheless, notwithstanding their ambiguity, GVCs are an important source of norm creation. This is especially true of the largest buyer firms.[9] This term – buyer firms – describes the relatively small collection of extremely large firms that comprise much of the world's GVCs. They are engaged in a process Dan Danielson refers to as 'supply chain capitalism';[10] the process through which buyer firms create competition amongst supplier firms, thereby funneling would-be profits and excess capital from supplier firms to buyer firms. Because in the largest GVCs, the former are overwhelmingly located in developing countries while the latter are overwhelmingly located in developed ones, supply chain capitalism undermines assumptions that legal instruments that liberalize the cross-border flow of trade and investment make any meaningful contribution to the 'development' of less economically powerful States.

The idea functions as follows. The largest buyer firms are those responsible for precuring the most cumulative contracts amidst the many fragmented firms operating within a given GVC. These firms create and sustain markets for smaller firms within GVCs that would likely not exist but for the GVC. As globalization progresses, GVCs create sub-competitive markets within the various States or regions composing a GVC for the commodities or services needed to feed the GVC of the larger buyer firm. This results in a status quo under which large buyer firms are best positioned to assume coordination of the GVC and to assume governance functions throughout a given GVC. For example, large buyer firms often organize their global corporate structures and the geography and structure of their supply chains to maximize chain efficiency, resilience and ultimately their own global returns. The process of organization takes place according to centralized plans within the buyer firm. At the same time, legal liability for any part of a GVC is almost invariably contained within the domestic system in which a given link in a GVC is located. While planning is centralized, 'control' and 'ownership' are easily dispersed. This broadly dispersed legal and geographic supply chain coupled with the interdependence of participants in chain structures – not to mention the dependence of suppliers and intermediaries on chain structures for access to markets – gives large buyer firms an immense bargaining advantage over States and firms alike. Both States and smaller firms need the buyer firm, and as a result, buyer firm directives have a significant impact on the business practices of the firms within the GVC as well as the law that governs the contexts in which they operate. Thus, categorically speaking, buyer firms are more economically and therefore legally powerful than developing States.

This power is evident in a few ways. For example, only buyer firms have the power to deploy law in a manner designed to direct the activities of chain suppliers and intermediaries such as supply contracts. Operating across jurisdictions, these ICP buyer firms can determine internal corporate codes of conduct, which can include policies regarding subcontracting by suppliers or intermediaries. Within those policies, these ICPs can unilaterally enact punitive commercial measures that punish noncompliant firms; they can multisource from supplier firms, thereby leveraging competitive pressure to induce supplier compliance; they can unilaterally impose limitations on supplier sourcing of production inputs; they can unilaterally create monitoring, reporting, auditing and due diligence requirements; and many others. In addition to these direct examples, the ICP also has the means to shape the firm relationships within GVCs through the designs and structures business operations detailed in the previous chapters. Some common examples include buyer firm strategies to maintain global proprietary control over innovation, intellectual property and brand assets through complex ownership and licensing structures, as well as inventory control and production management systems that minimize technology transfer to suppliers; or the use of complex corporate structuring to distribute buyer firm business functions and the recognition of revenues and profits geographically to minimize global tax liability and maximize global returns.

The power of buyer firms over chain operations and governance under supply chain capitalism shapes the strategic behavior of many developing countries and their domestic firms. To illustrate this, Professor Danielson has offered the following example from the ready-made garment sector.

> For domestic firms selling to global apparel brands concerned with reputational risk, national policy aimed at improving workplace safety and government oversight of labor conditions in garment factories may be important to retaining the business from those global brands. By contrast, for domestic firms selling to less reputation-oriented global brands or to buyer firms supplying low price markets, a policy change imposing additional safety regulations or government oversight of labor conditions would likely increase production and compliance costs, resulting in tighter margins for domestic suppliers or the loss of business if supplier firms cannot absorb these additional costs and buyer firms seek alternative sources of supply rather than pay higher prices.[11]

Such considerations show that both the national policy and the labor practices of supplier firms are determined with a view to their compatibility with the demands, requirements, and sourcing alternatives of the GVCs on which both the supplier firms depend. Once one considers the full scale on which such interactions occur across jurisdictions and industry sectors, it is easy to make the arguments that GVCs – governed by large ICPs – play a more significant role in establishing the business practices and competitive position of domestic supplier firms and the comparative advantage of developing States than the policy choices of domestic governments. The magnitude of this dynamic is compounded by the multitude of global supply chains in multiple export sectors.

All of this – in addition to the ICP constituency concerns raised in Chapter 4 – suggest that both supplier firms developing State policy makers are operating in a legal environment over which they have little or no control. Foreign firms create internal 'law' that determine domestic firm behavior, State policy caters to export led growth thus increasing dependence upon foreign buyer firms, buyer firm multi-sourcing tactics increases competition amongst supplier firms thus decreasing their ability to redirect capital gains to the domestic market, and the power of the State to change this dynamic is undermined by the weakness of domestic policy when it comes to the needs of its exporting firms: for example, a developing State that increases worker protection squeezes the ability of its supplier firms to compete with other supplier firms in other developing States and a State that decreases worker protection enacts policy that is irrelevant to supplier firms who enact internal policy with an eye toward compliance with the buyer firm that governs the broader GVC.

b. The ICP and CSR

Corporate Social Responsibility plays a key strategic role in the globalization of corporate personhood. As UN Secretary General Kofi Annan put it in May 1999 addressing business leaders at the World Economic Forum in Davos, and as U.S. President Bill Clinton put it one month later during his address to the ILO, CSR initiatives are desirable because they 'put a human face on the global economy'.[12] In many cases, CSR initiatives 'brands' an ICP's international behaviors in campaigns that take place alongside but distinct from the marketing of products; these initiatives are intended to convince the consumer that the ICP's existence is a net positive more than they are intended to convince the consumer to purchase any product linked to the ICP. But the human face achieved through CSR policies can also be used to replace or distract from policy spaces that are traditionally considered the 'public' sphere of the State. For example, where a State fails to provide universal and high-quality education to its public, an ICP's presence in that State might be considered a 'net positive' if it funds a handful of education programs. Through CSR, the ICP often presents its 'responsibility' not as one to share its spoils with the State (e.g., through taxation or joint ownership schemes) but to 'give back' to the public of the State by selecting a collection of programs to fund. Indeed, a visual survey of the CSR initiatives of Fortune 100 companies would suggest that the programs and initiatives chosen are often influenced by optics of 'human face'–producing considerations for the ICP in question.

To provide one industry-specific concrete example amongst many, for the past two decades, big tobacco companies have lobbied hard at the WHO in Geneva. As sales dropped in developed countries, tobacco sales became increasingly dependent upon developing countries, so when the WHO led a successful effort to establish an international Framework Convention on Tobacco Control (FCTC) in 2003, the world's four largest tobacco companies – British American, Philip Morris, RJ Reynolds, and Brown and Williamson – invested a vast quantity of resources into trying to convince States that accession to the FCTC was unnecessary. A complete record of these efforts is available from Weissharr et al;[13] John Ruggie has summarized that work as follows:

> The WHO's right to convene a treaty negotiation was challenged. Claims were made that the FCTC would conflict with other international treaties. Developing countries were warned that the treaty would undermine national sovereignty, good governance, and prospects for economic development. Even some of the scientific evidence of the adverse effects of tobacco was questioned – and some scientists willingly enlisted for this purpose. Specific national delegations were targeted for pressure in Geneva and national capitals. Alliances were sought with unrelated business associations that might have an interest in resisting the potential contagion effects of this instance of international regulation. Joint ventures with governments were proposed, weak national policies were encouraged, CSR initiatives were promoted as an alternative, and freedom of expression in labeling invoked.[14]

There are two CSR points here to which I wish to draw attention. First, the use of CSR as an alternative to the international adoption of evidence-based policies to address a public health issue that goes against commercial interest. The tobacco companies put forward a vision of CSR and corporate responsibility more generally that emphasized individual consumer choice and the importance of 'public-private' partnerships. And second, the capital required to engage in this effort helped sustain industries that directly undermine broadly accepted social goods. For example, the firms deployed to coordinate this lobbying effort specialized in such services; they were the same 'public relations and crisis management firms advocating climate change denial on behalf of their clients'.[15]

Thus, while the ICP's use of CSR can indeed put a 'human face' on the global economy, perhaps the issue is whether that face truly represents the multifaceted nature of a given ICP's legal, economic, and social actions. Indeed, as many passages have shown, the ICP's composition is more akin to a Matryoshka doll or Hobbes's Leviathan than to a human – within each face there are many faces, within each bodyless body many bodies.

III. Things as disenfranchised persons

Justifications for ICP treatment are inconsistent with the treatment of 'things' that either have agency or have bodies but not both; trends in international courts show tensions in the concept of personhood as accorded to corporations and the dissolving lack thereof with respect to nature, animals, and AI. This is because the concept of 'subjecthood' is so linked to the concept of agency that the 'thinghood' of nature is a feature almost fundamental to the ways in which most lawyers understand legitimacy in law (a). Because animals are not understood to have agency, they have historically reached only 'welfare' rather than 'rights' – a category that aligns more cleanly with 'thinghood' – in domestic courts. Meanwhile, AI is treated as a 'thing' and most of the legal debates revolve around its capacity to change human engagement with law rather than its capacity to be a subject of law, denying AI's capacity to act as an agent possessing active rights (b).

a. Nature

Even before the most famous corporate personhood cases of the modern era came down in the mid-2000s, efforts were bubbling by indigenous and environmental groups to attribute legal personhood to nature. For example, courts in the Netherlands and Pakistan have found that States have a duty under human rights law to protect the environment,[16] and that environmental protection falls within the human rights to life and dignity,[17] respectively. In Norway, the constitutional court found that, although the State had a duty to protect the environment for present and future humans, environmental damages that take place outside of State territory are not part of the State's duty, even if the company damaging the environment is a 'citizen' of the State.[18] And the constitutions of Ecuador and Bolivia recognize the rights of nature, at least nominally.

Internationally, as early as 2005, the *Intuit Petition* at the Inter-American Court of Human Rights unsuccessfully argued that climate change caused by U.S. corporate activity had resulted in a deprivation of various cultural rights of indigenous peoples in the Arctic.[19] And as recently as 2019, the Philippines' Commission on Human Rights found that carbon majors could be held accountable for violating the rights of its citizens for damages caused by climate change.[20]

A blind spot persists where nature meets the ICP. In some instances, because nature's rights are actually derisive of the rights of humans to enjoyment of nature, the rights attach only to humans within State borders. In others, because nature's rights are in reality the State's negative duties not to unduly harm nature, harm external to realms of State duties do not attach. There are no recognized rights inherent to the condition of being 'nature'. Even though nature can be said to have 'interests' in international legal outcomes, it is not typically regarded as a subject of international law because it is capable only of holding passive rights and is incapable of holding duties. Nature – indeed, 'the environment' – is therefore a 'thing'. And 'thinghood' in the eyes of international law has no place apart from regimes that define and sustain property. The concept of 'subjecthood' is so linked to the concept of agency that the 'thinghood' of nature is a feature almost fundamental to the ways in which most lawyers understand legitimacy in law. For those who understand 'legitimacy' as broader than 'human approval' – those who seek legal legitimacy in a system that understands humanity as one part of an ecosystem rather than as its central ends – an understanding of nature as a possessor of the 'passive' rights articulated in the previous chapter may provide an inroad to redirect existing law.

b. Animals and AI

Domestic courts have for centuries recognized corporations,[21] for decades recognized animals,[22] and very recently begun to grapple with artificial intelligence (AI) as 'subjects' of law.[23] The most contentious legal questions revolve around whether should attribute 'personhood' or 'thinghood' to these entities. While corporations have long enjoyed rights through the category of personhood, animals have historically reached 'welfare' rather than 'rights' – a category that aligns more cleanly with 'thinghood' – in domestic courts. Thus far AI has only been treated as a 'thing' and most of the legal debates revolve around its capacity to change human engagement with law rather than its capacity to be a subject of law or even an agent possessing active rights. With these points aired, international law is showing signs of change; it has demonstrated flexibility toward non-human persons as holders of rights in the past and a handful of decisions indicate that a broader variety of 'things' could become 'people' in the future.

On the subject of animals: domestic jurisdictions have 'slowly, nervously' begun to acknowledge animal rights. Courts in Argentina and Colombia have granted habeas corpus to apes and a bear, respectively.[24] The Indian Supreme Court recognized fundamental animal rights under the Constitution of India.[25] In a criminal trial against animal activists for trespassing, a German lower court has accepted self-defense in favor of farmed animals which could be creatively read as implying that these are 'persons' within the meaning of the law.[26] However, the pattern has not been one of unambiguous progress towards recognition of animal rights. In United States, American lower courts, judges have been hesitant to endorse animal rights. Rather, they have denied habeas corpus to chimpanzees and the standing of a macaque in a copyright suit.[27] Nevertheless, it is worth noting the trends with animals are consistent with the theory of the ICP set out in the previous chapter. Animals are gaining 'personhood' because they possess passive claim rights which can be exercised on their behalf by third parties and for their exclusive benefit. And a growing chorus of prominent international lawyers have noted that domestic law is insufficient to achieve consistent animal personhood precisely because of ICP behaviors. As Anne Peters puts it:

> The industrialised mode of meat, dairy, and pet production is now spreading to countries of the global south and to developing countries in which the demand and purchase power for animal products is steeply

> rising. Those industries have become globalised, with transnational supply chains. The manufacturing and trade conditions are leading to a dramatic increase of 'normal' violence against animals in sheer numbers (confinement, mutilation, killing). Also, the transnational dimension of these more or less violent activities has been intensified, it has become cross-border violence.[28]

On the subject of AI, it is worth first noting the impact AI has on the freedoms and rights thus far attributed to the ICP along with natural persons. Various governments have started to use AI-driven facial recognition software not only to identify criminal suspects but also to record patterns of life and monitor people quarantined with the novel coronavirus. This use implicates international human rights rules related to privacy, freedom of association, and freedom of expression. AI tools have the potential to complicate transnational law enforcement cooperation and compliance, such as where a state makes an extradition request that is derived entirely from probable cause determinations informed by opaque algorithms. And departing from such 'public' concerns to the 'private' sector, private corporations are developing self-driving cars and ships that ultimately may operate transnationally. Yet the international community generally, and States specifically, have not reached a common understanding about the extent to which existing international law suffices to regulate these developments. The most intensive AI-related international negotiations have focused on whether to ban lethal autonomous weapons systems, and this focus (while undoubtedly serious) has narrowed the discursive space on AI in international law to its effects on natural persons or corporate decision-making rather than its individual capacity for 'personhood'.

The increasing use of AI in ICPs implies a shift from viewing the enterprise as primarily private and facilitative, towards a more public, and regulatory, conception of the law governing corporate activity and capacity. Today's AI is dominated by machine learning applications which assist and augment human decision-making. These applications raise multiple challenges for business organization, the management of which we collectively term 'data governance'. The impact of today's AI on corporate law is coming to be felt along two margins. First, there is likely to be a reduction in costs across many standard dimensions of internal agency, coordination, and organization within firms. Second, the oversight challenges – and liability risks – at the top of firms will rise significantly. Tomorrow's AI may permit humans to be replaced even at the apex of corporate decision-making. This is likely to happen first in what we call 'self-driving subsidiaries' performing very limited corporate functions. Replacing humans on corporate boards by machines implies a fundamental shift in focus: from controlling internal costs to the design of appropriate strategies for controlling 'algorithmic failure', that is, unlawful acts bay an algorithm with potentially severe negative effects (physical or financial harm) on external 'third' (or second?) parties. Perhaps less severe, but also affecting human parties, is the growing use of AI for corporate goal setting; some have predicted that in the medium term this is likely to become the center of gravity for debate on AI and corporate law.[29] The implications of this are vast: every existing human job is potentially obsolete in some sense, even if not completely. The debates surrounding this and policies resulting from this will only flourish as technical progress moves toward the possibility of fully 'self-driving' corporations. Some scholars have already cautioned that current regulatory structure is inadequate to deal with this outcome: 'The potential for regulatory competition weakens lawmakers' ability to respond, and so even though the self-driving corporation is not yet a reality . . . the regulatory issues deserve attention' well before tomorrow's AI becomes today's.[30]

IV. 'The actual': liability

Dominant understandings of the ICP as para-individual or para-State have created and sustained international liability structures that do not reflect the legal reality of ICPs or MNEs more generally. Domestic systems can bring ICPs to account for negligence or fraud or other breaches of law, but these systems cannot reach beyond the borders of the State (a). The territorially bound nature of States also renders domestic systems inadequate to counteract complex transfer pricing transactions that erode the capital available for taxation revenue within each State – especially States with weaker enforcement mechanisms (b). By contrast, ICPs can construct and enforce private (internal) normative legal orders that concern and affect the external legal world, both international and domestic. In some instances, private normative orders have greater potential to affect international human behavior than any existing international legal personality (c).

a. Legal form and liability

The ICP and MNEs more generally are legal forms that reflect a total shift in the production process in many if not most sectors in the global economy. Hence, as this book has suggested, an important first step toward understanding the ICP within the international legal system is recognizing the fundamental dissonance between economic reality and legal form. This includes acknowledging that many of the classic theoretical justifications for legal form – whether the State, the corporation, or international legal authority – simply do not apply to the reality of the ICP.

In a recent article that illustrated the mismatch between economic reality and legal form, John Ruggie offered three examples. As an example of an 'actor-based' corporate form, he described the French company Total, which is the fourth largest publicly traded oil and gas company in the world. It 'operates in 130 countries and has 100,000 direct employees. Its business segments cover every aspect of the oil and gas industry, from exploration, development, production, refining, and petrochemicals to marketing, trading, and shipping. It is also active in specialty chemicals and aims to become a global leader in new energies'. The Total 'group' is composed of roughly 900 subsidiaries and equity affliliates, and each of these is composed of multiple properties and enterprises. Total's marketing division 'owns' over 16,000 service stations in 110 countries organized according to three legal ownership structures depending upon domestic markets and legal circumstances: 'owned and operated by an in-country subsidiary, owned by a subsidiary but operated by independent dealers, and dealer owned and operated'. All these entities carry the Total brand, but beyond these are a myriad of further private and public service and distribution contracts, amongst other legal relationships. Total is not just 'Total' – it is not a discrete and insular readily identifiable entity. And Total is the easiest type of ICP to identify.

More complicated legal forms emerge when one considers the entire GVCs within and amongst ICPs. Ruggie provides Starbucks as an example of a buyer-led supply chain network; that is, the buyer (Starbucks) creates a product and forms contract relationships with a network of suppliers all producing a similar commodity. Citing a 2013 UNCTAD report, Ruggie notes:

> [Starbucks] directly employs 150,000 people; sources coffee from thousands of traders, agents and contract farmers across the developing world; manufactures coffee in over 30 countries, mostly in alliance with partner firms, usually close to final market; distributes coffee to retail outlets through over 50 major central and regional warehouses and distribution centres; and operates some 17,000 retail stores in over 50 countries across the globe.[31]

To illustrate a producer-led GVC contract network, Ruggie offers the example of the Apple iPhone 6. Although the iPhone's components were produced by 785 suppliers in 31 countries, in 2014, the most crucial components were sourced from 60 US-based suppliers and 349 China-based suppliers. All of these suppliers were MNEs themselves, and many outsourced components of the production of the iPhone's components to 'companies in Japan, South Korea, and Taiwan', which in turn are sourced from yet other (and lower cost) locations in South East Asia. Thus, the producers of the components for the iPhone are responsible for the vast majority of the contract relationships along the GVC that enables Apple's final product. The legal effect of these contract networks is that the vast majority of the production chain is external to Apple and an ICP or MNE. In many cases – and in Apple's case especially prior to the company's internal efforts to increase transparency within these networks – it is not feasible to monitor the origins and labor conditions across all the firms involved in producer-led GVC.

These are a few examples of what Ruggie describes as 'mini – and in many cases not-so-mini – transnational economic systems. Product and process standards [that] are set by the lead firm and then cascade across its network and down the supply chains'. As noted in previous chapters, and also citing a 2013 UNCTAD report,[32] one consequence of these structures is that 'about 80% of global trade (in terms of gross exports) has become linked to international production networks of TNCs [transnational corporations]'.[33] That 80 percent is comprised mostly of what the ILO calls 'intermediate goods' – that is, not final products but components, produced in part here, assembled in part there, shipped and reassembled for a variety of legal and economic reasons (e.g., at least one international trade dispute broke out over the issue of whether a mostly assembled automobile imported into China and then fully assembled in China comprised a foreign or domestic automobile for international tariff purposes).[34] As the ILO noted in 2016, trade in intermediate goods is now greater than all other non-oil traded goods combined.[35] A year earlier, the ILO reported that at least one in seven jobs in the world is supply chain–related.[36]

These realities are not reflected in the law. A given ICP does not operate as a single entity with a single purpose, with unity of command, or with a single coherent strategy. As Ruggie explains:

> Where no equity nexus exists, as in the Starbucks and iPhone examples, relations between producers/buyers and their suppliers are governed by the private law of contracts. In the case of an integrated firm like Total, each of its 900 subsidiaries and affiliates is a separate legal entity, subject to the laws of the particular jurisdiction in which it is incorporated. Through equity relations they are ultimately linked to a 'corporate parent,' which is itself a separate legal entity.

In other words, although the ICP is composed of legal persons and that are economic actors organized as corporations, neither the ICP nor MNEs more generally are 'a corporation'. While they span multiple jurisdictions, they are wholly subject to no legal authority. Domestic – not international – law governs the multiple legal persons that compose the ICP, and the ICP's primary regulatory compass is therefore internal. Parent companies enjoy limited liability even if they wholly own all of their subsidiaries; they incur liability only to the extent of investment in the subsidiary, and often not even to that extent.

As this book has emphasized, domestic systems can bring ICPs to account for negligence or fraud or other breaches of law, but these systems cannot reach beyond the borders of the State. There are, as noted in Chapter 3, some notable exceptions, such as the FCPA or anti-trust law or DPAs, but these are often infused with the value and political interests of the State. In practice, this means only economically powerful States – those in which most of the world's ICPs are headquartered – can reach beyond their own borders to repatriate damages caused by corporate activity abroad. What many hoped to be an exception – the ATS discussed in Chapter 2 – has passed through 150 cases since 1997 producing a watered-down jurisprudence that favors ICPs.

It is indisputable that MNEs exist in fact. I believe that this book has demonstrated that ICPs exist as a subcategory of MNEs capable of accessing rights and privileges available only to the ICP. Nevertheless, these entities are all but invisible to international law. Again quoting Ruggie:

> The fact that public law (national and international) does not generally encompass the economic unity of the multinational firm is the single most important contextual factor shaping its power, authority, and relative autonomy. Twenty-first century corporate globalization is built on foundational principles of corporate law that date back to the 19th century when they were intended to facilitate capital formation among natural persons: attributing legal personhood to corporations, investors' limited liability, and permitting one corporation to own another while still construing them to be separate legal entities.[37]

Normatively speaking, if international lawyers believe that international law's role is to protect humanity rather than to encourage States to do so; that international law's role is to correlate rights with duties and power with liabilities; if international law's role is not only to increase the size of the economic pie but to ensure that increases do not harm humanity and are justly distributed amongst States, then the whole of the MNE must be retheorized so that the legal reality of these entities reflects their economic and social realities. In the categories of labor rights, economic redistribution, equitable taxation, and many others, meaningful change will only occur across State boundaries when the first principle of corporate representation under international law is corporate subjectivity to international law.

b. Territory and liability

States are territorially bound; as legal entities within the current system, they compete for investment from their geographically fixed vantage point. By contrast, ICPs have a multitude of locational options, even (in many instances) when it comes to extracting geographically fixed commodities. As one UNCTAD report puts it: 'For many GVC [global value chain] segments, tasks and activities, there are relatively few "make or break" locational determinants that act as preconditions for countries' access to GVCs'.[38] In addition, the legal technologies that govern private international commercial relations have expanded immensely, which in turn delocalizes both commercial transactions and lawmaking affecting enforceable dispute settlement.[39]

We have seen how this structural link to territory affects liability most clearly through international investment arbitration in IIL, which uses the category of 'investor' to collapse the ICP and natural persons into a single legal concept. To justify this system, many traditionally-minded commentators have pointed out that states win at least as many cases as MNEs in international arbitration suits; they argue that this fact suggests no structural power is in play.[40] But these observations downplay the fact that investors win in the jurisdictional phase of arbitration more than 70% of the time.[41] The fact that the jurisdictional phase represents a point of entry to litigation on the international level indicates a low bar to entry for the ICP, or the 'investor'. Once jurisdictional decisions against them are subtracted, ICPs actually win roughly 60% of cases at the merits phase. As Mann puts it:

> The combination of low bars to entry and high win rates . . . is perfect for motivating investors, counsel and third- party funders to initiate cases. Importantly, it also increases the effectiveness of threats by investors against states in response to potential measures states may be considering adopting – the regulatory chill impact of the investor-state arbitration system.[42]

On these grounds, Mann rightly notes that "states never win; they only do not lose."[43] That is, States cannot obtain an 'Award' under the IIL system; at most they can obtain costs of litigation. No wonder that China, whose outward foreign investment is on the verge of exceeding inward flows, has broadened the scope of issues it has agreed to subject to international arbitration in its most recent BITs.[44]

The territorially bound nature of States also renders domestic systems inadequate to counteract complex transfer pricing transactions that erode the capital available for taxation revenue within each State – especially States with weaker enforcement mechanisms. We have seen in previous chapters how transfer pricing may enable firms to create, administer, or negotiate prices that differ from those on the general market. The fact that ICPs can (and do) fragment production across jurisdictions to obtain economic benefits from a global pallet of jurisdictions in which each intermediate good can be produced results in an increase in the cross-border trade of intermediate goods. Naturally, this increases the opportunities for cross-border transfer pricing according to 'markets' created within each ICP.[45]

The official data on this are almost non-existent; most countries collect no data, and no countries collect good data. The reasons for this are unclear but the constituency concerns described in Chapter 4 are at least a plausible hypothesis. In any event, as described in Chapter 1, the present state of affairs when it comes to investigating transfer pricing is that the knowledge obtainable is largely derived from tracking arms-length market prices comparable to existing market prices, which often do not exist. Where market prices do not exist – that is, where IP is involved or where service is a primary product (in other words, almost always) – MNEs have a high degree of pricing discretion.[46]

From the data that is available, all signs suggest that intra-firm prices differ significantly from arms-length prices if major tax and tariff considerations are in play. Transfer prices tend to be higher for goods sent to jurisdictions featuring low corporate tax rates and high tariff rates.[47] Hence, unless tax and tariff rates are harmonized internationally – unless the powers that drive a globalized economic system can accept a centralized authority for global taxation – these intrafirm cross-jurisdictional legal realities will remain a source of structural power for ICPs and MNEs more generally.

c. Liability in private normative orders

A final 'actuality' element in the ICP liability landscape, repeatedly mentioned throughout this book, is the ability of ICPs to construct and enforce private (internal) normative legal orders that concern and affect the external world. Internal ICP law may take the form of CSR or ESG initiatives or it may be a matter of private (internal) policy with respect to a particular issue. The Bigtech firms provide prominent and visible example. The language of human rights concerns originates from and is defined in many ways by international legal instruments, but the form it takes at Facebook, for instance, flows from an internal norm-creation process. These private legal orders then become internationally enforced. The following paragraphs the process of determining exceptions to 'free speech' as understood by Facebook.

At Facebook, an internal Product Policy Team, which has grown immensely since 2016, establishes and amends Facebook's Community Standards – the content moderation policies at Facebook.[48] The content moderation policies form the basis for the content moderation training material that is developed to instruct content moderators on the ground. During the policy development process many internal and external players are involved. This includes the subject-matter expert, the heads of department within Facebook involved in the policy development process, the Director for Human Rights, and the Stakeholder Engagement team that coordinates interaction with external stakeholders.[49] Reacting to what Facebook calls 'signals', the Product Policy Team constructs its policies based 'on feedback from community representatives and a broad spectrum of the people who use our service'.[50] The process is meant to 'root [Facebook's] policies in sources of knowledge and experience that go beyond Facebook'.[51] Facebook defines the stakeholders as 'organizations and individuals who are impacted by, and therefore have a stake in, Facebook's Community Standards. . . . Our more than 2.7 billion users are, in the broad sense, stakeholders'.[52] But not all stakeholders. Only those who 'are informed about and able to speak on behalf of others'.[53]

Facebook's universally applied Community Standards are drawn primarily from 'civil society organizations, activist groups, and thought leaders, in such areas as digital and civil rights, anti-discrimination, free speech, and human rights'.[54] After conducting consultations and presenting at the Product Policy Forum, the Product Policy team creates policy that reflects the 'range and nature of engagement' embodying the 'rationale for [Facebook's] final decision.'[55] Although Facebook acknowledges that 'Freedom of expression is a fundamental human right,'[56] the process of amending or developing Community Standards does not directly link to any international legal order or refer to international human rights commitments. The process for determining violations – for example, which interests are weighed and how and which exceptions may apply – is not available to users or the public. In this way, Facebook's Community Standards can be seen as a private normative legal order that regulates public communication.[57]

Companies such as Facebook often utilize the concept of the 'platform' in a manner that both absolves the company of the responsibility to monitor what occurs on its site and shifts responsibility for consuming content onto the users. As the former argument goes, Facebook's responsibility stops where principles of freedom of speech begin – if a person is free to say something at all they are free to write it on the 'platform'. As the latter argument goes, Facebook's users do not need to consume content on Facebook; they choose to do so, and this choice incurs consumer responsibility for the content consumed. However, the social reality is that, in some countries, it is not possible to receive up to date government information or to operate some types of business without engaging with Facebook, which calls into question the degree of consumer 'choice' and the nature of the accompanying responsibilities involved. In recent years, Facebook's roles in, for example, manipulating election outcomes,[58] enabling revolutionary organization,[59] facilitating crimes against humanity,[60] and exacerbating the general spread of misinformation have pushed the company to increase regulation of the content broadcasted through its cite, yet as of early 2021, the transparency and legitimacy concerns raised earlier remain unaddressed. Although Facebook has established an independent content-oversight board to review Facebook's decisions to censor content, its rulings have yet to be published and the effect of the board on the transparency of Facebook's internal review processes remains unclear.

V. 'The possible': reform

This section focuses on proposals that would reform to some extent the textual basis on which certain international regimes and their doctrines are rooted. The orientation of existing proposals varies widely; here I briefly touch upon five that specifically address the issues raised in this book: (1) efforts to establish new international regimes in the image of existing ones (i.e., State accession to a treaty and the establishment of an international court) for business and human rights as well as the environment; (2) proposals for global, non-State based systems that could eliminate the ICP's ability to exploit differences amongst domestic legal systems (i.e., transnational or global law with primacy over the State); (3) methods through which ICPs and MNEs as lawmakers and rework international legal structures to keep the best features of these legal personalities while curtailing their potential for harm to humans and the environment; (4) insights from feminist political theory that expose and challenge one dominant perspective from which concepts such as 'legalness' and 'valuableness' are constructed; and (5) reactions to evolutions such as the ICP and AI given the anthropocentrism of law generally and the state-anthropocentrism of international law specifically.

a. Establishing new regimes: human rights and environment

Two largescale efforts are underway to shift the manner in which international law addresses ICP behavior with respect to human rights and environmental degradation. The first of these, the Draft Instrument, was discussed at length in Chapter 3. While negotiations surrounding the draft instrument are ongoing, and while there is a reoccurring flirtation with the idea of an international business and human rights court,[61] at this stage it seems likely that the instrument will require domestic law to adapt and enforce the provisions and principles of the instrument with no independent judiciary charged with interpreting the terms (and therefore compliance) with the instrument. Thus far, State responses to the instrument are varied,[62] but there is already substantial commitment from G-77 States and resistance from private sector representatives. As of October 2019, sixteen States have participated and tentatively committed to guaranteeing individuals whose human rights have been harmed by businesses in their territories access to a remedy through State systems adhering to the instrument's terms.[63]

The second major effort is an international environmental court: The International Rights of Nature Tribunal. While it is (in my view) a theoretically elegant project, it is unfortunately toothless for pragmatic purposes. It is theoretically elegant in part because it does not root its authority in State accession; it is an ecocentric Court that views humanity as one part of a broader environmental system, and it is this system the Court sees as its primary rights holder and end. It is toothless for the same reason: States are not bound by and often do not participate in its pronouncements, and therefore, it is impractical as a venue to address immediate harms. Nevertheless, the project is valuable in that it sparks the legal imagination; it creates a normative surplus through its non-binding judgments that may serve to create a discursive space from which a new trajectory of eco-law can emerge. Indeed, the Court's judgments live up to its goals. According to the Earth Law Center, the Tribunal 'generates sophisticated legal analysis of diverse cases; recommends mitigation based on rights of nature, educates governments, advocacy groups, and the interested public on the tenets of the rights of nature and how they can be applied; [and] enables others to develop legal structures that recognize the inherent rights of nature'.[64] The rights of nature it recognizes and adjudicates are those flowing from one fundamental core: the idea (or the recognition) that nature has an inalienable 'the right to exist, persist, maintain and regenerate its vital cycles'.[65]

b. Global economic law: taxation and wealth registration

In Chapter 3 of this book, I sketched a rather bleak view of international law's ability to curtail the ability of ICPs to displace what is meant to be public wealth (in the form of taxed revenue) to private organizations and accounts within a given ICP. The core of this problem is that, because there is no unified system of global corporate regulation or taxation, each State is positioned to compete against others for corporate tax revenues by offering systemic advantages that enable ICPs to move assets, transfer revenues, or channel income through a variety of jurisdictions (e.g., offshores with anonymous accounts), legal fictions (e.g., trusts and mailbox companies), and internal strategies (e.g., transfer pricing, circular ownership, and capital flow structures that, *inter alia*, reduce what is in reality 'management' to 'services' such as consulting). In his seminal 2014 book *Capital in the Twenty-First Century*,[66] economist Thomas Piketty suggests that a collection of global progressive tax rates would be the most manageable and equitable legal method through which to curtail *inter alia* corporate exploitation of the fragmented international taxation system. Piketty of course assumes that law's purpose is to resolve human problems, and the problem he aim at in *Capital* is that of global distributive inequality. Piketty's proposal in *Capital* derives from an historical analysis of wealth inheritance across multiple jurisdictions over time; this aspect is more thoroughly hashed out in a 2013 paper with Emmanuel Saez, A Theory of Optimal Inheritance Taxation.[67] In that paper, Piketty and Saez note the dual dimensionality of individual inequality: persons differ both in their labor earning potential and in their inherited wealth. Piketty brings this observation to *Capital* where he suggests that global tax rates on global activities should progressively attach to different types of inequalities amongst individuals and across jurisdictions.[68] Thus, just as inheritance and income should both be taxed progressively but both have different optimal progressions, the same can be said of the ICP's accumulation of wealth. Like inheritance, in which individuals have access to a variety of legal technologies (e.g., trusts, various 'fees', and even 'gifts') to channel accumulated wealth to destinations of benefit to the family, the ICP 'parent' can channel wealth and income to offspring 'subsidiaries'. The principal components of a more equitable global solution are global progressive taxes tailored to specific areas of capital accumulation and transfer coupled with greater democratic control over where and how wealth is accumulated and transferred. Piketty argues that global taxation would be most effective but does not detail the sort of centralized institution that would be responsible for collection and redistribution. Rather, he seems to suggest regionalism is a more effective regulatory avenue. Building off this, one could imagine a trajectory that included a regionalism of cooperation on corporate taxation. For example, the EU or the OECD or ASEAN could commit to standards on behalf of their member states and could form a joint collection and redistribution institution. The problem would of course be that not every State is a member of a regional regulatory body and very few of the existing regional bodies have the legal capacity to commit states to schemes of taxation.

On the specific issue of corporate use of tax havens, Gabriel Zucman – an economist and former Piketty student – offers a global solution similar to Piketty's, but one focused on data disclosure as a means to address 'public theft'.[69] For Zucman, tax havens persist in part because of the anonymity granted in many havens either officially or through lax registration requirements (e.g., in Switzerland one can use a hotel address to open a bank account which means unknown quantities of offshore wealth are recorded as 'Swiss'), the ease with which shell or pass through companies can be created in offshore jurisdictions and the ease with which those companies can in turn create new companies in their name, and given these and other factors, the impossibility of distinguishing legitimate from evasive transactions in real time.[70] The massive amount of wealth kept offshore – roughly 20% in the United States alone[71] – places the burden of public costs largely upon middle-class taxpayers while companies that benefit from the systems and workers who use those systems avoid paying a fair share. Moreover, where corporate revenues that are taxed benefit only the jurisdictions in which they are posted, which deprives workers all along the GVCs and supply chains which created corporate profit of profits derived from their efforts. So while source base taxation works fine for corporations that operate in only one or two States, it fails in the face of greater corporate complexity. And where the arm's length principle can solve the problem of distributing corporate tax revenues in proportion to various States in which they operate, in the modern world of trusts, shells, and an increasing array of securities, treating various members of an ICP family as if their financial activities are distinct distorts reality to the detriment of most natural persons and States.[72] Nevertheless, the unlikelihood of States ever collectively committing and (much less) adhering to a centralized authority regulating transactions within and amongst States calls for more creative thinking. Zucman provides just this: States can place the onus on their own treasuries and on corporations, financial management firms, and banks without curtailing transactional freedom. The solution Zucman offers is the requirement of disclosure of all known wealth to be centralized in a global registry. According to Zucman, this would remedy problems created by the ALP (which treats different subsidiaries of a single ICP as if their incomes are unrelated) and would provide regulators with a figure of the total amount of wealth available for taxation; regulators could work backward from there according to various principles of redistribution, such as market-share redistribution or various forms of labor-based redistribution.[73] This would still require international cooperation, perhaps in the form sanctions, to pressure States that benefit from the status quo to adopt disclosure policies. It would also depend upon States to enforce penalties for breaching those policies on banks and wealth management firms that conceal assets from the registry.[74]

Along similar lines, recent trajectories in international law have opened discursive spaces to include the idea of 'global law': law rooted in humanity or human problems rather than State interests, which might run counter to the interests of their publics – international economic law has succeeded in increasing the size of the global pie but has left redistributing its pieces to the States; international human rights law also neglects redistribution.[75]

c. *Structural reform: governance and forbearance*

Because corporate activity is often considered the realm of private rather than public law, international lawyers have often neglected means through which reforms on corporate governance – particularly within ICPs – could serve many of international law's economic and social goals, perhaps even diplomatic ones. The following is a sampling of some of the corporate governance models that, unlike the dominant U.S. shareholder-driven model, arrange 'control' through means that ensure employee involvement in management decisions, at the very least indirectly through significant board membership. These are not 'new trajectories' strictly speaking but samples to inform conversation on broader MNE/ICP governance reform.

Codetermination

The German codetermination model provides for a two-tier board structure for all listed companies. Under this model, the management board consists of managers and deals primarily with strategic and operational issues. The supervisory board, like the board of directors of a U.S. corporation, includes only nonexecutive directors and is elected by shareholders. Members of the management board are appointed by the supervisory board. For companies with more than 2,000 employees, German corporate law requires that one half of the supervisory board must comprise employees (one-third for companies with 500 to 2,000 employees). These representatives are chosen and elected by the employees according to procedures designed and supervised by employees; trade unions can also seek representation by nominating candidates.[76]

Collective decision making

Nordic states with the largest economies – Norway, Sweden, Denmark, and Finland – have long been defined by a model of collective decision making among labor, owners, and the government. This model extends to the boardroom, with a mandate for employee representation on corporate boards. In 2015, France expanded the obligation for companies with 1,000 or more employees in France or more than 5,000 worldwide to have employee representation on the board of directors.[77]

Keiretsu

Japan's corporate governance practices are viewed as protecting managers from shareholder pressure. Managers are seen as having an obligation to all stakeholders in a company, including employees, customers, banks, and suppliers. Ownership of corporations is often (though not always) characterized by the *keiretsu* system – a web of cross holdings across group companies, often suppliers and customers of one another, with a finance bank in the middle as a significant owner of the group companies.[78] The finance bank is a dominant governance force that approves significant investments and can intervene to discipline managers.[79] The cross-holding structure prevented hostile takeovers. When Shinzo Abe became prime minister of Japan in 2012, however, he introduced reforms meant to change Japanese corporate governance, including erosions of key *keiretsu* tenets, such as systematic cross holding.[80]

At least one vein of new trajectories in corporate governance comes from private sector rather than government initiatives to address the 'purpose' void arising amid growing acknowledgment that shareholder profit as a legal mandate is either ambiguous or non-existent.[81] The most influential of these is a private certification issued by B Lab – a global non-profit with presence in most of the world's major commercial jurisdictions.[82] B Lab issues 'B Corporation' certifications to applicants who receive a minimum score on an online assessment attempting to measure 'social and environmental performance'. It is a self-selected group of companies that self-report compliance with B Lab standards; there is no legal liability attached to deviance from the activities reported to attain B Lab status, but companies do have to pay fees and recertify on an annual basis to maintain the status. The fees are progressive based on the size and revenue of the company.[83] On the legal front, B Corporations are required to integrate certain stakeholder commitments into their governing documents;[84] in this sense, it resembles the commitments of States to non-binding declarations in international law, such the UDHR. Given the self-committing nature of the certification, its function is primarily one of signaling. B Corporations and similar certifications signal to customers and other stakeholders that a company holds certain values and governs itself internally in a manner that holds social and environmental goals as priorities alongside profitability. As of late 2019, there were almost 3,000 certified B Corporations in 64 countries.

A similar State-sanctioned trajectory is the United States' Benefit Corporation. These are for-profit entities that include positive impact on society, workers, the community, and the environment as legally defined goals alongside profit. Benefit Corporations do this by including such requirements in their bylaws, which in 35 States are legally recognized as a clarification to the typical corporate law requirement that management act 'in the best interest of the corporation'.[85] As such, switching from a traditional corporation to a Benefit Corporation typically requires only a change to a company's bylaws. It is unclear whether this corporate form has much of an impact, but at the very least, like the B Corporation, the status has signaling value.

d. Feminist political theory and the ICP

In an age of increasing polarization, the idea that politics and law are 'impartial' is viewed by many as an illusion, and with good reason. Fresh thinking is needed to address the tension between multiple reasonabilities and to better place the reality of emotional life in civic and legal engagement – thinking that breaks free of slavish adherence to divisive fictions, such as the public–private delusion detailed in Chapter 4. In my view, feminist legal theory offers just such an approach. In volume that challenges many of the orthodoxies of political life in 'modern' democratic societies, Iris Marion Young offers a particularly enlightening feminist critique of the public–private divide. She argues that emancipatory politics – those movements which seek emancipation through political and legal means – assume that 'normative reason' is 'impartial and universal'.[86] (As I have written elsewhere, as late as the mid-1950s, Western politicians found it completely acceptable to label political movements 'emotional and therefore unreasonable'.)[87] She calls for a new trajectory in law that does not deny and repress difference through the supposedly universal ideal of 'impartiality' – an ideal that generates an opposition, indeed a hierarchy, between reason and desire.

Young takes aim particularly at Rousseauian and Hegelian insistence that the 'public' realm of the State is the realm of impartiality, universality, or normative reason.[88] The theoretical bedrocks these thinkers (building on Kant) set forth have so informed our understanding of civic duty that it seems almost 'natural' to have a rigid artificial barrier between public and private life that claims thought and reason belong to the former and the body and emotions belong to the latter.[89] Taking inspiration from Young, the 'ethics of care' suggests the need for a new trajectory of legal thinking that reclaims the 'historical' meaning of 'public':[90] The "meaning of public is what is open and accessible."[91] Rather than elevating a false universalism through the idea of 'universal impartiality' embodied through a temporally bound conception of normative reason, Young suggests a trajectory that recognizes that '[e]xpression and discussion are political when they raise and address issues of the moral value or human desirability of an institution or practice whose decisions affect a large number of people'. To Young, this expression becomes a public political act when it is communicated to any audience and diverging views have an opportunity to respond. Rather than conceptualizing 'private' as that which the 'public' excludes, 'private' should describe those things from which a person should have a right to exclude the public.

Placing this discussion in the context of the ICP and drawing from the proposals put forward by Piketty and Zucman, at least one typically 'private' area from which ICPs should not exclude the public is disclosure of wealth, as the public has a direct interest in ensuring ICPs that benefit from presence in a jurisdiction pays its fair share of taxes there. The idea of the ICP as residing in some 'private sector' sections off liability for ICP behavior to other private actors and excuses States from holding ICPs accountable to the public. Typically, the public sector is ultimately accountable to a State's citizens; the private sector is accountable to other parties (private or public) with which it sustains contractual commitments.[92] The private–public divide is in this sense fundamentally concerned with locating responsibility, accountability, and ultimately, liability. While ICPs certainly engage in private behavior by this definition (i.e., commercial contractual behavior), the financing, revenue, and capital flows (internal and international) are of paramount public concern insofar as each public from which an ICP shifts profits also incurs the burden of its tax missed as a result of the ICP's profit shift.

e. *Anthropocentrism, sovereignty, and the ICP*

Law is in some sense invariably anthropocentric; humans make law to organize humans and to reach toward solutions to human problems. But even if human generation of law is an inevitable fact of law, law does not need to understand humanity as its primary beneficiary. It could quite easily understand humanity as one sub-beneficiary and pursue as its primary beneficiary an ecosystem. This is a rough sketch of ecocentrism: a trajectory in law once banished to the fringes but a trajectory that is steadily gaining ground amongst progressive thinkers. International legal regimes that regulate climate change – much like those that regulate water, air, land-based pollution control, and fisheries – are based on a flawed premise. As noted in Chapters 2 and 3, these regimes proceed from the assumption that resources are to be harnessed for and consumed by humanity. Thus, the only 'management' involved is in regulating how much will be consumed and how soon. While these regimes are addressed to States, they assume that the public is best served when it caters to (yet curtails) development of the private sector. Increasing the consumption of nature – a goal traditionally relegated to private actors – is assumed to serve the public if done so responsibly. None of these regimes ever hint at one glaringly obvious option (increasingly so in the era of COVID-19); namely, the 'no consumption' or 'no development' option. The assumption so prevalent in international treaties that proper resource management will beget infinite supply is one entirely based on faith. By contrast, there is hard evidence to suggest that many global environmental crises, past and ongoing, are *caused* by humanity's development-focused relationship with the environment. If the status quo persists, law's role will continue to be reactive rather than preventative; treating the symptoms rather than the cause. A theoretical shift toward the ecocentric rather than anthropocentric could reorient international law especially in ways that could move toward solutions. Scholars in the TWAIL and CLS movements have amply demonstrated in many times over the ways in which law 'speaks' from a perspective of power or interest[93] – that the language of 'reason' or 'neutrality' just as often suppresses as it liberates. I envisage an ecocentric reorientation as pushing toward a project similar to these scholars,[94] especially those that understand international law as rooted in humanity rather than States.[95] I would suggest ecocentrism pushes a similar re-appropriation of law but takes issue with either (1) the elevation of humanity above all other forms of life, animal and otherwise, or (2) the assumption that humanity's interest in law is something distinct from the environment which provides the most essential contextual elements for any human interests to exist. Or (3) both. I hope to push discussions along this trajectory further in the future.[96]

But let us for now depart from what could be and return to what is, and in the process, return to two primary themes of this book: sovereignty as a potential hindrance to more equitable arrangements for natural persons, and corporations as international legal personalities that are more effective than traditional 'sovereigns' when it comes to achieving the goals of constituents. Core to international law's approach to environmental regulation is its uncompromising emphasis on the concept of sovereignty; one can see this plainly in the records of three decades worth of diplomatic Conferences of the Parties meetings.[97] This emphasis casts international regulation of ICP environmental damage alternatively as an infringement on regulatory autonomy or as a regulatory responsibility placed on individual States rather than as a regulation on ICPs as entities separate from States.

Determining the place of regulation in framing the ICP has profound implications for a theory of the ICP. The former method of framing regulation is rooted in the principle of non-intervention and therefore calls for State resistance to regulation. The latter method of framing regulation is rooted in the prevention of global harm and thereby calls for regulatory intervention. In this way, the theoretical primacy of States rather than individuals in international law limits the text, and this in turn limits the discourse on what international lawyers perceive as possible through international law. At the same time, because the international legal personality that is most engaged in shaping the individual's interaction with international law is the ICP, non-binding legal strategies associated with CSR and ESG tend to set the international regulatory agenda. Fresh thinking is needed to meaningfully address these issues.

Notes

1 See TRIPS example in Chapters 3 and 4.

2 'Governance' is an interdisciplinary concept. In legal literature, it is used as a shorthand for the public (municipal, state, supranational) and private (e.g., through private standard-setting and certification) regulation of the GVC. But here, 'governance' is used to refer to the shift from traditional toward more sophisticated regulatory techniques which gain traction through knowledge and markets rather than legal sanctions. For a comparative view, see P Zumbansen, Governance from an Interdisciplinary Perspective, in D Levi-Faur (Ed.), *Oxford Handbook on Governance* (2012). The GVC literature speaks of the 'governance' or management/coordination by the lead firm of the chain. Unless reference is made to the multiple normative layers shaping GVCs, this book will use the term in the latter meaning.

3 Kevin Sobel-Read, Global Value Chains: A Framework for Analysis, *Transnational Legal Theory (*2014)

4 IGLP Law and Global Production Working Group, The Role of Law in Global Value Chains: A Research Manifesto, *London Rev. Int'l L.* (2016).

5 D Schneiderman, Power and Production in Global Legal Pluralism: An International Political Economy Approach, in A Perry-Kessaris (Ed.), *Socio-Legal Approaches to International Economic Law* (2013).

6 Larry Catá Backer, Economic Globalization and the Rise of Efficient Systems of Global Private Lawmaking: Wal-Mart as Global Legislator, *U. Conn. L. Rev.* (2007) and A Beckers, *Enforcing Corporate Social Responsibility Codes* (2015).

7 For the text, see Bangladesh Accord on Building and Fire Safety, available at www.bangladeshaccord.org. For an analysis, M Anner, J Bair & J Blasi, Toward Joint Liability in Global Supply Chains: Addressing the Root Causes of Labor Violations in International Subcontracting Networks, *Comparative Labor Law and Policy Journal* (2013) and Haar & Keune, One Step Forward or More Window-Dressing? A Legal Analysis of Recent CSR Initiatives in the Garment Industry in Bangladesh, *International Journal of Comparative Labour Law and Industrial Relations* (2014).

8 David Kennedy, The Mystery of Global Governance, *Oh. N. U. L.* Rev. (2008): '[A]s the world is re-ordered, law will be there, imagining it, making it, writing it down, consolidating and contesting the new arrangements'.

9 G Teubner, *Global Bukowina: Legal Pluralism in the World Society*, in G Teubner (Ed.), *Global Law Without a State* (1997) and P S Berman, *Global Legal Pluralism: A Jurisprudence of Law Beyond Borders* (2012). For an illustration from the global toy industry, F Snyder, *The EU, the WTO and China: Legal Pluralism and International Trade Regulation* (Hart, 2010) 44–88. See, e.g., E Pashukanis, *Law and Marxism: A General Theory* (1978, originally printed in 1924). Pashukanis argues that the very form of law follows the commodity form.

10 Dan Danielson, Trade, Distribution and Development Under Supply Chain Capitalism, in David Trubeck, Alvaro Santos & Chantal Thomas (Eds.), *Globalization Reimagined: A Progressive Agenda for World Trade and Investment* (Anthem 2019).

11 *Id.*

12 William Jefferson Clinton (1999), Address by Mr Bill Clinton, President of the United States, 16 June 1999. International Labour Organization.

13 H Weishaar, J Collin, K Smith, T Grüning, S Mandal & A Gilmore (2012), Global Health Governance and the Commercial Sector: A Documentary Analysis of Tobacco Company Strategies to Influence the WHO Framework Convention on Tobacco Control. PLoS Med

9(6): e1001249, available at https://doi.org/10.1371/journal.pmed.1001249 (accessed 20 November 2020).

14 John G. Ruggie, Multinationals as Global Institution: Power, Authority and Relative Autonomy, 12 *Regulation & Governance* 317 (2018).

15 *Id.*

16 Dutch Supreme Court, Urgenda, ECLI:NL:HR:2019:2007.

17 See Parvez Hassan, Environmental Jurisprudence from Pakistan: Some Lessons for the SAARC Region. This is a paper presented at the South Asia Conference on Environmental Justice organized by the Supreme Court of Pakistan on 24–25 March 2012, at Bhurban, Pakistan, available at www.iucn.org/sites/dev/files/import/downloads/pk_1_environmental_jurisprudence_from_pakistan___some_lessons_for_the_saarc_region__d.pdf (accessed 2 June 2020).

18 A summary of the judgment in English is available at Sabin Center for Climate Change Law, Greenpeace Nordic Ass'n and Nature and Youth v. Ministry of Petroleum and Energy (Climate Change Litigation Database, 2018), available at http://climatecasechart.com/non-us-case/greenpeace-nordic-assn-and-nature-youth-v-norway-ministry-of-petro leum-and-energy/ (accessed 2 June 2020).

19 Inuit Petition and the IACHR, all documents available at www.ciel.org/project-update/inuit-petition-and-the-iachr/ (accessed 2 June 2020).

20 See Amnesty International, Philippines: Landmark decision by Human Rights Commission paves way for climate litigation (9 Dec 2019), available at www.amnesty.org/en/latest/news/2019/12/landmark-decision-by-philippines-human-rights-commission-paves-way-for-climate-litigation/ (accessed 2 June 2020).

21 See Adam Winkler, *We the Corporations: How American Businesses Won their Civil Rights* (2018).

22 See e.g., Anne Peters, Liberté, Egalité, Animalité: Human – Animal Comparisons in Law, *Transnational Environmental Law* (2016).

23 Roman Dremliuga, Pavel Kutznetcov & Alexey Mamychev, Criteria for Recognition of AI as a Legal Person, *Journal of Politics and Law* (2019).

24 For the ape, see Argentina: Tercer Juzgado de Garantías Mendoza, case no. P-72.254/15, 3 November 2016 – *Chimpanzee Cecilia*. For the bear, see Colombian Supreme Court of Justice, AHC4806–2017, Radicación n.o 17001–22–13–000–2017–00468–02, 26 July 2017 – *bear Chucho*. The bear decision was overturned by the Constitutional Court with a public hearing on 8 August 2019.

25 Supreme Court of India, *Animal Welfare Board of India v. Nagaraja and others*, Civil appeal no. 5387, 7 May 2014. See most recently also High Court of Punjab and Haryana at Chandighar, CRR 533–2013, judgment of 31 May 2019, esp. para. 29: 'The entire animal kingdom including avian and aquatic are declared legal entities having a distinct personality with corresponding rights, duties and liabilities of a living person'.

26 L G Magdeburg, Az. 28 Ns 182 Js 32201/14 (74/17), 28 Ns 74/17, judgment of 11 October 2017; OLG Naumburg (Saale), judgment of 9 May 2018 rejected self-defense but not because the pigs were not 'others', but rather because the act of trespass did not avert an imminent danger for those same pigs.

27 U.S. Court of Appeals (9th Circ), *Naruto v. Slater*, No. 16–15469 D.C. No.3:15-cv-04324-WHO, judgment of 23 April 2018.

28 Anne Peters, Toward International Animal Rights, in Anne Peters (Ed.), *Studies in Global Animal Law* (2020).

29 Nicol Turner Lee, Paul Resnick & Genie Barton, Brookings Institute Report: Algorithmic bias detection and mitigation: Best practices and policies to reduce consumer harms (22 May 2019).

30 John Armour & Horst Eidenmueller, Self-Driving Corporations?, *Harv. Bus. L. Rev.* (forthcoming).

31 United Nations Conference on Trade and Development [UNCTAD] (2013), p. 142.
32 UNCTAD, World Investment Report 2013: Global Value Chains: Investment and Trade for Development, p. 135 (2013).
33 *Id.*
34 See WTO, Appellate Body, *China – Measures Affecting Imports of Automobile Parts*, WT/DS399/AB/R; WT/DS340/AB/R; WT/DS342/AB/R (2008).
35 International Labour Organization (ILO), Decent Work in Global Supply Chains (2016). Report prepared for 105th Session, International Labour Conference, 8 April 2016.
36 ILO, World Employment and Social Outlook (2015). International Labour Organization, Geneva.
37 John G. Ruggie, Multinationals as Global Institution: Power, Authority and Relative Autonomy, 12 *Regulation & Governance* 317 (2018).
38 UNCTAD, World Investment Report 2013: Global Value Chains: Investment and Trade for Development, p. 144 (2013).
39 See A Claire Cutler, *Private Power and Global Authority: Transnational Merchant Law in the Global Political Economy* (CUP 2003); Saskia Sassen, *Territory, Authority, Rights* (Princeton 2006); Gralf-Peter Callies & Peer Zumbansen, *Rough Consensus and Running Code: A Theory of Transnational Private Law* (Hart 2010); and John Ruggie & John Sherman, Adding Human Rights Punch to the New Lex Mercatoria: The Impact of the Guiding Principles on Business and Human Rights on Commercial Legal Practice, 6 *Journal of International Dispute Settlement* 455 (2015).
40 E.g., Susan Franck, Development and Outcomes of Investment Treaty Arbitration, 50 *Harv. Int'l L. J.* 435 (2009).
41 See e.g., Howard Mann, ISDS: Who Wins More, Investors or States?, IISD, *Investment Treaty News* (June 2015), available at www.iisd.org/itn/wp-content/uploads/2015/06/itn-breaking-news-june-2015-isds-who-wins-more-investors-or-state.pdf (accessed 20 November 2020).
42 *Id.*
43 *Id.*
44 Qianwen Zhang, China's "New Normal" in International Investment Agreements, Columbia FDI Perspectives, No. 174 (23 May 2016), available at https://ssrn.com/abstract=2783740 (accessed 20 November 2020).
45 Christian Aid, False Profits: Robbing the Poor to Keep the Rich Tax Free (March 2009), available at www.christianaid.org.uk/sites/default/files/2017-08/false-profits-robbing-the-poor-to-keep-rich-tax-free-march-2009.pdf (accessed 20 November 2020); UNCTAD, World Investment Report 2013: Global Value Chains: Investment and Trade for Development, p. 156 (2013).
46 See generally UNCTAD, World Investment Report 2013: Global Value Chains: Investment and Trade for Development (2013).
47 Ranier Lanz & Sébastien Miroudot, Intra-Firm Trade: Patterns, Determinants and Policy Implications, *OECD Trade Policy Papers*, No. 114, OECD Publishing, Paris. http://dx.doi.org/10.1787/5kg9p39lrwnn-en (2011).
48 Facebook, Product Policy Forum Minutes, 15 November 2018, available at https://about.fb.com/news/2018/11/content-standards-forum-minutes/ (accessed 20 November 2020).
49 Kettemann, Matthias C. & Wolfgang Schulz, Setting Rules for 2.7 Billion, A (First) Look into Facebook's Norm- Making System: Results of a Pilot Study, HBI Works in Progress 2020.
50 Facebook, Stakeholder Engagement. How Does Stakeholder Engagement Help us Develop our Community Standards?, available at www.facebook.com/communitystandards/stakeholder_engagement (accessed 20 November 2020).
51 Kettemann, Matthias C. & Wolfgang Schulz, Setting Rules for 2.7 Billion, A (First) Look into Facebook's Norm-Making System: Results of a Pilot Study, HBI Works in Progress 2020; referring to: Facebook, Stakeholder Engagement. How Does Stakeholder

Engagement Help us Develop our Community Standards?, available at www.facebook.com/communitystandards/stakeholder_engagement (accessed 20 November 2020).

52 *Id.*

53 Facebook, Stakeholder Engagement. How Does Stakeholder Engagement Help us Develop our Community Standards?, available at www.facebook.com/communitystandards/stakeholder_engagement (accessed 20 November 2020).

54 *Id.*

55 *Id.*

56 Kettemann, Matthias C. & Wolfgang Schulz, Setting Rules for 2.7 Billion, A (First) Look into Facebook's Norm- Making System: Results of a Pilot Study, HBI Works in Progress 2020.

57 *Id.*

58 See e.g., Matthew Kushin, Masahiro Yamamoto & Francis Dalisay, Societal Majority, Facebook, and the Spiral of Silence in the 2016 US Presidential Election, *Social Media + Society* 1 (2019).

59 See e.g., Luis Fernando Baron, More than a Facebook Revolution: Social Movements and Social Media in the Egyptian Arab Spring, 18 *International Review of Information Ethics* 86 (2012).

60 Christina Fink, Dangerous Speech, Anti-Muslim Violence, and Facebook in Myanmar, 71 *Journal of International Affairs* 43 (2018).

61 See Chapter 3 of this book for a thorough discussion on these points.

62 For an overview, see e.g., Sharan Burrow, UN Treaty on Business and Human Rights Vital for Economic and Social Justice (28 Oct 2019), available at www.socialeurope.eu/un-treaty-on-business-and-human-rights-vital-for-economic-and-social-justice (accessed 2 June 2020).

63 Fifth session of the open-ended intergovernmental working group on transnational corporations and other business enterprises with respect to human rights, available at www.ohchr.org/EN/HRBodies/HRC/WGTransCorp/Session5/Pages/Session5.aspx (accessed 20 May 2020); see also 2019 Draft, Section II, Art. 4, par. 8 (October 2019).

64 Earth Law Center, Rights of Nature Tribunals, available at www.earthlawcenter.org/rights-of-nature-tribunals (accessed 2 June 2020).

65 *Id.*

66 Thomas Piketty, *Capital in the Twenty-First Century* (2013).

67 Thomas Piketty & Emmanuel Saez, A Theory of Optimal Inheritance Taxation, *Econometria* (2013).

68 Thomas Piketty, *Capital in the Twenty-First Century* (2013).

69 Gabriel Zucman, *The Hidden Wealth of Nations: The Scourge of Tax Havens* (2015). See also Thomas R. Tørsløv, Ludvig S. Wier & Gabriel Zucman, The Missing Profits of Nations, National Bureau of Economic Research (NBER), Working Paper No. 24701 (2019).

70 Gabriel Zucman, *The Hidden Wealth of Nations: The Scourge of Tax Havens* (2015).

71 *Id.*

72 These last points are League of Nations–era policies to address tax evasion of MNEs; they are still the primary bedrocks of many international taxation agreements. See also Gabriel Zucman, *The Hidden Wealth of Nations: The Scourge of Tax Havens* (2015).

73 *Id.*

74 *Id.*

75 The Amsterdam Center of International Law aims to address this issue through a new project entitled Sustainable Global Economic Law. Information and latest updates on research available at https://sgel.uva.nl (accessed 2 June 2020).

76 This paragraph derives from Aline Conchon, Norbert Kluge & Michael Stollt, Worker Board-Level Participation in the 31 European Economic Area Countries, European Trade Union Institute, August 2015; and Board-Level Representation: France, European Trade

Union Institute, 2016, www.worker-participation.eu/National-Industrial-Relations/Countries/France/Board-level-Representation (accessed 10 January 2020).

77 *Id.*

78 On trust versus legends and on details re. perceptions as well as disclaimers, see Yoshiro Miwa & J. Mark Ramseyer, *The Fable of the Keiretsu: Urban Legends of the Japanese Economy* (2006).

79 Yutaka Tajima & Misako Inagaki, *The Impact of Globalization on Japanese Banking Law* (1998).

80 Tomoshita Shinoda, *Contemporary Japanese Policies: International Changes* (2014).

81 The idea that corporations are legally required to maximize profits for shareholders is simply a belief, rooted in cautious interpretations of judge-made law. More discussion on this can be found in the Introduction, Conclusion, and Chapter 4 of this book.

82 For more information on 'B Corps', see B-Lab's website, available at https://bcorporation.net (accessed 4 June 2020).

83 *Id.*

84 *Id.*

85 *Id.*

86 Iris Marion Young, Impartiality and the Civic Public: Some Implications of Feminist Critiques of Moral and Political Theory, in Seyla Benhabib & Drucilla Cornell (Eds.), *Feminism as Critique* (1987).

87 See the *Le Monde* articles quoted in Kevin Crow, Bandung's Fate, in Ingo Venzke and Kevin Jon Heller (Eds.), *Contingency in the Course of International Law* (2020). See also Kevin Crow, *'Acceptance': International Law in Post-Colonial Asia, 1955–1995* (book forthcoming hopefully in late 2022).

88 Iris Marion Young, Impartiality and the Civic Public: Some Implications of Feminist Critiques of Moral and Political Theory, in Seyla Benhabib & Drucilla Cornell (Eds.), *Feminism as Critique* (1987).

89 *Id.*

90 On care ethics, see e.g., Virginia Held, *Ethics of Care: Personal, Political, Global* (2005).

91 Iris Marion Young, Impartiality and the Civic Public: Some Implications of Feminist Critiques of Moral and Political Theory, in Seyla Benhabib & Drucilla Cornell (Eds.), *Feminism as Critique* (1987).

92 Mortin Horowitz, *The Transformation of American Law, 1780–1860* (1977).

93 See seminally, Joseph Nye, The Changing Nature of World Power, *Political Science Quarterly* (1990).

94 See e.g., Antony Anghie, *Imperialism, Sovereignty and the Making of International Law* (CUP, 2005); José-Manuel Barreto (Ed.), *Human Rights from a Third World Perspective: Critique, History and International Law* (Cambridge Scholars Publishing, 2015); Sundhya Pahuja, *Decolonizing International Law: Development, Economic Growth and the Politics of Universality* (CUPT, 2013); Balakrishnan Rajagopal, *International Law from Below: Development, Social Movements and Third World Resistance* (CUP, 2020); B S Chimni, *International Law and World Order* (CUP, 1993); Duncan Kennedy, *A Critique of Adjudication* (HUP, 1997); David Kennedy, *The Dark Sides of Virtue* (Princeton, 2004); Rose Parfitt, *The Process of International Legal Reproduction: Imperialism, Historiography, Resistance* (CUP, 2019); and Adom Getachew, *Worldmaking after Empire: The Rise and Fall of Self-Determination* (Princeton, 2019).

95 In this statement, I am thinking along the lines of B S Chimni's approach in his TWAIL-era classic *International Law and World Order* (1993), advancing a view of the future of international law that removes it from the coercive power of State political elites and roots it in service to peoples. But see also Ruti G. Teitel, *Humanity's Law* (2011); while it is a valuable contribution, I take Teitel's approach with a grain of salt for reasons raised by Martti Koskenniemi in his critical review, Humanity's Law, *Ethics and International Affairs* (2012). Teitel's reply to Koskenniemei's critique was published a year later in the same

journal: Ruti G. Teitel, A Response to Martti Koskenniemi's Review of 'Humanity's Law', *Ethics and International Affairs* (2013).

96 One major forthcoming effort is an edited volume, *International Law and 'The Natural'*, which will likely appear around 2025. I have organized an initial discussion group, postponed because of COVID-19, but to convene at the ICON-S Conference in Wroclaw 2021 'Public Law, (Dis)Trust, Dissent'. The working group is called 'International Law and "The Natural"'. Stay tuned for a first effort in this vein to be presented at the ESIL Research Forum in 2020, Solidarity and 'The Natural', programme available at https://esil-sedi.eu/wp-content/uploads/2019/07/Draft_Program_Catania_2020_RF_ESIL_v.1.pdf (accessed 4 June 2020).

97 These and other UN Climate Change records are fully searchable on the UNFCCC's 'documents' webpage, available at https://unfccc.int/documents (accessed 4 June 2020).

Conclusion

Beyond sovereignty, beyond the veil

Whereas sovereignty is often understood in terms of State authority, many passages in this book have suggested it is an invisible boundary through which accountability, responsibility, and ultimately liability are assigned. On the international stage, the Sovereign is understood to be an entity representing the persons within a given geographic space, through democratic processes or by some other right. Its functions relate primarily to the preservation of the State. The State thus operates in a discursive space in which the reasons it must give for its actions to be considered 'legitimate' often derive from some 'public' benefit, as traditionally conceived in broad utilitarian terms. Corporations, by contrast, are thought to be the 'private sector' – they seek profit, incur liability through transactional arrangements, and have employees rather than citizens.

As we have seen, the ICP blurs these lines considerably. While there is no official 'international corporate law', the unofficial international corporate law created by ICSID tribunals, various OECD texts, the TRIPS, and decisions from the ICJ, WTO, ECtHR, and ICC reveal a fragmented legal landscape in which ICPs can both dodge and create international law by framing both capital and activity alternatively as domestic or international, as public or as private. While particularly egregious examples of international crime, theft, and exploitation often meet with penalty, the reality of the international corporate legal landscape is that whatever teeth it has blunt and sharpen along scales of power. Put another way, the more economic and political power a corporation has, the more able it is to seamlessly shift between the private and the public to pursue its purposes and without international legal liability, both through geographic prevalence and through influence upon the State legal systems in which it operates. Thus, in this way, State sovereignty caters to the needs of the very largest ICPs: it geographically and legally compartmentalizes duty, liability, and redistribution, so ICPs bear no international responsibility for what States permit at the same time as ICPs are empowered to influence what States permit.

The status quo with respect to the ICP is not something that can solved, regulated, or addressed by within one State or group of States. Indeed,

State sovereignty prevents solutions to ICP regulation in the same way as it prevents solutions to many problems that can truly be characterized as 'global problems'. Space law, cyber law, environmental law, and international corporate law (re. the ICP) have this tension with sovereignty in common. The international construct – the understanding that law is rooted in defined geographic and political territories – is inapposite to address such problems and to seize opportunities that transcend physical and conceptual borders.

Parent corporations also have access to a status of immunity analogous to sovereignty; it is an analogy with historical roots so close and legal privileges so similar to sovereignty that it has inspired more thorough investigations than the one I offered here, authored by lawyers, historians, and political scientists alike.[1] The sovereign's geographical legal exceptionalism has analogies in special economic zones and offshore drilling sites; the sovereign's political immunities have analogies in the immunity from liability granted to corporate parents for the actions of their subsidiaries. But, as I have shown in Chapters 3 and 4, direct analogical reasoning with other international legal personalities tends to mischaracterize the issues raised by the ICP.

In response to the ICP's use of 'corporate sovereignty as sword' and 'State sovereignty as shield', this book has stressed that neither sovereignty nor veil, neither public law nor private, should stand in the way of resolving the human problems generated by ICPs. If ICPs have acquired new rights – such as access to deferred prosecution agreements, the layered rights of multi-jurisdictional taxation, and the right to set pricing for services in intrafirm transactions – direct liability (sans veils) for breaches of obligations should be available under international law, especially if we adopt Orts's view that corporations are not merely creatures of the State but entities that can exist outside of the law of any one particular State (as I have suggested in Chapters 1 and 4).[2] This means that the global public must rely not only on international institutions as loci of ICP regulation and governance, but also on ICPs themselves; the law's role in this understanding should promote ICP aspirations beyond profit such as inter-jurisdictional accountability, financial transparency, compliance with ethical best practices, and efforts to promote redistributive justice. In many ways, the ICP is the international legal personality that is most flexible and most adaptable, and therefore, best suited to react to the world's greatest challenges. But the status quo of ICP constituency leaves its interests unaligned with anything that might approach a 'global public good' (e.g., a global human interest in maintaining a healthy planet). The ICPs interests would align more closely with global public goods if international legal institutions mirrored domestic ones but sought protection of global rather than local 'goods'. Thus, in relation to the ICP, an international tort law should address obligations and criminal law should address aspirations, both international and domestic.

What does it mean to say that tort law should address obligations? It means that if an actor engages in action that increases the likelihood of harm to others around the actor, questions arise as to whether that actor owes certain duties – duty of care, duty to warn, duty to mitigate – in order to justify the increased likelihood of harm. The law steps in not to attribute moral wrongness to the actions of the actor, but rather to ensure that others who bear the risk imposed by the actor have recourse against breaches of any duties generated by its actions.

What does it mean to say that criminal law should address aspirations? It means that if an actor engages in an action that breaches a legal community's ideals of what *ought* to be, breaches the fundamental values common to a given legal community, actively obstructs the ability of others to live their values, or intentionally causes harm, questions arise as to whether that actor should face punitive consequences. The form of such consequences can be retributive or redistributive (rehabilitation is an uneasy fit with ICPs); consequences should be transparent so as to serve as a deterrent to prevent future harms from other actors. Ultimately, aspirational law should express the values of the community from whom the law flows and for whom the law exists. On the international stage, aspirational law should resist universalizing impulses. Although some champions of universalizing values such as human rights dismiss its critics as 'relativist', these dismissals are often based on the shallow and somewhat irrelevant counterargument that because many delegates participated in the creation of certain human rights treaties, human rights must surely be universal.[3] The empirical evidence and lived experience suggest that claims to substantive universal rights will invariably encounter a vast array of complex problems and contradictions, and these in turn will lead to resistance. International law's legitimacy depends on its ability to drop impulses toward moral coercion; it is strongest where it ensures that both humanity as a whole and regional groups of people can voice and enact value preferences. Thus, international law's aspirational arm should stick to procedures that ensure various legal communities can express their version of what *ought* to be, with perhaps the substantive exception of the assumption that resolving disputes through non-violent means is desirable.

When it comes to ICPs, creating law that responds to regional and human aspirations beyond sovereignty could come in two forms. One is the form described previously: Law that expresses the values of the communities it serves is justified in coercion insofar as it expresses the values of those communities. The other form has been noted in many sections of this book: The ICP is itself a creator of law – business norms and internal 'soft law' governance systems and networks as well as binding 'hard law' through TRIPS and various BITs. This book has tried to address this dimension through critical discussion on corporate purpose; it has pointed out several times that profit is more of default assumption of purpose than a legal requirement. But with this point aired, it is more difficult to address the question of what a given business's purpose should be or, indeed, whether businesses should have any legal purpose at all.

Perhaps it is easier to start with a question such as: what would a business's primary purpose be if not profit or wealth maximization? Over the years, various scholars have offered new orientations. Some suggest that creating and keeping customers responds to social needs; customer creation is a symptom of meeting human desire, and meeting human desire is the purpose of business.[4] Others have suggested that putting workers first rather than demand (i.e., the customer) is the primary purpose of business; providing meaningful employment to as many humans as possible, which presumably also responds to human desire.[5] Another view is that the idea of 'purpose' does not necessarily need to favor any particular group but that businesses should rather consider all relevant stakeholders, that is, those who are affected by the business. This is often referred to as stakeholder theory or stakeholder primacy; it takes issue predominantly with the shareholder primacy theory embraced by Friedman and his followers. Still other contemporary commentators seek to revive Dodd's 1932 position that, as a creature of the State, a corporation's primary purpose is to serve the interests of the State,[6] that is, the public or common good. All these views take the corporation as responding to various group desires, and in some sense, the real debate is over how to determine the contours of the group whose desires hold the most 'legitimate' place as the corporation's master. In this way, the entire debate immediately abandons liberal individualist concepts of economic interest at the same time as it retains the anthropocentrism that runs through much of the law surrounding business, rights, torts, and crimes. And most of the views that would have corporations consider a broader range of 'stakeholders' enter waters that get murkier as corporate engagements with domestic, regional, and international legal systems compound. Asking a corporation to 'balance' stakeholder needs thus incurs a sense of subjectivity that pushes stakeholderism toward the realm of lip service. All of this occurs against the background fact that, for the ICP, multiple publics are stakeholders even as the States shape public desire through ICP interests.

With this book, I have clarified the parameters of the ICP (amorphous as they are) and identified many of the exclusive rights and privileges it enjoys. I have also offered a two-tiered solution for courts and lawyers concerned by the status quo – the ICP's lack of accountability and often unchecked power – in an effort to shape the ICP's future trajectory in international law. International law should provide 'passive' procedural rights to ICPs that correspond directly to universal duties – those that concern the environment, global public health, and global distribution of capital. And international law should avoid the impulse to universalize 'active' substantive rights, rights that require and can be shaped by corporate agency, such as political rights, religious rights, or rights that assume qualities 'intrinsic' to agents or groups.

The picture is complex, but for the ICP, the veil is often a shield and sovereignty is often a sword. A law beyond sovereignty, beyond the veil, one legitimated by service to humanity – but one that understands humanity as part of a broader ecosystem to which it owes duties – could bring humanity toward solutions.

With an eye toward a global law that embraces the passive claim rights of the ICP while delegating its active rights to regional governing blocs, with an eye toward a global law that embraces claim rights to redistributive justice but delegates allocative justice to regional governing blocs, with an eye toward a global environmental law that recognizes passive claim rights of nature which can be exercised on its behalf for the benefit of nature without needing to square those rights with the political agendas of regional blocs, international lawyers can reimagine how international law might move beyond the limits of sovereignty. In stark contrast to what global constitutionalists often suggest, if international law is to retain its legitimacy in years ahead, its lawyers must re-imagine the global institution as one designed to recognize, respect, and represent multiple ideologies and international legal personalities at the same time.

Notes

1 Joshua Barkan, *Corporate Sovereignty* (2013); Doreen Lustig, *Veiled Power: International Law and the Private Corporation, 1886–1981* (2020).
2 Eric W. Orts, *Business Persons: A Legal Theory of the Firm* (2013).
3 See Diane Desierto, The Myth and Mayhem of 'Build Back Better': Human Rights Decision-Making and Human Dignity Imperatives in COVID-19, EJIL: Talk! Blog (25 May 2020), available at www.ejiltalk.org/the-myth-and-mayhem-of-build-back-better-human-rights-decision-making-as-the-human-dignity-imperative-in-covid-19/ (accessed 6 June 2020), citing Steven L. B. Jensen, *The Making of International Human Rights: The 1960s, Decolonization, and the Reconstruction of Global Values* (2016).
4 Theodore Levitt, *The Marketing Imagination* (1983).
5 Norman Bowie, Empowering People as an End for Business, in Georges Enderle, Brenda Almond & Antonio Argandona (Eds.), *People in Corporations: Ethical Responsibilities and Corporate Effectiveness* (1990).
6 Robert Bellah et al, *Habits of the Heart: Individualism and Commitment in American Life* (1985).

Index

Page numbers in *italics* indicate a figure and page numbers in **bold** indicate a table on the corresponding page. Page numbers followed by "n" indicate a note.

For Product Safety Concerns and Information please contact our EU representative GPSR@taylorandfrancis.com
Taylor & Francis Verlag GmbH, Kaufingerstraße 24, 80331 München, Germany

www.ingramcontent.com/pod-product-compliance
Lightning Source LLC
LaVergne TN
LVHW021126300926
849160LV00010B/874

* 9 7 8 0 3 6 7 6 9 4 9 4 4 *